# DRIVER #8

## DALE EARNHARDT, JR.

### WITH JADE GURSS

## VISION

NEW YORK    BOSTON

*Cover design by Flag*
*Cover photo by Harold Hinson*

Vision
Hachette Book Group USA
237 Park Avenue
New York, NY 10017
Visit our Web site at www.HachetteBookGroupUSA.com

Vision is an imprint of Grand Central Publishing. The Vision name and logo is a trademark of Hachette Book Group USA, Inc.

Printed in the United States of America

Originally published in hardcover by Hachette Book Group USA
First Paperback Printing: December 2002

15  14  13  12  11  10  9  8  7  6

To my dad, Dale Earnhardt

# Acknowledgments

Big thanks go to Bill Kentling, who edited, prodded, and encouraged me for months and months while this thing took shape. He deserves some sort of "ultimate editor" title. I also offer thanks to Harold Hinson, whose photos document Dale Jr.'s efforts each weekend, to Richard Abate and Robert Lazar at ICM, and all of my friends and family who suffered through endless e-mails and discussions about each chapter along the way.

Big props to Tim Schuler at Anheuser-Busch, who gets the credit for teaming me with Budweiser and Junior and then giving the OK for this project to go ahead. Thanks to all of the Budweiser sports marketing guys, Sponsor Services, and everyone at Dale Earnhardt Inc., who were nervous about the book but supportive all the same.

The guys on the No. 8 team are the greatest. I'm looking forward to watching you guys win championships in the future. And most of all, thanks to Dale Jr. As he says, he lived it, I just typed it. Dude, the future is limitless.

Thanks,
JADE

# DRIVER
## #8

# The Ride of a Lifetime

I hop through the right-side window of the Budweiser Chevrolet race car. Unlike a typical racer that has only a driver's seat, this car has been prepared by the Richard Petty Driving Experience (a leading race-driving school—like a sports fantasy camp on four wheels) to give fans a feel of what it's like to go 160 miles per hour with a professional driver behind the wheel. I am strapped snugly into the passenger seat and take a deep breath.

Today the driver is no mere Petty school instructor, but one of the finest drivers in the world. Dale Earnhardt Jr. gets an ornery grin on his face as he hits the ignition switch and then throws the car into gear. Soon we are hurtling toward the high-banked Turn 1 of Lowe's Motor Speedway near Charlotte, North Carolina. From this angle, it looks like we are about to be launched up the side of a three-story building.

Dale Jr. is here today to shoot a segment for a documentary about his life that will soon air on MTV. Before he agreed to participate in the video shoot, he insisted that the Petty school allow him to take several of his buddies for the ride of their lives. I am on that short list of passengers. Through a contract with Anheuser-Busch, my company, fingerprint inc., has been in charge of Dale Jr.'s publicity for the past fifteen months. It has been the busiest, and the most eventful, time of my life.

"I want you guys to have an appreciation for what I do," Dale Jr. tells us. "I think our friendship can have another level if you understand more about what it's like out there. . . ."

I have that thought in my mind as we careen through the first corner of the 1.5-mile oval track. The G-forces while cornering in a 3,400-pound race car at more than 160 miles per hour are immense. My pelvis is forced downward into the form-fitted racing seat. My head, encased in a helmet that seemed to weigh next to nothing while I was sitting on the wall along pit lane, suddenly feels like it weighs two hundred pounds as it tries to launch itself off of my head and fly out the passenger-side window. While I'm trying hard to look cool and relaxed, I have to brace myself with both hands. My feet involuntarily slide toward the right side of the car. My brain flashes to scenes from NASA videos of astronauts being spun around at high rates of speed in G-force tests. While many astronauts become disoriented or sick, I am exhilarated.

On the back straightaway, I look over to see Dale Jr. still smiling broadly. Before I can turn my head forward, he shoots hard into Turn 3. He keeps his right foot pressed on the accelerator pedal while using his left foot to lightly brush the brake pedal. The brake pedal is used more to help balance or position the car for the corner rather than to dramatically slow the hurtling beast. At these speeds, physics dictate that a sudden jerk of the steering wheel or on the brakes can have dire consequences. The car seems to rotate on a center of gravity located immediately beneath my ass. *So this is why they refer to a scary moment on the race track as having a "high pucker factor,"* I think to myself. Even if I had wanted to say it out loud, the wailing engine would drown out my screaming.

In the midst of the third turn, we travel over a series of ripples in the track surface. You would not feel these bumps in a passenger car, but in a car designed for the NASCAR Winston Cup series, they produce kidney-jiggling, teeth-rattling vibrations. As we increase speed, the track, which seems so wide from the relative safety and comfort of the grandstands or pit lane, suddenly looks to be razor thin. *How in the hell can he do this while battling forty-two other cars and drivers?*

As the car swings onto the front straight, the outside wall approaches fast. I wonder if Dale Jr. realizes that I am on the side that will impact this concrete barrier if we slide one or two inches closer. Both sides of my brain begin a frantic argument: the emotional side screams in equal parts terror and joy, while the rational side is comforted that one of the best drivers in the world is only twenty-four inches to my left, artfully pulling at the wheel as we hurtle toward the start/finish line.

After three laps, he slows on the backstraight, and I give him a big-ass thumbs-up. Two thumbs up, in fact. We both continue to smile as we roll slowly into the pit lane. I am confident that our high-speed laps have eclipsed the Winston Cup track record that Dale Jr. himself holds, but when we arrive in the pits, he points out that our lap times were more than three seconds slower than the pace he would maintain during a race such as the Coca-Cola 600, held here every May. His one-lap record is 29.027 seconds, an average of more than 186 miles per hour. Our best lap today is 33.4 seconds, or an average speed of slightly more than 161 miles per hour.

After three laps (less than five miles) of doing nothing but holding on, adrenaline is shooting though my veins as if propelled by a high-pressure fire hose. My ears are ringing from the heavy-metal volume inside the car, and my eyes are scratchy from the fumes and grit as I climb from the car delirious with joy. I am completely worn out. I refuse to believe that Dale Jr. has the strength, the stamina, and the concentration to do this for six hundred freakin' miles—four hundred laps—while fighting the rest of the aggressive pack of drivers who want nothing more than to get past him. There are no time-outs in racing, no time to rest or catch your breath. The ride has further convinced me what I had already suspected: this is the *ultimate* extreme sport.

My position as the publicist for Dale Jr. gives me unequaled access to all the action as it happens, but I have tried to keep myself out of the stories as much as possible to keep the focus on Dale Jr. and the team.

This book, though, is not a biography of Dale Jr. His life story will have to come several years from now. It is a behind-the-scenes look at his first full season on the biggest stage in American motor sports. This book looks at one year in the life of this young star, as he grows and becomes more of an adult every day. One year in his life—starting the season as a timid rookie and ending it as one of the most outspoken role models in the sport.

One year after his first Daytona 500, he returns as a confident veteran, only to see his sparkling second-place finish, indeed his entire life, turned upside down by the tragic death of his father on the final lap of the race.

No matter how many races Dale Jr. wins in the future, or how many championships he grabs, there will always be only one rookie season. Only one first win. One first all-star race. And only one first motorized bar stool (but we'll tell *that* story later).

Jade Gurss<br>
Charlotte, N.C.<br>
January 2002

# Contents

Intro                                    xxiii

Daytona Beach, Florida                      1
*The Daytona 500*
The Future Has Arrived

Mooresville, North Carolina                34
There's No Place Like Home

Rockingham, North Carolina                 53
*DuraLube 400*
Get a Grip

Las Vegas, Nevada                          57
*CarsDirect.com 400*
Like a Rolling Stone

Atlanta, Georgia                                      67
*Cracker Barrel 500*
No Brakes! I Have No Brakes!

Darlington, South Carolina                            76
*Mall.com 400*
We Need a Driver . . .

Bristol, Tennessee                                    84
*Food City 500*
Living Up to Our Fathers' Legacies

Fort Worth, Texas                                     94
*DirecTV 500*
Victory!

Martinsville, Virginia                               111
*Goody's 500*
The Greatest Two Hours of My Life

Talladega, Alabama                                   120
*DieHard 500*
Over before It Began

Fontana, California                                  128
*NAPA 500*
I Have to Deliver Beer

# Contents

Richmond, Virginia     134
*Pontiac Excitement 400*
I Love You . . . Now Find Your Own Way Home

Charlotte, North Carolina     149
*The Winston*
Here Comes This Red Thing

Charlotte, North Carolina     167
*Coca-Cola 600*
A Hottie

Dover, Delaware     179
*MBNA 400*
Juniormania

Brooklyn, Michigan     182
*Kmart 400*
Not Drinking Enough . . . Water

Pocono, Pennsylvania     186
*Pocono 500*
I Guess I Was Just in Dad's Way

Sonoma, California     190
*SaveMart 350*
I Am NOT Riding That Thing

Daytona Beach, Florida                              198
*Pepsi 400*
I Want to Emphasize BIG Curves

Loudon, New Hampshire                               204
*New Hampshire 300*
Tragedy . . . Again

Pocono, Pennsylvania                                209
*Pennsylvania 500*
Junior, Are You OK?

Indianapolis, Indiana                               217
*Brickyard 400*
A Lesser Driver Would Have Finished a Lap Down

Watkins Glen, New York                              227
*Global Crossing at the Glen*
A Video Game?

Brooklyn, Michigan                                  234
*Pepsi 400*
Big E, Little E, and Now Middle E

Bristol, Tennessee                                  240
*Goracing.com 500*
Poisoned and Pained

Darlington, South Carolina 245
*Southern 500*
Losing Is So Damn Cruel

Richmond, Virginia 253
*Chevrolet 400*
We're Gonna Lap Everybody

Loudon, New Hampshire 261
*DuraLube 300*
Like Paying to Drive a Go-Kart

Dover, Delaware 270
*MBNA.com 400*
Note to Self: Don't Cuss at Stiffy

Martinsville, Virginia 278
*NAPA 500*
Like Some Sort of Stunt Show

Charlotte, North Carolina 282
*UAW-GM 500*
Seems Like It Was Five Years Ago

Talladega, Alabama 294
*Winston 500*
The Big One

Rockingham, North Carolina                    310
*Pop Secret 400*
I Know a Man and Leave That Kid Alone

Phoenix, Arizona                              323
*Checker 500*
I Admire Your Style

Homestead, Florida                            333
*Pennzoil 400*
Too Sexy for One Page

Atlanta, Georgia                              342
*NAPA 500*
Put Us Outta Our Misery, Know What I Mean?

Epilogue                                      348

# Intro

Hey, everyone, this is Dale Jr.

I want to tell you straight up that this book is not my life story, or about my life with my dad (Maybe I'll write those books in the coming years). Instead, this is the *real* story of my first season as a driver in the biggest race series in the country: NASCAR Winston Cup. It was one helluva rookie season, and my team and I experienced tons of emotions: exhilaration and exhaustion, fun and fear, triumph and tragedy, and everything in between.

This project began early in the 2000 season. The goal was to tell the story of one year in my life, beginning with my first Daytona 500 through to the finish of the same race in 2001. The last lap of the 2001 Daytona 500 turned into a nightmare for me, my family, and race fans everywhere. It didn't take me very many days to decide to finish this book in honor of my dad. He was not only my father and friend, but he was also my boss, the guy whose name was on the door of the race car I drive. I miss him every day.

Sit back and enjoy the year 2000 behind the wheel with me.

DALE EARNHARDT JR.
*December 2001*

# DRIVER
## ═══ #8 ═══

# Daytona Beach, Florida
## The Daytona 500

## The Future Has Arrived

The Daytona 500 is known as the Great American Race. Some insist on referring to it as the Super Bowl of racing. I like the Super Bowl, but I think that having every team and every NASCAR superstar in one race is more compelling than a game with only two teams. No matter what you choose to call it, the 500 is the biggest race of the NASCAR Winston Cup season.

I am Ralph Dale Earnhardt Jr., driver of the No. 8 Budweiser NASCAR Winston Cup car. The 2000 season is my first in American racing's biggest league. I drove five races in the Winston Cup series as a practice run last year, but now an entire season looms ahead for me and my team. Some of the media and fans are calling me the most heralded and hyped rookie in NASCAR's fifty-plus–year history. That kind of crap puts a lot of pressure on me, but no more than I put on myself.

Call me what you want. Most call me Dale Jr. Or Dale. Or Junior. Or Little E. My dad started calling me

Junebug when I was young. Hell, I'll answer to any of
'em.

I am the second-oldest son of a racing legend, seven-
time NASCAR Winston Cup champion Dale Earnhardt,
whose skill behind the wheel and an ironhanded, com-
monsense approach to life created a huge self-made
success on the track, in the boardroom, and in the family
room.

My life is full of contradictions. On the one hand, if
you believe everything you read, I'm some kind of rising
superstar; I've even been called the future of NASCAR.
But on the other hand, I'm really just a normal guy. I was
born October 10, 1974, and like most other guys in their
twenties, I like nothing more than to chill out at home,
have a cold beer and hang with my buddies. Some people
think of me as a hell-raising partyer, known to occasionally play the drums on stage with famous rock bands.
Truth is, much of the time I'm quiet, introspective, and
sometimes almost painfully shy. I think I'm a lot like
other people my age, and I hope I'm also growing to be a
lot like my dad. If I can ever come close to my father—
being successful on and off the track and with my family—I'll be all right.

My dad has won thirty-four races here at Daytona—
more than twice as many races as anyone else—including
wins in the Daytona 500, the 125-mile qualifying races,
the International Race of Champions, the Busch Clash,
the Firecracker 400, and the Busch Series races. Yet he
lost the Daytona 500 nineteen times before winning in
his twentieth start in 1998. I thought Dad was just as
great before he won that race as he was after he won, but
some say your career is incomplete without winning it

at least once. It's like someone saying an athlete was unsuccessful in their career—no matter how great their stats were—if they didn't win the Super Bowl, World Series, or Olympic gold. I guess, because I saw Dad try so hard and still not win it so many times, I feel differently. Sure, I want to win it right now, but it's not everything.

When Dad finally won the Daytona 500, it was one of his greatest victories. People remember that race for the way every crew member from every team ran out on pit lane to give him a high five after he had won. I think that showed how much he was liked and respected among his competitors despite his "Intimidator" nickname and reputation. After slapping hands with hundreds of crew guys, he went out in the grass and did donuts for a few minutes. It was a great moment and I remember how happy he was afterwards.

This is my first Daytona 500. Literally. I've never even seen one in person. I was always in school each February and couldn't travel to watch my dad race until the summer months. Just driving into the infield of the track through the tunnel underneath Turn 4 is exciting. The history and the prestige of this place are just so immense that I can't wait to say I've raced in the Daytona 500. No matter what else I do in life, no one can ever take that away from me.

Or, should I say, I *hope* this is my first Daytona 500. As a rookie driver with a rookie team, there is no guarantee at all that our car will even be in the starting field. More than fifty teams are trying to gain one of the forty-three starting positions, and just because my team and I have won the last two Busch Series championships

(NASCAR's version of Triple-A baseball), that doesn't help us at all now.

I can't imagine *not* making the starting lineup. There has been so much buildup to this one event that the pressure is immense on the whole team. It's the first race of the year, and people have been talking about Daytona since an hour after the 1999 season ended. Hell, for me it goes back more than eighteen months to the day that we announced to the world that Dale Earnhardt Inc. (DEI) was pairing up with Budweiser to move up to the Winston Cup series in the year 2000. It was exciting and terrifying at the same time.

Every sponsor makes big plans for this race, and every team spends the entire off-season preparing their best new cars just to make it into the starting field. Anything the crew can imagine (or purchase) is put into the car to win this one race. I have a good team behind me, but strange things can happen, so you hope and hope and hope that all goes well. I don't know how I could face my fans and my sponsors if I failed to qualify. I may as well take the rest of the year off.

In the Busch Series, we always had a fast car here, but I never finished better than fourteenth place in the two races at Daytona. My first race was in 1998, and it ended with my car flipping down the back straightaway at something like 170 miles per hour. As I was flipping, all I could see was earth, sky, earth, sky, earth, sky. . . . When I flipped for the final time, the ground looked as if it was being thrown at me like a giant prop from the movie *Twister.* Only after the car came to a stop did I realize I had landed upside down. It was as wild and exhilarating as any ride I've ever taken. When you clear your head and realize you're not seriously hurt, you think, *Hell yeah! That was wild!*

The Daytona 500 is the climax of two weeks of practice and qualifying, as well as other special races like the Bud Shootout (reserved exclusively for last year's Bud Pole position winners), two 125-mile qualifying sprints, an IROC race, which is a fight between twelve champion drivers in identical cars (I'll be racing against Dad in that one, too), a 300-mile Busch race, a NASCAR truck series race, and a helluva lot more.

The track seats almost 170,000 people and you can add about half that many in the infield as well. (Let's see the Super Bowl try to match that.) Many of those people are around for the whole two weeks, living in their RVs, cooking on the grill, drinking Bud, partying, watching the races, buying souvenirs, and trying to get close to the drivers.

Being a Winston Cup driver means being accessible to the fans. This accessibility is the basis of NASCAR's popularity, and a huge tradition that goes back to when there was no fencing around the garage area and fans were able to wander around and talk to the drivers before the race. This still happens, but you need to know someone who is a sponsor or on a race team to get a garage pass. I cannot imagine any other professional sport that would allow you into the locker room or dugout so close to the start of the game.

The drivers have known for years they weren't anything without the fans. So they signed autographs, they did interviews, and they let the fans get close and see them. The fans felt like they knew the drivers personally, and the result was fan loyalty. This continues today.

When a lot of other sports see declining loyalty among fans and players, NASCAR fans remain faithful. Young drivers learn early to treat the fans right. I learned it from being around racetracks for my entire life.

There is no telling how many autographs a NASCAR driver will sign during Speedweeks. Thousands, for sure. And someone like my father or Richard Petty will sign millions in his career. In fact, I often joke that Richard Petty ruined it for all of us because he was known to sign anywhere and anything for anybody. Now fans expect that from all of us! I say that half-jokingly, because I'm happy to sign most of the time, but sometimes the constant crush gets overwhelming.

I used to feel strange about signing autographs, because I thought people were just asking because of who my dad was. But sometimes it's really cool to sign an autograph. For instance, Kenny Mayne of ESPN's *SportsCenter* interviewed me on the day before the 500. He teased me that I looked like some college kid on spring break and then he asked me to sign the cover of his copy of the latest *ESPN* magazine. (It didn't hurt that my photo was on the cover, along with my buddy and longtime rival Matt Kenseth.) Mayne meets all kinds of athletes but he still wanted me to sign the magazine, and he even asked me to go out and race karts with him after the race. I thought he was just kidding, but I heard later he was pissed off that I didn't show up.

One of the first nights in Daytona, I did a radio show at the local shopping mall with Benny Parsons, a guy who went from driving a taxi in Detroit to winning a Winston Cup championship. Benny is a good guy and everyone likes talking to him, so I enjoy doing his show.

The producers told all of the drivers that they didn't have to sign any autographs for the hundreds of fans packed into the mall for the show. Some guys took that seriously, and walked in and out of the security entrance without signing a thing.

I'm not comfortable just walking past, especially since there are many people packed three, four, and five rows deep along a roped-off area behind the stage. They couldn't see or hear the radio show—they are there for one thing: autographs.

They are all holding or waving something to be signed: a die-cast collectible of my race car, life-size cardboard cutouts of me that they "borrowed" from their local bar or convenience store, T-shirts, hats, trading cards. Hell, I have signed just about everything except checks or money orders.

I have fun on the air with Benny, but I'm tired. I'm in a bad mood. I just want to get back to my own motor coach for some peace and quiet and video games. But these fans are the people who pay my salary, so I remember Richard Petty and I venture out into the middle of the walkway. Somehow, especially early in his career, Dad has always been able to walk right through a line like this without signing a thing. He'd say, "I gotta go! I'm late for [insert excuse here]!" and the crowd would go crazy. "Go get 'em, Dale!" or "Kick their ass, man!"

Nowadays fans are much more aggressive and much more demanding. They think you *owe* it to them to stay and sign every last one. If I walked out without signing, they'd all yell, "Fuck you, Junior!" and "You suck!"

So I take out a black Sharpie—it's the NASCAR tool of choice for this job—and I start signing. My dad and Petty use a long, complex signature to sign their names, but I prefer the immediate approach. I almost always sign "Dale Jr." and sometimes I'll put a small "#8" below it. Tonight there are so many people here, I can't possibly sign for everyone, so I look for the official merchandise first—my hats, jackets, T-shirts, model cars—because I know the fans with that stuff had to go find it and buy it and that they are really my fans. (Plus I get a few nickels and dimes from that stuff too.) I always try to seek them out first.

The biggest secret to signing autographs in a big crowd is to keep moving. While I sign (left-handed of course), I keep moving slowly toward the door. When you stop moving, the crowd can surround you and things can get out of hand. As I inch closer to the exit, the people at the back get more impatient and start pushing. This is when it gets tense and I worry about people getting knocked over—especially little kids.

I sign for about thirty minutes, when my publicist Jade Gurss and I finally reach the doorway. When we turn to leave, the ones who got an autograph are cheering and the rest are saying, "Fuck you, Junior" and "You suck!" See, I told you so.

In a perfect world, I could sign for all of them, but it's late and I have to be in the race car early the next day.


At Daytona, being a rookie dictates many things, including your location in the garage. Teams are placed according to their position in the point standings in last year's Winston Cup, and since we ran only five races in 1999, we didn't accumulate many points. The top ten point-earners get the biggest garage stalls as well as other perks. Each team uses stacks and stacks of Goodyear Eagle racing slicks, and it takes a lot of time and effort to mount all of those tires for each of the teams. They are mounted for the successful and winning teams first, so we have to wait patiently for them to stack our tires.

My team is parked way down in one of the last garage stalls—all dusty and cramped. Right next to us is Matt Kenseth, who is driving a Ford for team owner Jack Roush. Matt and I became buddies off the track during the last two years, when we were both running the Busch Series and competing hard for the championship. He was always my toughest competition and for some reason I think it made us closer. Matt is a good guy and a great driver, and the media who cover NASCAR are saying that the two of us are natural rivals for the Rookie of the Year award. As much as I like Matt and enjoy hanging with him, I really want to beat him. I know he's also gunning for me, since I won the last two Busch titles. NASCAR rivalries and friendships are like that. When you are out on the track, it doesn't matter who is in the other car—you want to beat him. I feel that way when the guy driving the other car is my friend, like Matt, or when the other car is a black No. 3 and the driver is my dad. I want to beat him and I know he wants to beat me. Badly.

Having Matt so close in the garage is cool because it gives me someone to talk to and relax with. Because we are both new and have similar backgrounds, we learn a lot from each other. I'll talk with Matt about a lot more things than I will with my father. Dad is one of those guys who doesn't give detailed lessons or tips. But Matt and I can ask, "Is your car doing this?" or "What did you do here in Turn 3?" We even discuss off-track pressures and expectations. Our motor coaches (our homes-away-from-home) are parked side by side in the drivers' lot, so we hope to talk at night.

I don't want to make it sound like my dad doesn't offer any advice, but he always wants me to learn things for myself. When I was getting started in racing, he'd tell me things like "Be smooth" or "Be careful," but he really didn't give me a lot of specific racing hints. The one I remember most, though, is when I was just getting started in late-model stock cars at a small local track in Myrtle Beach, South Carolina. For three Saturday nights in a row, the same guy had spun me out. Each week, I'd try to pass him on the inside and he would cut across the track and spin my inexperienced ass around. I told Dad that the same damn guy had wrecked me three times and I was beginning to wonder if I would ever pass anyone ever again. Dad asked for more specifics about each incident. He thought for a second, and then he turned and said, "Here's what you do. The next time you come up to pass him, you know he's going to do that to you. And he will keep doing it as long as you let him do it. So you come up on the inside like before, but when he starts to cut across, you put on the brakes and keep your steering wheel straight. That should do it."

I was pumped up and ready the next week. A little unsure of the move, but I was ready. In the feature race, I was zooming along and there he was—right in front of me. I got a good run down the inside, and just as he was ready to cut me off, I put on the brakes and kept the wheel straight. When I opened my eyes, sure enough, he spun up into the wall and I cruised along just fine. Thanks, Dad.

But, of course, that move won't work here at Daytona, and I still have to make it into the race, and that's no sure thing regardless of how much advice Dad gives me. Actually, I worry a helluva lot more about making the starting field than how I'll do once we're in the race. There is a lot riding on just being in the race. No one wants to have to load up the entire team and go home three days before the race. No one wants to face several hundred VIP guests on race morning to tell them why they won't be seeing *their* car take the green flag.

Not making the race would be agonizing. Agonizing because all of the preparation and hard work and practice would be wasted. Agonizing because I'd feel like I let down my crew, my sponsors, my dad, and my fans. After all of the preseason hype, magazine covers, and sponsor dollars . . . it's almost too much to imagine. The worst is wondering if I'm really ready for this, if I really belong in Winston Cup.

I believe I do belong. But I still have to go out and prove it to myself—and to everyone else, especially the veteran drivers. They don't give a damn that I won two Busch titles. That would be like Michael Jordan worrying about a rookie who won an NCAA title or two. I have to make the right decisions and earn respect every lap of every race.

The qualifying system for the Daytona 500 is pretty complicated. The front two positions are determined by the Bud Pole qualifying session. Cover the thin ribbon of 2.5 miles of asphalt in less time than anyone else, and you are given the number one starting position. The

Bud Pole session (one car runs at a time for two timed laps; only your best lap counts) takes place eight days before the 500. The team that wins the pole position gets to hype the media for the entire week leading up to the race. The rest of the forty-three-car field is determined by qualifying times, or where you finish in one of the 125-mile qualifying races the Thursday before the 500, or even where you ranked in last year's Winston point standings. It's difficult to understand, but the important thing—for me, anyway—is to make it into the starting field, no matter what.

There are fifty-six cars going out separately for Bud Pole qualifying, one by one, to clock their best lap time. We draw the forty-eighth spot, so we have to wait for several hours before it's our turn. It feels like a month. I can't stand waiting in the garage or my motor home watching on television, so I help the guys push the car to its spot in the qualifying line.

While I am standing there, Dad comes over to give me a little pep talk and some tips about the track conditions. He looks strange in a different uniform for this race. Chevy has paid big money to paint his car in a special "Tasmanian Devil" scheme that is a big part of their Monte Carlo advertising campaign. He has been in a black car with a white driver's uniform for so long it's jarring to see him in a different uniform for just one race. Dale Jarrett, the current champion, and Jeff Burton both come by and wish me well. It feels weird to be racing against guys who I had looked up to for so many years.

Alone in my thoughts in the middle of all of the noise and hoopla, I wait my turn to qualify. There are an unbelievable number of photographers and video camera crews on the other side of the pit wall and a huge group of fans. I try to tune it all out and relax. But my gut is full of nervous rumbling. I notice one of the fans wearing one of my new souvenir T-shirts. The shirt says, *The future has arrived.* Damn right.

Yes, sir. The future will arrive real soon. Finally.

When I get out on the track for my qualifying laps, all I think about is driving the car. At Daytona, you can keep your foot on the throttle all the way around, so it's more about the car and whether the team has set it up to slice through the wind as efficiently as possible. The driver is just a passenger for much of the lap. We were looking for a particular lap time, and we managed to knock a half second off of that, but my qualifying time is only twenty-second fastest. Good but not great. I still might be able to finish poorly in the 125-mile qualifier and make the 500 on that lap time, but it's no sure thing and we don't want to take any chances.

I know that I have to run a good qualifying race on Thursday. That means a finish of at least fifteenth or better to ensure a spot in Sunday's lineup. But the most important thing is to finish. You don't want to get too aggressive, wreck the car, and not make the 500 at all. Sometimes it's totally out of your control. Someone else crashes and you get swept up into the accident. Or maybe a piece of the car—a two-dollar part that never failed before—breaks apart and you drop out of the race. It's not your fault, but you are still going home heartbroken.

Before Thursday's qualifying race, there is more waiting to do. There are two 125-mile qualifying races on the same day, and I'm in the second one. So I get to watch the first one and maybe learn something. I watch from the top of the transporter that the team uses to haul our race cars and a garageful of parts, pieces, and tools from track to track. The view from there is great and I get a feel for how huge and impressive the track is. The banked turns are three stories high from top to bottom and banked at 31 degrees. They call this a "self-cleaning" track, since most of the debris from a wreck will just slide down to the apron below.

When fans see that high banking for the first time—in person, instead of on television—they get a little dizzy. Then they start thinking about the great racing with lots of passing that they're going to see here. At least they used to. In recent years the races at Daytona have been boring because it has become so hard to pass. For the last ten to fifteen years, NASCAR has used restrictor plates to reduce the horsepower of the engine—slowing the cars down so they don't take off and fly through the air or into the grandstands. These plates restrict the power and make it very hard to pass unless you are a master at "the draft."

The draft occurs when cars are pulled along by the vacuum that is created by the car in front. Working together, two or more cars in the draft can all go faster than any one car alone. A car going nearly two hundred miles per hour makes a big hole in the air, and if you get inside of that hole, you have very little air resistance to move through and you get pulled along at a higher speed. You also give the car in front of you a push. Even if you are many yards behind, the draft helps your car speed up and catch the car or cars in front of you. The problem is, if you pull out to pass the car in front, your car suddenly drops out of the draft and is hit by a huge wall of air. It's like having a parachute on the back of the car.

Dad always hated the restrictor plates. He hates the reduced power because it takes away a lot of things that a driver can do to get to the front. Or maybe he just wants us to believe he hates them, because he has won a lot of restrictor-plate races and is considered the very best that ever raced with the plates. Some people claim Dad can "see the air" in the draft, but I think he just has a deeper understanding of how to use the airflow to his advantage. He knows how to use it to help his car or to mess with another car. He also has great peripheral vision, so he can see what is happening around him and is able to react quickly. Sometimes he makes moves where I think he must be able to see behind him.

After the first qualifying race, I spend a little time listening to the drivers who have just finished. A lot of them are talking about how their cars didn't handle right once the tires wore out. This might be something we can use in our race. Mainly, I need to be conservative with my tires so they will last the full distance. I'm thinking about that as I climb in my No. 8 Chevrolet. I want a top-fifteen finish to guarantee me a spot in the big race. But today my motto is Better Safe Than Sorry. If I can get into the starting field on Sunday, then I can really hang it out.

When the green flag drops, I run cautiously for the first few laps. I try to get the feel of the track and stay up near the front. The team has done a great job of setting up the car, and it flows in traffic. I'm in eleventh position but I'm faster than a lot of the cars around me. I start passing people, moving up on the leader and exciting the crowd. At one point my car handles so well that I go up high near the wall in Turn 3 and get three-wide with two other cars and pass them both. My crew insists the people in the stands were gasping for air when I made that move. *You aren't supposed to do that at Daytona! Especially not if you're a rookie!* But if you're a racer and you've got a car that can pass people, what you do is . . . you pass 'em. That's what I'm paid to do.

The move gets me into fourth place, and although I want to move up a few more spots, time runs out and I finish the race there. I am not just happy with the way I ran; I'm overwhelmed.

"We're in the *Daytona 500!!!*" I scream into the radio as I come across the finish line. "We're in the *Daytona fucking 500!*"

You just can't grasp what a great feeling it is. Not just an entire winter of working and worrying—it's a lifelong dream for me and my crew. It's like the weight is lifted off my shoulders, just like that, in a single moment. We are in the race. Mission accomplished!

The crew is just as happy as I am, and everybody is celebrating when I get the car back to the garage. I'm the top-qualifying rookie out of seven other rookies who'll be starting the race on Sunday. I'll be in the outside position in the fourth row, starting eighth overall. Matt Kenseth will start behind me in the twenty-fourth position. I'm happy that he made it safely as well.

I'm so happy, but I'm also relieved. I've been trying to stay cool this week and remain unfazed by all the attention and everything that surrounds this race. Sometimes I even got a little sick to my stomach before practice because I was so nervous about qualifying. I just didn't want to hurt the car or smash it up today. Thankfully, I'm in the Daytona 500!

The starting grid is set for Sunday's race. But this doesn't mean that Friday and Saturday are quiet. There aren't any of those days during Speedweeks. It's flat out the whole time. That's part of what makes it special. On Friday we run practice laps, trying to get the car set up just perfect for the race. I also run in the first race of the International Race of Champions (IROC) series.

The IROC is a series of four 100-mile races with twelve identical cars. It is designed to find the ultimate champion among drivers from different racing series. It started out with drivers from all disciplines running on different tracks. Now, though, there are usually a couple of Indy car drivers in the field, but it's mostly NASCAR drivers, and the races are on the big ovals during Winston Cup weekends. The field has changed but the racing is still . . . well, the best word to describe it is "insane."

And a lot of fun. There's no pressure in thinking about how you stand in the points for the season or if your sponsor will be pissed off if you make a wild-ass move that fails. You can just go out on the track and have fun, beat and bang, and let it all hang out. It's like driving a go-kart against your buddies.

Even though I'm in Winston Cup, I'll be racing in IROC this season as the 1999 Busch Series champion. Last year I ran the series as the 1998 Busch champ—and people still talk about the race we had at Michigan. It came down to the last lap between my father and me—

Big E and Little E side by side, banging fenders all the way across the finish line. I had him beat, but his fishing buddy, Rusty Wallace, came up at the end and gave him a big push. They're big rivals when there's Winston Cup points on the line, but that day they were like ol' buddies. It was a photo finish and they wound up calling my father the winner by a coat of paint. When we goof around, we still argue about it. It was one of the most exciting and fun races we ever ran in. The race was only one hundred miles, but I don't think I've ever felt so drained after a race. It was incredible.

This race starts out like it might be more of the same. I get out in front of the other eleven guys and I lead for a few laps with my father trying to get by and the two of us swapping a little paint. Near the end of the race, I just miss getting taken out when Indy Racing League (IRL) driver Greg Ray gets sideways and causes me to lose a whole lot of ground to the field. I start working my way up toward the front but the race ends with me running fifth. Dad takes the checkered flag. One more victory for the winningest driver in IROC history. And one more for the winningest driver in Daytona history.

I get out of my car and run over to Victory Lane so I can congratulate him. We hug each other and pose for pictures with him holding the trophy. My father sees Bill France Jr. sitting off to the side of the stage, where people won't notice him. France is the son of the founder of NASCAR, Big Bill France, the man who made all of this possible. Big Bill took the Daytona race from an event that was run on a track that was half on the highway and half on the beach to what it is today. Big Bill turned over the reins of NASCAR to his son, Bill Jr., who has masterminded NASCAR's growth since the 1970s. When my father sees Bill Jr., he stops the Victory Lane activities and goes over to sit with him. France, who is battling cancer, manages a smile when Dad hands him the winner's trophy.

A little later, after I'm done with the television interviews, I check out my father's car and I find a scrape of paint on the back bumper. Dark green paint. My color. So I borrow a Sharpie from someone and draw a big circle around the scrape and write, "Hi Dad! Dale Jr." next to it in big letters.

Somebody asks me if I think he will be mad about the scrape.

"Naw," I say. "It's cool. We were racing for the lead at the time."

That gets a couple of laughs. In fact, the whole scene is pretty much like that, just some racing people hanging around the track, having fun.

But you can't ever forget that this is a serious business. Earlier in the day, there was a horrible crash that involved Geoffrey Bodine, one of the top drivers in Winston Cup for many years and one of Dad's main rivals. (Bodine was especially good when he was driving Winston Cup cars prepared by my grandpa Robert Gee, my mom's dad. He's not as famous as my other grandpa, Ralph Earnhardt, but he's still a legend in the garage.) Bodine was running in the NASCAR Craftsman Truck race when he got hit by another truck. He was on the front stretch at the time and the other truck just punted him into the air and up against the fence. He hit so hard, flames and debris went into the first rows of seats and injured some fans. Fortunately, none of them were severely hurt. Meanwhile, Bodine's truck cartwheeled and rolled down the track. The engine separated from the rest of the truck and finally came to a stop hundreds of feet from where the chassis ended up. It looked like a smoking pile of junk. Bodine has some broken bones and minor burns, but looking at the crash, you have to think he was lucky to get off that light.

Some of the worst-looking wrecks are the kind drivers survive. Sometimes they aren't injured at all. The car and the roll cage take all the damage, and the driver gets out and heads to the infield medical center—not because he's hurt but because the rules say he has to. The worst crashes are the ones where the car doesn't come apart. The parts and pieces that fly off help lessen the impact the driver absorbs. The cars have "crush zones" that are designed to collapse, dissipate energy, and protect the driver inside the protective cocoon of the seat and roll cages.

But a wreck like Bodine's is a horrible thing to see, and it makes you think. The IROC race was a lot of fun, but racing these cars at high speeds is still a serious business and you don't ever want to forget it.

Saturday, the day before the big race, is a strange day. I feel a mix of emotions. It's the last day of practice for the 500, so I'm thinking about all the final adjustments that we need to make to the car. It's also the day of the Busch Series NAPA 300. This is a great race, and it's kind of like an opening act before the headliner at a big concert. For the last two years, I was the Busch champion and there is a big part of me that really misses being out there. But the man who owns the team I'm driving for says he wants me to skip the Busch races so I can concentrate fully on Winston Cup.

Dad told me I need to "worry about red, not blue." Red is the predominant color for Budweiser, while blue is the color of Busch. I figure he knows what he's talking about, so when the race starts, I'm in the Budweiser hospitality suite, high up over the front straightaway, meeting and greeting VIPs.

When they announce the starting field, I stare down at the track like a kid looking through the fence at a field where his best buddies are playing ball. It's like I moved away from a school that I really liked. I know I'll learn to like my new school, but right now I sure miss my old friends down there having fun. Matt Kenseth is running in some of the Busch races this year, including this race. Matt runs a good race and wins it. This makes me wish that much more I'd been down there running with him. It has to be a big boost to his confidence going into tomorrow's race. I'm envious as hell.


I'm gonna see my first Daytona 500 from the outside of the fourth row. That's my first thought when I wake up in the morning.

Several hours before each race, NASCAR holds a mandatory meeting for all of the drivers and crew chiefs to go over the details of today's event. (If a driver misses one of these meetings, he loses his starting position and has to start from last place.) I'm excited about the day, so I hop out of the motor coach looking stylish in some freshly pressed khakis and my favorite brown suede jacket. Stylin'!

"Let's go," I say to my publicist as we begin the walk to the garage area for the meeting. When I'm pumped up, I just wanna get there without delays or distractions.

As I walk toward the garage, there are more fans than I've ever seen waiting for the drivers to arrive at the meeting. The Daytona 500 is like the Kentucky Derby—even if you are not a devoted fan, it's *the* place to see and be seen. I speed up my pace, and Jade is forced to become more of a bodyguard than a publicity dude. He sucks at the bodyguard part, but he's still new and he promised me he's working on it. He's too damn nice, so it's hard for him to be the hard-ass that yells at people to get the hell outta the way.

"Let him walk!" is his theme, screamed loudly above the fans' shouts of "Dale!" . . . "Junior!" . . . "Sign this! Sign this!" "One more! Just one more!"

"Stand to one side or the other, please!" Jade yells with little or no impact. "Walk with us! Please don't stop in front of him! Let him walk. *Please!* One side or the other! Let him walk! He has to get to the drivers' meeting!"

I sign as many as I can, as fast as I can, but I feel like a slow-moving ship with raging seas around me. The swirling crowd of people surrounds me, thrusting their souvenirs in my direction, each fan yelling my name and hoping that I choose their item from among the many others being pushed at me. The crowd only seems to bring more and more people into the scrum, like lemmings into the sea. They see the commotion from a distance and decide they have to join in as well to try and get an autograph. Often the crowd becomes so big, no one can see who is in the center of the mess. "Is that Gordon?" they ask, craning their necks. "Earnhardt?" "It may be Junior? Is that him? Who is it? *Juniorrrrrrrrrrrrrr!*"

Some fans come equipped with huge bags or boxes full of souvenirs from nearly every driver—just in case. We call these folks the Bag People. As they see a driver approach, they reach for their stockpile, yelling at their companion in a frenzied, high-pitched squeal. "Hurry it up, honey! It's Ricky Craven! Hurry! He's getting away! C'mon! C'mon! Get his 1995 trading card out! I know it's there *somewhere*! Hurry! Hurry!"

While the rush of fans can be exhilarating (and I do enjoy the attention at times), it can also be intimidating. Just like at the mall a few nights ago, I have to keep moving, especially when the shoving begins. Most fans carry their own Sharpies with the top opened—poised for easy signing. This is a problem today, as several overzealous fans mark all over my suede jacket.

Once we fight our way into the relative calm of the garage, I curse at Jade even though it's not his fault. "Damn, man! Look at this shit on my jacket," I tell him, pointing at the stray, permanent black marks across the suede. So much for my favorite jacket.

Rookie Lesson Number One: Don't wear your really cool clothing to the drivers' meeting.

While I'm in the meeting, the crew swarms over the Bud car like a team of surgeons in the operating room. Following Saturday's final practice session, they began checking every piece of the car. They replace many key parts with brand new components, while tightening and retightening every screw, bolt, nut, and fastener. On race morning, they double- and triple-check each part, marking each step off of a 150-item prerace checklist. With millions of dollars on the line, something as simple as a loose bolt or the failure of a ten-cent part can cause a race-ending failure or, even worse, a huge crash.

No detail is ignored. As an example, one crew member takes a pink Day-Glo marker and draws bright lines on each wheel spindle—pointing directly to the five bolts that hold each wheel to the car. This makes it visually easier for the tire changers to loosen and then tighten the lug nuts on each pit stop. A typical pit stop for four new tires and up to twenty-two gallons of racing fuel takes less than sixteen seconds. A good stop is less than fifteen seconds. A mistake that costs the team one second during a pit stop translates to a distance of more than one hundred yards on the racetrack at top speed. Anyone who says that racing is not a team sport has never spent a morning in the garage or watched a pit stop up close.

When the car is finally ready for action, they push the shimmering waxed red machine through the final inspection line, where NASCAR officials confirm that the car meets a long list of regulations. We call the inspection garage the Room of Doom. If the car passes inspection, it is pushed gingerly to the pit lane like a newborn being wheeled into the nursery. The team rolls it into its place on the starting grid along pit lane. Forty-three cars will start today's race, lined up two-by-two. My car will start in eighth position.

•   •   •

The hour prior to the start of any race is electric: everyone's nerves are on edge, and each of us still believes that he is going to win the race. Once the green flag falls, a huge dose of reality may be dealt to many of us, but for now, nervous, jittery optimism reigns supreme. The crowd begins to fill each of the 170,000 seats in the gigantic complex; thousands more will watch from the infield from atop their own recreational vehicles. The infield at most NASCAR events is like a campground with a full-time spring-break tailgate party mixed with standing-room-only viewing. The Speedway is more than a sports arena; it becomes a medium-sized city on race day. The complex covers more than 480 acres, with a 44-acre lake in the infield.

After the drivers' meeting, I slip into the team transporter to change into my work uniform. The uniform (red with black stripes, just like my race car) is equal parts fireproof safety shield/embroidered sponsor billboard (logos cover the chest, collar, sleeves, back, and even the Velcro-equipped "belt")/formfitting jumpsuit. (The ladies say the suit looks sexy. Something about the way it makes my butt look. I pretend that that embarrasses me.)

I lace up my custom, thin-soled driving shoes with the silver coating like a space suit. The coating prevents my heels and the soles of my feet from being broiled by the heat of the 750-horsepower engine. The final piece of the uniform is a Budweiser hat. While the hat is a sharp-looking new design, I'm just not happy with the comfort.

"It feels like I'm wearing a damn cardboard box on my head," I complain to no one in particular. But I have to show the logo of the company that writes the biggest check and makes it financially possible for me to do what I love to do.

My helmet, goggles, and fireproof gloves already rest inside the race car, awaiting my arrival.

When the race starts, Dad and I will join four other father/son combinations to race together in the 500 since it began in 1959. The others—legends all—were Lee and Richard Petty, Richard and Kyle Petty, Buck and Buddy Baker, and Bobby and Davey Allison.

After I'm introduced, I stroll to the car and begin the intricate process of strapping myself into my office. The world now moves in slow motion. Everything is quiet. I'm focused totally on the job ahead and I'm oblivious to the colorful prerace activities. National anthem. Prayer. Military jet fly-over. Crazed cheers from the stands. I don't notice any of it today.

I kneel down to strap on additional heel protection, a soft pad that insulates my feet in addition to the silver shoes. The floor of the car transfers much of the heat that is rushing through the exhaust pipes that run underneath my ass. The cockpit air temperatures can reach to 140 degrees Fahrenheit or more. How's that for working conditions for the next four hours?

I lift my right leg and slide through the driver's-side window (no such thing as an opening door on these hand-built machines) and into a seat crafted for my support, safety, and comfort. Driver comfort is essential when you have to drive five hundred miles without a restroom break or a chance to stretch your legs. The Budweiser cap comes off, and I slide it down the gearshift knob. It will ride along with me until the race ends. I can grab it and put it on quickly when I jump out. I put my custom-designed sunglasses in their own holder on what would be the passenger side of a street car.

I strap myself in with the help of Brian Cram, the crew member responsible for my comfort and safety. The seat belt is much more than a simple lap belt and shoulder harness. It is a five-belted system that wraps through the seat, with one harness over each shoulder, one across each side of my torso, and the fifth coming up between my legs (the "crotch belt") to prevent me from sliding forward out of the harness in a head-on collision. All five belts meet in the middle near the center of my belly, connecting with a deceptively simple latch. The connector is designed with a quick-release latch just in case I need to make a quick exit. Once I'm fully strapped into this harness, I feel as if I'm part of the car—almost as if I'm the heart and brains of this machine.

Communication is essential once the race is under way, and I will talk with every member of the team and my spotter via a two-way radio system. (The spotter is usually located somewhere high above the circuit with a clear view of the entire track. He helps me keep track of the traffic and avoid accidents.) To block out the extreme noise, I use form-fitted earpieces. I put them in before I slide on my old-school–style bubble goggles, just like Dad wears. The day is bright and sunny, so I choose goggles with a dark lens. Then the open-faced helmet goes on (also old school). It's painted with some cool-as-hell skulls and eight balls. It's badass! The radio is connected to a cable and microphone on the right side of the helmet, my chinstrap is secured, and I'm ready.

"Gentlemen . . . start your engines!!"

The huge crowd roars, drowning out forty-three rumbling, snarling engines as we roll down the pit lane. At the end of five hundred miles, forty-two drivers will come back losers, and one driver will place his name into racing history as the winner of the 2000 Daytona 500. I'm usually pretty calm once I'm inside the car, but today I'm unbelievably anxious.

Waiting. Waiting. Waiting.

The slow pace laps seem to take forever, just like the rest of the buildup to this season. Then, *finally*! The green flag is waved by honorary starter Jackie Joyner-Kersee, a track-and-field star and new NASCAR team owner.

Once the race starts, it's like a hyper rush replaces the slow-motion buildup. It's as if it's happening with the fast-forward button mashed down hard on your VCR. Guys jockey for position, and I'm pretty happy to leap into the top five, working in the lead draft, using the cars ahead of me to slice through the air. The wind is swirling much stronger today than at any time during the month, which makes the cars do things that they haven't done before. It's disturbing to the car and the driver, but the conditions are the same for everyone, so you get used to it.

The entire pack of cars seems to be running in one large lump, almost as if they are connected by one big tow chain—the first-place car towing the others behind. Things quickly become tense and the traffic around me goes to two- and three-wide, everyone dicing hard for position.

I really don't say anything on the radio for the first twenty laps or so, as I'm just trying to comprehend everything around me. Dean Middlemiss, my spotter, is doing his best to help me move through traffic. He says, "Outside . . . outside . . . ." when another car is running on the right side of my car, or "Inside . . . inside . . ." when there is one on the left. Sometimes he says, "Three-wide, you're in the middle . . ." when it gets really hairy.

The spotter keeps his eye on the action ahead. When the cars are running in large bunches so close together on the high-banked turns, it is impossible for me to see beyond my own bumper, so the spotter is a necessary second set of eyes. He is also an amateur psychiatrist, helping me balance my emotions. The rapport between the two of us is critical to a smooth race.

Many fans bring their own scanners and listen in to the radio chatter between the drivers, teams, and spotters. It really gives them a much better insight into the race. It's like eavesdropping on the huddle in football.

However, the 2.5-mile oval is a huge track, and my spotter becomes confused when the several similar-looking red cars run close together. Several times he calls out commands while watching the wrong red car. It sounds like the tension of the biggest race of the year has gotten to him.

"What the fuck are you doing, man?" I scream into the radio when I narrowly avoid making some serious contact with several other cars. "What car are you watching? You're gonna get me killed out here! . . ."

I calm down, and as the race progresses, my confidence grows with each lap. I declare some new goals near the halfway point of the race. "Guys, I am so happy to make this race, but my goals have kind of changed. We can race at the front. We gotta shot here."

As the race continues, I make contact with other cars several times—it's part of the game when you're running so close together—but I'm being raced hardest and treated roughest by the man in the No. 3 car—my car owner. I end up with a few "donuts" on the side of my car—black circles left on the sheet metal when another car's tire rubs against it.

Rookie Lesson Number Two: Don't mess with Dad.

As we pass three hundred miles, I struggle a little bit and drop as low as fourteenth position. I'm fighting with a race car that doesn't want to turn into the corners. When a car is "tight," the front end of the car resists turning into the corner, so I have to let off the throttle earlier than usual in order to get the front tires to turn. We need to make a change to the air pressure in the tires during the next pit stop to help correct the situation.

In addition to an ill-handling car, my aggressive style is no longer working as well as the race gets close to the final one hundred miles. Superspeedway racing requires teamwork of sorts, as cars work best when running with two or three cars nose-to-tail to better slice through the wind. It begins to look like I'm running out of dancing partners. It seems no one wants to race with a rookie.

The key moment comes on Lap 156 (of 200) when a yellow flag flies, slowing the action and sending all of the teams to pit lane. My crew chief, Tony Eury, who happens to be my uncle and the man in charge of our pit strategy, makes a bold decision.

"Two tires! Two tires only, guys!" he screams into the

radio as I roll down pit lane. He hopes that the two new tires will correct the tight-handling race car.

However, it's a gamble because even though we make our pit stop much quicker and gain a few positions, cars with four fresh tires are almost always faster than cars with just two new tires.

We restart the race in second place. In our first Daytona 500, we have victory in sight with less than one hundred miles to go. Could it be this easy? I take a deep breath and tighten the shoulder harnesses.

When the green flag falls, I am right behind the leader, Johnny Benson (who is in a strange-looking all-white car with sponsor decals that look like they were put on just this morning. It turns out that they had signed a new sponsor the night before the race). Before we are even back at top speed, Mark Martin dives inside of me, making it three-wide, and I'm shuffled backwards like a stone through water.

Shit.

From that moment on, I feel more like a pinball than a race driver. I can't find drafting help from anyone in the final laps, even from my dad! He and I bump and bang and it's like we're both trying too hard to beat the other. It doesn't work for anyone except the guys passing me. I am shuffled, bumped, and pushed around. I drop spot by spot helplessly until settling into thirteenth place on the final lap. Despite running among the leaders all day, many spots ahead of all the other rookies, the final laps drop-kick us behind Kenseth, who gets a late-race push to finish tenth. He is the top rookie finisher. Score round one for Matt.

Dale Jarrett, who won the Bud Pole and the Bud

Shootout last weekend, grabs the clean sweep by taking his third Daytona 500 victory. Jeff Burton is second, followed by Bill Elliott in third.

Dad was shuffled back after contact with the wall late in the race, falling all the way to twenty-first. It is the first time that I've finished a Winston Cup race ahead of him, and he is not happy with his finish or with his son. And he tells the media. Loudly.

"He didn't work with anybody," he grumbles about me as soon as he is out of the car. "He wanted to pass. That's all he wanted to do, so that's why he finished where he did."

I pull into the garage and hop out to find a huge crush of media pushing to talk about my scrapes and bumps with the Intimidator.

"I had some fun racing with everyone, and with my dad," I say. "He was damn tough on me—tougher than anybody—no help at all! I was hoping we could work together in the draft more, but I had to fight for everything when he was racing with me. My car has some dents on it, and I tell ya it wasn't my preference to have been near some of those dicey moves near the end of the race. Everyone just got real antsy there and it got insane with people crashing and goin' everywhere.

"When the 88 car [eventual winner Jarrett] came up through there [with less than forty laps to go], he was a lot faster than me, but I would have appreciated it if he would have helped me out a little bit," I say naively. "My dad too. I thought he would be the first one to help me, but he was the last person who wanted to stay behind me. I wanted to stay with him and behind him.

Everybody got to racing behind me, and it was either pass or be passed."

I guess my frustration and impatience cost us some positions on the track. All day I tried to be patient, but I just kept thinking, *Get outta the way! Get outta the way!* I wanted to pass those guys, but it just doesn't work like that. I wanted to get to the front so bad, but on a track like Daytona, you just can't do it on your own, you need someone to help you.

I'm pretty happy overall but of course I'm not going to be truly happy unless I win. I'm not happy to finish thirteenth, but I have to say I had a good week and the team met some high expectations. We finished on the lead lap and ran with the lead draft for most of the day. And despite my disappointment at falling behind Matt Kenseth at the finish, I'm glad he got a top-ten finish.

The Daytona Speedweeks are now over, and the adrenaline rush that has sustained me is now gone. It feels like a hangover as all of the drivers, crews, and thousands of fans head back home. Next week, the normal, week-after-week-after-week NASCAR Winston Cup grind continues. Thirty-four events in the next thirty-nine weeks lie ahead like some sort of endless marathon.

# Mooresville, North Carolina

## There's No Place Like Home

Mooresville, North Carolina, is a twenty-five-mile drive north of Charlotte along Interstate 77. In cultural terms, it may as well sit fifty years away.

Charlotte is the sleek, modern business and cultural hub of the Carolinas, whereas Mooresville is a quiet town of seventeen thousand residents that is an echo of a distant America. The local radio station, WHIP-AM 1350, plays golden oldies, and if you close your eyes, it sounds just like it did back in the 1950s.

After Daytona—and after every race when my schedule allows—I head back to Mooresville. It is my home and I love it. The Mooresville Chamber of Commerce calls the town Race City USA, referring to the growing number of racing-related shops and businesses that are located here. The biggest one, the one I work for, is the one owned and operated by my dad and stepmom, Teresa. Dale Earnhardt Incorporated is a huge complex that has grown from a simple farmhouse into a modern race shop, museum, office building, and souvenir store.

Steve Crisp, my right-hand man, likes to say, "You can't swing a dead cat in this town without hitting a race shop." NASCAR is everywhere. From the race shops to the big houses that successful drivers have built along the shore of Lake Norman, affectionately known as the Redneck Riviera.

In the midst of all this, Mooresville is a great place to be. Small towns suffer what I have heard called brain drain—where teens grow up in a sleepy lil' town, then move away to college or move to the big city for a high-paying, high-tech job or some other turn-of-the-millennium career path. Some of my friends did that too, but not me. I like it here. Mooresville is an old-school small town and a lot like Mayberry, North Carolina, the fictional town where *The Andy Griffith Show* took place.

In Mooresville, the main street is called, well, Main Street. You can eat pizza downtown at a place called Pie-in-the-Sky, or you can get a hamburger in your car at a genuine drive-in restaurant called What-A-Burger. There is a place outside of town called the Coddle Creek Country Store with a sign out front that says, *Come on in, I need your money.*

Then, just past the Country Store, on a 350-acre plot of ground, there is this complex of low-slung, sprawling, mirror-windowed buildings known as DEI. When you first see it, you think it must be a mirage. Darrell Waltrip, who won the Winston Cup three times before he retired and went into broadcasting, calls the complex the Garage Mahal. It's that unbelievable.

It is hard to believe, even if you grew up here like I did, just how big DEI is. There are other race shops within the region that are similar, but this was the first of its kind. When Dad began, he worked out of a tiny garage behind his mom and dad's house, and now you walk through the various areas of DEI thinking, *I could eat off this floor.* This is *not* your father's backyard garage. There are no oil spills or random tools lying around. This is a state-of-the-art facility where there aren't any shade-tree mechanics.

There is a high-tech engine shop where experts like Richie Gilmore urge the last bit of gut-pounding horse-power out of each and every good ol' American Chevro-let V8 racing engine. For the 2000 season, the complex houses the complete shops for my team, the No. 1 Pennzoil team for whom Steve Park drives, a Busch Series team with Ron Hornaday driving, plus a full body shop where the Monte Carlo bodies are crafted and fab-ricated by hand, one thin sheet-metal panel at a time to strict aerodynamic specifications.

The shop looks more like NASA than anything else, and there seems to be no piece missing that could im-prove the performance of the DEI race cars (at least not within the restrictive NASCAR rules and regulations).

DEI isn't just for testing, building, and working on cars. There are offices, conference rooms, a museum, an auto showroom, a gift shop, and an executive dining room (known as the Trophy Room) with big, heavy fur-niture and rich, dark paneling just like you would expect to find at an investment banking firm. But that's the kind of money that my dad—and NASCAR—has generated. (There's a line you hear around here: "How fast you go depends on how much money you got.")

NASCAR is rich because it is popular—not the other way around. NASCAR hasn't outgrown Mooresville, even if DEI and the Garage Mahal make it look that way. And, I suppose, you could say the same for me. This is home. I'm from here and I can't imagine living anyplace else. My roots are here. My friends are here in the place we call Dirty Mo. My house is just a short ride down the road from DEI.

But the house, like me, probably isn't what you expect. There used to be (and maybe there still is) a stereotype of the NASCAR driver—a tobacco-chewin' good ol' boy who likes to hunt and fish and listen to country music. A throwback Southerner who is not too tolerant of others (especially of different races) and who still flies the rebel flag on his truck.

Well, that stereotype doesn't fit anymore, especially if I have anything to do with it.

My small house is equipped with the latest and loudest big-screen televisions, video games, a computer room, and a basement that has been made into a full-scale nightclub, complete with a sound system, dance floor, drum set, and—to top it off—a cooler that will keep up to eleven cases of beer cold at all times. We call it Club E.

My idea of fun is to party with some friends and sleep late. I like surfing the Internet, playing computer games, and hanging out at the mall. I like whatever is the newest, the latest, the loudest, the *coolest*. What I am, I guess, is a normal guy who wants to stay that way. I like to drive around town, listening to music—everything from rap to alternative to Elvis or Merle Haggard. It might even be something like Fleetwood Mac that I remember my mother listening to on the car radio when I was little. I love music and I can't imagine my life without it. I have more than five hundred CDs in my ever-growing collection.

Being normal, being able to go out in town, go to the movies, or cruise the mall is important to me. I don't want to get to be where I can't go out and do what I want to do. That's what happened to my dad. He got so famous that there are very few places he can go without being mobbed by fans. He won't even go to the grocery store. I don't want to get like that. I guess if all the people in Mooresville get used to seeing me at Wal-Mart at 3 A.M., then that's cool.

I'm a member of my own generation, but I never forget I am also the son of a racing legend and grandson of another famous racer, Ralph Earnhardt. Being the son and the grandson of these two tough guys definitely hasn't hurt my career. And you will *never* hear me complain about being brought up with the name Dale Earnhardt Jr. But don't for one minute believe that I had everything handed to me, though. If you knew my father, you would never think that.

I understand my grandfather was the same way. Ralph was a tough racer in a time when racing was a rough way to make a living regardless of how good you were. And he was good. He won the equivalent of today's Busch Series title in 1956, run mostly on short tracks in places like Monroe and Hickory in North Carolina, and Columbia and Greenville in South Carolina. He won more than 250 races, but the cash he took home was usually no more than $150 or $200. The other racers called him Ironheart because of his dedication and because he was always tougher than anyone. When NASCAR produced a list of the top fifty drivers during its first fifty years, Ralph Earnhardt was on the list.

My grandfather died of a heart attack in 1973, so I never knew him. But I know quite a lot from the stories everyone has told me. Especially from my grandmother Martha, who has an extensive photo collection, not to mention a photo of my dad every time he won a race. She's also doing the same thing to chronicle my racing career.

Racing actually brought my dad and my grandfather closer together. After Dad dropped out of school in the eighth grade to pursue racing, Grandpa wasn't pleased. But not long after, the two began working together. My grandfather worked on the engines, and Dad handled the chassis setups. With Dad driving, they began winning races on the short tracks. They say my grandfather was a man of few words, but one piece of advice he did give my father was, "Establish your territory." Anyone who has done business with my dad or even watched him drive knows he followed that advice.

After my grandfather died, Dad struggled to stay in racing while supporting his family, including his mom and his brothers and sisters. He worked at installing insulation and in a paper mill, even though he hated every single minute of it. But he needed the money. By this time he was already divorced from two wives—the second of which was my mother.

Luckily, Dad got his big break in 1978 when he got a chance to drive in the NASCAR Winston Cup race at Atlanta. His teammate was Dave Marcis, who would become a close friend. It was my father's ninth start in a Winston Cup race but the first time he'd been in a decent car. He ran hard and finished fourth. The next year, he won four poles and his first Winston Cup victory at Bristol, Tennessee. He was in the top ten in seventeen of twenty-seven starts and was named Rookie of the Year. The next year, he won the Winston Cup championship, his first of seven titles. He was awesome and fearless in those days—it seemed like he would win or crash trying.

At this time my sister Kelley and I were living with our mother, Brenda, after she divorced my father. My mom is the daughter of Robert Gee, a famous mechanic and fabricator who was considered one of the finest craftsmen ever. (Fortunately, I get my racing genes from more than one side of the family.) The three of us lived in a small old mill house with shitty wiring. One night the wiring caught fire and the house burned down. There wasn't enough money to rebuild it or buy another place, so Mom did the only thing she could do. She moved to Virginia to be near her family and sent my sister and me to live with our dad. Dad was on the road a lot, of course, and by then he was married to my stepmom, Teresa, who grew up as a part of the Houston racing family. Teresa is great and she helped raise Kelley and me while Dad was away racing most of the time. He was so focused on winning that even when he was at home between races, his mind was still at the racetrack instead of at home with us.

My mom and stepmom have been wonderful and I love them both very much. When I talk about either of them in interviews, I always feel like I should bring up the other so that I don't risk offending either of them. I would never want to upset them.

My childhood wasn't anything special. The Earnhardt name didn't carry any weight at school. Back then nobody cared too much about who Dale Earnhardt was, although sometimes I got teased on Monday if Dad did something like crash or run into another driver. I was a small kid, an Opie, only five foot four or five foot five until I graduated high school. I was shy and didn't have the greatest luck with girls. This is kind of funny considering the attention I get from women now. The way they carry on when I make appearances or sign autographs and the stuff they say about me—or to me—on the Internet still embarrasses me. I'm a lot taller now (the bio says an even six feet, so we'll go with that), but I know there's more to it than that, which is why I am always leery about their interest in me.

My racing career started when I was twelve years old. Dad thought racing a kart would be fun, so I got one and went out to set the world on fire. But karts don't have roll cages or seat belts, so most of the time I was being run over by or thrown off my own kart. After a few races, Dad decided that karts weren't safe enough (or maybe it was *me* that wasn't safe enough), and my karting career was over. (Though I did run a few national karting events in secret a few years later. Shhhhhh! I didn't want the family to find out!)

My half brother Kerry and I didn't meet until I was in my mid-teens. Dad and Kerry's mom didn't have the best relationship after their divorce, so it wasn't until Dad urged me to race at a local track that Kerry and I got to know each other. Kerry was going to race there as well, so I think this was Dad's way of making an introduction and helping us get closer and making up for those years we didn't know each other. Before I knew it, we decided to sell the go-kart for five hundred dollars and bought a

1979 Monte Carlo. We raced that car on local short tracks like Concord Speedway, with me behind the wheel one week and Kerry driving the next. We didn't have a lot of success but we certainly learned a lot—especially about how to repair crash damage.

Not long after, Kerry and I were able to start our own race teams, driving late-model stock cars. Even though I had my own car and my own unpaid crew, I also volunteered to be crew chief for my sister Kelley. Even though she shared the same last name, there were fewer people willing to help her work on the car or even offer her a few sponsor bucks here and there. Rumors still float around that Kelley was the most promising driver among the three of us, and I'm not afraid to say that, yes, Kelley was the best of us kids by far. She was tough as nails and did the most with little help or cash behind her. She's really a lot like Dad in and out of the race car—so stay outta her way. She decided to stop driving to go to college and became a top executive with Action Performance, Inc., the company that produces collectible souvenirs for Dad and me. (Now she works for my company, JR Motorsports.)

Eventually I reached a point where I was racing regularly, mostly at places like Myrtle Beach, where the parties and the fun off the track equaled the fun we had on the track. During this stretch of my career, I was a one-man team. I always drove my own equipment and did much of the work myself, so it's no surprise that I was only able to get three feature wins in more than one hundred races. In those days, fun was the key, and winning was a sort of freak, unexpected bonus.

I also went to Mitchell Community College (we called

it MIT for "Mitchell In Town") for two years and got an automotive degree and then I went to work at Dale Earnhardt Chevrolet in Newton, North Carolina. I was the fastest oil-change man they had. I really enjoyed it, and I had a clear idea that this was a much more realistic career path than driving a race car. I mean, I saw myself working my way up the ladder through the service department and having a good life. But being the owner's son didn't prevent me from getting my ass fired. The guy running the dealership asked us to stay after work for some meetings, and I was brave (or stupid) enough to ask if we would be paid for the overtime. When he told me there was no extra pay, I walked out. I told him I had other shit to do. He didn't agree with my point of view, so I was fired. But I still treasure those days and I take comfort that if this driving thing doesn't work out, I can always go back to being the fastest oil-change man in Newton.

Meanwhile, I was living with Kerry in a double-wide trailer (on the same land where my house now sits), and we were partying hard. We'd wake up some mornings and the doors would be missing off the hinges and shit like that. But even though I was partying and working, I was still driving and still learning how to be a racer. Most of all, I was still struggling.

Dad would come by the shop back in those days and watch me work on the car. The only time he would give me any advice was regarding the safety of the car. He was always making sure our roll cages and safety gear were done right. Other than that, I was on my own. He did let me work on my car in the "deer head shop" behind DEI. (It's called that because the walls of the entire shop are covered with the preserved heads of the animals Dad shot during his frequent hunting trips.) Anyway, he'd come by the deer head shop in the evening to relax and we'd get to spend time together.

He'd stop in and I'd be struggling with something on the car. I knew I wasn't doing it right. I knew that there was a better way of doing it and that he knew what it was. But he wouldn't tell me anything. Damn! That pissed me off. In the end, I think this was best for me because I learned from making my own mistakes. This helped me as I moved up into Winston Cup because things probably wouldn't have turned out the way they have if I'd come to depend on someone else, especially my dad, to fix things for me.

It was one of those times when I was working on the car that I gave him the nickname that stuck and eventually earned me my own nickname. I'm a big Elvis fan and I loved it that all his cronies would sit around and call him "E." You know, like "Hey, E, let's go get some dinner." Or "Hey, E, let's shoot some guns," and shit like that. So one night at the shop, when Dad came by and we were just having fun, I started calling him "E." Then it became Big E, because when he'd leave we'd all be saying, "Big E-go." Then, when I started finding some success, it seemed to make sense that people started calling me Little E, and the name stuck. (Now, some even call Kerry Middle E.)

One of things I admired most about Elvis Presley was the longevity of his career. He had a lot of setbacks but he always came back strong and always cooler than before. I think Dad is the same way—he's been at the very top of the sport for more than twenty years. Michael Jordan can't claim that and Tiger Woods has a ways to go before he even comes close.

I am anxious to see how my own career longevity plays out. Times seem different now than when Dad started. I guess I can't imagine still doing this when I'm nearing fifty years of age. I guess I'm like most twenty-five-year-olds beginning a new career. I'm dependent on my father in many ways, but at the same time I'm trying to emerge with my own distinct personality. Sometimes it's hard, because a lot of people expect me to be just like him. I understand that I carry my father's name and that I've chosen to follow his career path and that I'm employed by the race team he owns ("Dad, can I borrow the car? I promise not to drive over two hundred miles per hour. . . ."), but I'm my own person, and no matter what, I will never be Big E. But make no mistake, I'm proud to be a continuation of three generations of racing Earnhardts.

My Winston Cup car number is 8 (and it's not just *any* number 8—the numeral is a registered logo with an exact shape, angle, and drop-shadow). It's the same number used by Grandpa Ralph throughout his career, and even by Dad early in his Winston Cup career. But one day I hope people associate that number with me after I've won a few races and maybe a championship or two.

While I was racing my late-model team in 1996, DEI put together a car to give me a chance to drive one race at Myrtle Beach in the NASCAR Busch Series. The open spots are very limited. Not everyone who tries succeeds, but this was a great chance at a track I knew very well. I think I surprised everyone, including myself, by qualifying seventh. I did pretty well in the race too, finishing fourteenth, only one lap behind the winner.

The next year, I struggled to put together several Busch rides with a couple of low-budget teams and an old car that DEI had lying around. I got to run eight Busch races in 1997, including a high point of qualifying second at Bristol.

Not bad, but nothing to get too excited about.

My dad had a lot of success in the Busch Series as a driver and then as a team owner. In 1997 his Busch team won several races with Steve Park, a young driver from New York. Before that, my dad had a lot of wins running a limited schedule for many years, including winning the Daytona Busch race five straight years. For all of that time, his right-hand man was crew chief Tony Eury. Tony and Dad were longtime buddies, and they were so close that they even married sisters. (This is why Tony Eury Jr.—my current car chief—and I are cousins.) Uncle Tony is like a second father to me, and he also made sure Dad's Busch cars were always the fastest out on the track. When Dad decided to stop driving the few races each year in the Busch Series to concentrate fully on Winston Cup, Jeff Green was hired to drive for several years before Park was brought in and started winning races.

Park did so well that he was chosen as the driver for the first full-time Dale Earnhardt Inc. Winston Cup team. So, beginning in 1998, while Dad continued to drive for the team owned by his longtime friend Richard Childress, he raced against a team that he owned—a yellow Pennzoil-sponsored DEI car driven by Park.

This meant the seat in the Busch car was open. One

day Dad asked if I would like to drive it. I couldn't believe it! I was excited, but I was also worried. I mean, I hadn't really set the world on its ass, and now Dad wanted me to be the driver for a team that had been winning races for years. Talk about pressure. If the team struggled and didn't win, the fingers would be pointed straight at me, because the crew had proven they could prepare winning cars.

I couldn't pass up the chance, and from the start, we clicked. With Uncle Tony in charge of the crew and Cousin Tony Jr. making many of the decisions about how to set up the race car, we launched into the season.

In our first race at Daytona we qualified third and were in contention until I got into a bad crash and ended up flipping down the backstretch. Welcome to Daytona.

It took only six more races for everything to gel. I won my first Busch Series race at the fast new Texas Motor Speedway near Fort Worth. What a day, as I passed Joe Nemechek for the win with Dad talking to me on the radio throughout the race. He was so happy in the winner's circle I could hardly believe it. From then on, I wanted to keep winning just to see how happy it made him. I was relieved. I had proven I could win. I didn't have to worry about finger-pointing anymore.

After that, there was no stopping us. We won six more races that year, and I managed to survive the points battle with Kenseth to win the Busch Series championship. I became the first third-generation driver to win a major NASCAR title.

About the same time, there were rumblings of a possible second Winston Cup effort in the future at DEI. Soon it became known that Anheuser-Busch, which had a close business relationship with Dad for more than a decade, was interested in sponsoring a DEI Winston Cup car with me driving. Whoa! Did they know I'd only had one year of big-time racing?

Anheuser-Busch is a giant in American business, primarily with their Budweiser beer brand that has been the King of Beers for more than one hundred years. There were many similarities between the Busch family and my family. Just like the Earnhardts are to racing, the Busch family is to beer. The business has been handed down from one generation to the next.

Bud had been a sponsor for many years, but it seemed their Winston Cup sponsorship had lost its luster. A Bud-sponsored car had not been in the circle since 1994. They decided they had suffered for too many years without visiting Victory Lane, so in a brainstorming meeting at the corporate headquarters in St. Louis, they discussed removing themselves from their existing contract with Hendrick Motorsports. They had a good relationship with Hendrick, but they had become a part of a forgotten, unsuccessful third Hendrick team, while the two other teams were winning championships with Jeff Gordon and Terry Labonte.

The Bud image is built on pride and quality, and their deal was not working. They admired the way my dad approached anything that he was involved with, and they seemed to think I was showing some signs of being a good driver with my wins and the Busch Series point lead. They believed the combination of Dad's visibility and his track record of success mixed with my pedigree, youth, and energy would be the right combination to take them back to the top in Winston Cup racing.

August Busch IV, the top marketing man for Bud, who had watched his father grow Anheuser-Busch into a business powerhouse, said, "Let's go after Junior." So the sports marketing team, led by A-B vice president of sports marketing Tony Ponturo and group director Steve Uline, attempted the delicate negotiation of signing a multi-year sponsorship deal with DEI while at the same time continuing the Hendrick relationship for one more season.

So with time ticking and rumors beginning to fly about several other major sponsors that were courting my dad and me, a small team of Bud sports marketing staff traveled to Charlotte to open discussions with both Hendrick and DEI. They visited Hendrick for a sensitive meeting in the morning, getting permission to talk with DEI that afternoon.

"We are interested in sponsoring a DEI Winston Cup team with Dale Jr. behind the wheel," Ponturo explained in the DEI conference room. "We would like to be able to energize our customers and employees with a car that has a chance to win and run up front every week with a driver that we can promote. We've been missing the excitement and enthusiasm for several years, and we would like to schedule a meeting in St. Louis as soon as possible to put this deal together."

My dad's sponsorship guy for many years was Don Hawk, and it probably took him a millisecond to book the plane for a trip to St. Louis. He and the Bud people huddled in a conference room, and in one day they produced an agreement that Hawk brought back for my dad and Teresa to sign.

It's a deal. The King of Beers and the son of the Intimidator. A match made in heaven. The urgency from Budweiser was warranted, because the very next weekend at the track, one of the top executives at Burger King attended the race to speak with my dad to try to convince him that their company was a better match for his team and his son. But it was too late. I would not be Burger Boy, I would be the Bud Man.

Bud hoped that the entire combination would blend perfectly: huge support from the largest brewer in the world, complemented by my hipper, younger image that would reach a wide variety of twenty-somethings. Even if they didn't know about NASCAR or racing, I might be able to get publicity from magazines or television shows that no NASCAR driver had ever done before.

Soon after we signed the deal, Budweiser and DEI made a huge media announcement at the shop, complete with a full team of the Budweiser Clydesdales. And free beer too. I thought, *I can definitely get used to this!*

It was announced that we would do five races in a Budweiser car in the Winston Cup series in 1999 with the same team of guys that would also be trying to win a second straight Busch title.

Although we ran well at times in early 1999, we got off to a slow start in the Busch Series. Some whispered that the pressure of the five Winston Cup races had drained our focus, but once we got it rolling, we won our first race of the year at Dover in June and then ripped off two more wins right away. Three wins in a row put us into the point lead, and we didn't look back. We won a total of six races and our second Busch Series title in two years. In 1998 and 1999, we won thirteen races and more than $3 million in prize money and finished in the top five more than half the time.

We didn't do too badly in our five Cup races either. "Countdown to E Day" was a media promotion started by Bud to mark my debut at Charlotte. We ran both the Busch and Cup races that weekend, starting eighth and finishing sixteenth in the Coca-Cola 600. The rest of the races showed mixed results, but we finished tenth at Richmond and then led at Atlanta. Well . . . OK, we led only one lap, but we did lead.

Now here we are. Ready to move up to the big time, the Winston Cup series, with the biggest sports sponsor of them all, Budweiser. If this were basketball, imagine being the son of Michael Jordan and then becoming a number one draft pick (chosen by a team owned by your father) after winning two consecutive NCAA titles. Imagine the expectations of the fans and media as you joined the best league in the world. Because I will be surrounded by the same team, led by Tony and Tony Jr., that propelled me to the Busch titles, it is almost as if we are a starting five that won two college championships and are moving as a complete unit to the NBA level. We have a good relationship and a long history together, but we're entering a new world where everything is bigger, louder, and faster. Leave the old trophies home, because they mean nothing.

The college-to-pro transition also applies to the schedule. College players get used to eleven or twelve football games per year, but the NFL plays sixteen games plus the pre- and postseason. In basketball, the number goes from thirty-five games to more than eighty. In the Winston Cup series, there are thirty-four points-paying events plus two all-star races. While the Busch Series now has more than thirty races, most of those take place on Saturday, leaving Sunday as a day off nearly every week. In Winston Cup, a day off is a very rare thing once the season starts in early February and continues until the Sunday before Thanksgiving.

As the season approaches, I display almost a split personality, swinging wildly between supreme self-confidence and deep depths of self-doubt. My left foot is still planted in my youth—parties and playing with my buddies—while my right foot is planted hard on the gas pedal. I'm told I have a long career ahead of me with unlimited potential and possibility. I just want to keep my job by the end of the year.

It is a fear of failure that drives me. It's like a beast that haunts me. Perhaps this is why I am rarely alone, choosing to surround myself with friends and acquaintances as often as I can.

"C'mon in," I'll say. "Let's just hang for a while," as if the physical presence of my friends will keep away the demons.

Sometimes, when I'm out on the road, and the pressures of everything that goes with being a racer—the constant demand for autographs and media interviews and sponsor appearances and celebrity events and all the rest of it—start getting to me, I think about being back in Mooresville. Back home. It's where I can be myself and hang with my friends and let the other stuff just slide. That's why its so good to get back home after Daytona Speedweeks—even if it's just for a couple of days before we pack up and go racing again. We beat the demons at Daytona. Now we try again this week. This time in Rockingham. Fasten your seat belts; keep your hands inside the vehicle at all times. It's going to be one helluva rookie ride.

# Rockingham, North Carolina
## DuraLube 400

## Get a Grip

The fans call it the Rock. It is one of the oldest NASCAR tracks, and the original owners had to sell shares to the locals for a dollar to make it happen. The first race there was in 1965, when it was a flat track. Then, in 1969, they rebuilt it and made it a banked oval a little more than a mile long—1.017 miles if you keep track of those things.

The track is about two hours east of Charlotte, in the sand hill part of North Carolina. The wind blows the sand around until the surface of the track is literally sandblasted. This makes the surface rough and hard on tires. This part of North Carolina is more rural and blue collar than Charlotte, and you see it in the faces of fans. A lot of them have the look of hardworking, country people, and a lot of them look like they too are sandblasted. After the stress and never-ending hype at Daytona, it is a chance to buckle down and concentrate on nothing but racing.

The rough racing surface treats the Goodyear racing

tires like sandpaper across a soft eraser, making for some interesting racing. For several laps, fresh tires mean high speeds, but then the effects of the rough surface mean the tires and therefore the speeds dramatically go away. The result is a race based more on tire conservation than pure speed or aggressiveness. I hope the members of the Bud pit crew got a good night of rest prior to today's race, as we will likely make pit stops at nearly every yellow flag opportunity in order to keep fresh rubber under the car.

We're confident but . . . well, OK, maybe not totally confident. There are some doubts.

Last year, in the Busch race, we won the pole. But then we finished thirty-fifth in the race. I've never finished well here. But I finished better in Winston Cup at Daytona than I ever had in a Busch race there. After qualifying on Friday in the seventh position, I'm hoping I can keep that trend going. That's the way I'm thinking, anyway.

Early in the race, it looks like more of the same for me at the Rock. I'm okay for the first eighteen laps, but then there is a yellow and a lot of the cars behind us stop for fresh tires. We stay out, looking for track position and gambling that the cars that did pit will wear out their new tires fighting through the crowd to get back up front.

It works that way for a few laps, but then for eighty frustrating laps I drop back through the field helplessly. My tires are worn, so I'm not able to drive hard into the turns, especially when I try to fend off guys who have brand new tires. By the time we pit, I'm down to forty-third—running dead last.

I drop more than a lap behind and as Jeff Gordon

comes around the outside to lap me, my car gets really loose and I slide up the track into the side of his car. Both of us are able to gather it up and continue, but it's a close call.

A few laps later, Dad comes flying by. As he pulls alongside, I see him shaking his finger at me. I know he saw me run into Gordon, but at this point I'm not sure if he's being just another competitor saying "Stay the hell away from me," or if he's my car owner saying "Don't tear that car up," or if he's my dad telling me to "be smooth, be careful."

When you race against and for your dad, those lines are often blurred.

With fresh rubber, I start making my way back up to the front, passing the same cars that were passing me not too long ago. More than halfway through the race, I'm back up to twentieth when Dave Marcis hits me from behind and I come up with a bent rear wheel and have to pit again. With fifty laps to go, I'm twenty-ninth and charging like a mad bull. Trying to get as far forward as possible.

I make good progress again, and so does Dad. Like mine, his car is great on short runs but not so good on longer ones. We both sort of run out of laps when Bobby Labonte takes the checkered flag. The difference between Dad and me is that he is near the front and finishes second on a track where he's won three times, while I'm driving my ass off only to get to nineteenth. Frustrating, but it's still a top-twenty finish. One other bright spot is that we're the highest-finishing rookie team, which gives us the most points in the rookie battle today. We'll need to keep doing that all year to stay ahead of Matt and his team.

I learn a lot about how a Winston Cup car eats up tires on this track. Busch cars are lighter and underpowered and don't spin the tires as much, but a Winston car is heavier and more powerful and requires a different driving style. You can run hard for only a short time before the tires really lose grip. Imagine the car is a teeter-totter. When braking, the Cup car feels like it is falling forward twice as hard as the Busch car. Then, when you accelerate, the added power sends the teeter-totter backwards twice as hard. It's something that I have to learn as a driver and the team has to understand so we can be competitive for more than a few laps at a time.

But the car was just dynamite for the second half of the race. We fell back after the early yellow flag and then had to make an extra pit stop for the bent wheel. After we got new tires, man, we were able to run with any-body. (Of course, that applies to the other forty-two guys as well, I suppose.) Since this has never been one of our better tracks, I'm happy to come out of here with a top twenty and a car with all four fenders still attached.

Now it's on to Vegas next week. My kinda town. Talk about a complete change of scene. From coastal sand dunes to desert sand dunes all in one week. Bring on the lights.

# Las Vegas, Nevada
## CarsDirect.com 400

## Like a Rolling Stone

Two races into the season and we aren't doing too badly. But Tony Eury believes we should win the race every week—and that's the kind of thinking I like because it keeps the team pushing hard. I know it's still early—really early—but there's no getting away from the pressure. The team feels it and I feel it.

I also feel the pressure to impress my sponsors. In order to maintain their market dominance and to regain a hip and cool image, Budweiser wanted to try and attract young male adults. So if my personality or winning track record influences these guys and gets them to choose Budweiser, then the program is a success. If guys that drink beer see me on television or in a magazine or in person, and they feel like I'm a guy they'd wanna hang out with and have a beer with, then I'm doing my job. If the ladies see me, well, I suppose they'd want to have a beer with me as well. As long as it's Budweiser.

From the start, there was a plan to target media outlets

that appeal to males in the twenty-one-to-thirty-five age group. Several preliminary phone calls by my publicist to the *Rolling Stone* offices were met with a polite response but no commitment. So it was a big surprise when we got a call from the magazine after Rockingham saying they were doing an issue with a car theme and a writer would be in Charlotte on Wednesday to spend the rest of the week with me.

I couldn't believe it, and I was excited, but I also wasn't sure it was the right time. This was a once-in-a-lifetime deal. I didn't want to blow it by doing it too soon. *Rolling Stone* has a big audience and a lot of the people who read the magazine aren't familiar with me or with NASCAR. A positive story would be great for the program. But a negative story might be a disaster. The story could do wonders for my image, but it could also demolish it. It's risky. But just like when I got the offer to drive Dad's Busch car, I see no reason why I shouldn't go ahead and take the chance. And besides, man, it's *Rolling Stone*. It's almost too much. My first Daytona 500 and then, less than a month later, an article about me in one of my favorite magazines.

*Rolling Stone* sent one of its top feature writers, a guy named Touré. He has written profiles of musicians and celebrities like D'Angelo and No Doubt, but he knows nothing about NASCAR. But he's eager to learn. So right away we take him on a tour of the DEI facility to get him up to speed. Like everyone who sees the complex, he is impressed. What really gets him is seeing the way we build the cars by hand.

"You mean these don't start off as real Monte Carlos?" he asks, eyes wide. And he is knocked out when he sees that the headlights and taillights on the cars, that look so real, are just decals. You don't need lights to race, I explain to him, and he seems to really understand each item we show him.

When the tour is complete, it's on to my house, where I show him the cars I drive and the stereos and computers. Then I take him down to Club E, where we relax and kick back. We talk about all kinds of things, from cars to music, and it's like we've known each other for years. There are some good journalists that cover racing, but this is the first time I've been able to sit down with one who is the same age and enjoys a lot of the same shit that I do. Every forty-five minutes or so, he flips the tape in his recorder or puts in a blank one so we can keep going. He fills a box of those things before the week is out.

Touré shows up in Mooresville on Wednesday, and the next day we fly off to Las Vegas, where we'll be racing this weekend. Thursday night is the grand opening of the Las Vegas NASCAR Café, an operation that is a lot like the Hard Rock Café or Planet Hollywood. Instead of some rock star's underwear or guitar, the NASCAR Café sports some wicked driving suits and other memorabilia. For tonight's grand opening, there's a red carpet entrance for the drivers in front of the club and the usual crowd of fans who have come to get a look at their favorite personalities and maybe get an autograph.

Touré and I go in through a back entrance and we're escorted upstairs to the VIP seating area. Dad is there too, and even though I don't think he's ever read the magazine, he knows what a big deal the *Rolling Stone* thing is to me. So when he sees Touré with me, he throws an arm around his neck. It's his trademark embrace. My father isn't especially big, but when he throws that arm around your neck, you feel like you are completely enveloped. For someone who doesn't know my father—even for some people who do—it can be intimidating as hell.

"I hear you're writing about my boy," he says to Touré with his trademark smile as if he's teasing someone. He pulls Touré close and whispers a subtle threat. "Write good stuff about my boy, all right?"

He laughs, releases Touré, and goes on to his next stop.

After a while, it is my turn to be introduced to the crowd. I'm escorted out of the back of the restaurant and into a limo. Even though I arrived an hour ago in some cheap-ass rental car, the limo circles around to the front so it looks like we just pulled up and I can make the grand entrance on the red carpet. This is Las Vegas–style cool: a long red carpet complete with blaring music, spotlights, and screaming fans. Somebody has given me a beige shirt to wear with the NASCAR Café logo on the chest.

"My big Hollywood fashion moment," I say, "and I gotta wear *this* thing." But I put it on anyway for my walk down the carpet. While the fans crowd in, Touré interviews some of them. He wants to know what makes me so popular.

"He kicks ass," someone says.

"He's so hot," one girl adds.

Touré gets it all down on tape.

When the event is over, I ask him if he wants to head back to the speedway. We can talk in my motor coach. He's cool with that and when we get there, the stadium-style lights are still on and the track is brilliantly lit. It's quiet in a way that it almost never is once the event starts.

Touré has never seen a racetrack, and because I want him to understand what I do, I ask him if he'd like to walk around the track. This is my world and I want him to understand it and feel it. It's a mile and a half around the track and we walk in the quiet with him asking a few questions and me answering. I'm in a mood to talk and tell stories and try to explain who I am, which is good because a lot of what I say actually makes it into the finished story. Then, just as we come around the fourth turn, the lights go out. We keep walking in the dark, him asking the questions and me talking. A lot. And then we head back to the motor coach, where we stay for another couple of hours, and Touré keeps on filling up those tapes and putting them in the box. I guess I didn't know I had so much I wanted to say.

Now it's Friday morning and time to go to work. The No. 8 car is fast. Very fast. Everyone on the team is pumped and feeling optimistic about qualifying. We're hot in Vegas.

We're one of the first cars out for qualifying and rip off a lap that is quick enough for the track record. Damn! It feels good when the car is so nimble and so fast. Back in the pit, I tell the crew, "No matter where we end up in the final lineup, let's be thankful for that lap and this car. That was awesome."

Then it's high fives all around.

I'm still pumped, even after Ricky Rudd lays down an even quicker lap. I pull the top half of my uniform down to cool off, and I start down pit lane looking for Dad.

"I bet he asks me why Rudd beat me," I tell Touré.

When I do see Dad, leaning against his car waiting to qualify, he has already seen the No Fear T-shirt I'm wearing under my uniform. No Fear is a competitor of Chase Authentics, a company that makes a lot of the souvenir shirts and hats for my father and me. I usually don't wear any of it because a lot of it is pretty lame quality and not too cool. Before he says a word, Dad whips out a Sharpie and starts marking all over the No Fear logo. Then, just like I knew he would, he needles me, "Why weren't you first? How could you let Rudd beat you?"

When I don't answer right away, he keeps up the ribbing. "Tell me about that lap. What were you doing? How can I do that too?"

Just to keep up, I try to think of a smart-ass answer. "Run deep, brake hard, and then turn left."

Pretty fucking lame comeback.

Dad laughs, and the ends of his moustache curl up, the way I've seen them do a million times. Then he grabs Terry Labonte, one of the other veterans, and says, "Hey, Terry, c'mere and listen to this."

He makes me say it again, and this time I don't sound quite so sure of myself. They both laugh.

Before I leave, my dad gives me a pat on the shoulder. I know that's his way of offering an "attaboy." It tells me he's proud of me. I feel pretty good about it too.

At the end of the day, I have the third-fastest qualifying time. I still have a lot to learn about Winston Cup, especially long runs where I need to get better about protecting my tires. But I've got a good feeling and I really like my chances, especially since we had a good test here in the preseason.

The test session was a particularly special one for me. Big E had been suffering from the effects of a neck injury for several years, so at the end of the 1999 season, he opted to have surgery to repair the damage. He took some time off over the holidays and returned to the cockpit for the preseason test at Las Vegas.

Between the two of us, we share nine NASCAR titles. We also share the same name. But, until the test at Las Vegas, we had never shared our race cars.

I was fast from the very start, and Dad was trying to get his own car to match the speed we were showing. Dad just kind of ambled over during the test and asked to drive my car. Hell, he owns the team, so he didn't have to ask. In return, he was willing to let me fulfill a longtime dream by jumping into that black No. 3 Goodwrench car for a few fast laps.

"Man, I drove Big E's car!" I told Tony Jr. after I got out of the car. "It's been a dream of mine since I was ten years old playing with Matchbox cars. I always wanted to drive that black No. 3 car. That was pretty cool!"

It was fun, but really it was a chance for two drivers to give their opinions about each other's cars. Drivers don't really jump back and forth like that a lot, but I think we were able to give some good feedback to his team, and he helped my Bud guys with his comments. I mean, we're still a new team, so it may have taken us weeks to try something that he suggested in only a few laps.

It was fun for the crew guys as well to have their boss hop in the red Bud car. "We'll keep Dale Jr.!" joked one crew member (but only after Big E had walked out of earshot).

Word has gotten out since yesterday about Touré and the *Rolling Stone* deal. He has things pretty stirred up. The publicity reps for all the other teams are falling all over themselves, trying to get an introduction. Maybe they can get *their* driver and *their* sponsor mentioned in the magazine. They want to know why the magazine chose me instead of their driver. It's kind of funny.

What isn't funny is the way some people are reacting to the fact that Touré is from a magazine that doesn't normally cover NASCAR . . . and that he's African-American. They're worried because NASCAR is still trying to overcome the view that it is only a white man's game for the drivers and fans. Things seem to be improving all the time, but not fast enough for some, and the sport has taken some hits in the media and from sponsors for its lack of diversity. Some officials are concerned that this hip young writer might be here to do a hatchet job on NASCAR rather than write a positive personality profile of me. Everyone at NASCAR remembers what happened when John Rocker, the Atlanta Braves reliever, shot off his mouth about New York in *Sports Illustrated*. One NASCAR staffer even warns me to be careful about what I say. I've been talking to the man for almost a week about my love of hip-hop music and black culture and a thousand other things in the world, and she wants to tell me to be careful to avoid a "Rocker incident." She insists it's only because she's my friend and doesn't want me to get burned by the big-time media. If she knew me at all, she would have known a lot better. I've been around for a few years, winning races and championships, and it seems like some people still don't get who I am. It really pisses me off.

That woman, by the way, isn't with NASCAR anymore.

On Sunday, Las Vegas isn't the warm, sunny place it normally is. The weather turns cold and nasty with a real strong chance of rain, which changes everyone's thinking. The race is scheduled for five hundred miles, but it's considered an official race if it goes at least one lap past the halfway point. Teams are monitoring the weather and trying to decide whether to gamble on letting it all hang out early, in case the rains come and the race is shortened, or whether to play it safe for the long haul.

My goal is the same as always: go forward and race hard. When the race starts, we jump into the lead. It is the first time I've run out front for more than one lap in Winston Cup, and Touré is watching from the pit, getting it all for *Rolling Stone*. How cool is that?

After only twenty laps, I'm sailing along but the rains come in and the race is stopped. Rain delays are always tough but I think they're toughest early in the race and especially for the leader. All that adrenaline is flowing and, just like that, you have to stop and wait.

After the delay, the race restarts and I'm running in the top five until the tires start to wear down and I drop into the back half of the top ten. By the end of a long green-flag stretch, I'm down to tenth. We're planning on several changes, including tires, in the next pit stop that should make the car faster and improve it on long runs. But the team can't do anything about the weather, and when the rains come again, on Lap 148, the race is stopped again. It continues to rain and the race never restarts. Jeff Burton and his team seem to make a habit of winning rain-shortened races. Burton won the last two rain-shortened races, and he's first in this one too. He also won the Busch race on Saturday, so I guess it was just that kind of week-end for him. I hope he takes some of his luck to the casino tonight. I run tenth when the race is called. Our car is faster than that, but we just didn't make the necessary adjustments soon enough.

Still, it's our first top ten of the season and we led 41 of the 148 laps. It's satisfying but also frustrating at the same time. Now that we have shown we can run up front, we've gained some more confidence, but you keep thinking, *What if?*

Touré and I say our farewells. He's a great guy and it has been fun hanging with him. I feel like I have a new friend. Now I have to run to catch Dad's jet and fly back to North Carolina. Dad also ran well and finished eighth. The rest of the team will be along later, in a slower, larger prop plane. Tomorrow morning we start getting ready for Atlanta.

## Atlanta, Georgia
## Cracker Barrel 500

## No Brakes! I Have No Brakes!

The whole team has a good feeling when we unload the car at the Atlanta Motor Speedway on Friday morning for the Cracker Barrel 500. Atlanta is a big, fast track that's very similar to Las Vegas. We ran here last year in the final Winston Cup race of the season, and I led one lap and finished fourteenth. But even more important, we're familiar with the track, so we're not totally running in the dark. Because of the restrictions on engines and aerodynamics at Daytona and Talladega, the Atlanta track is the fastest on the entire circuit. Pushing the car hard into Turn 3 at the speeds we'll be going takes a lot of bravery or a lot of balls. It's one of those gut checks that take a while to get used to.

We use the same chassis that we used at Charlotte last season in the first Winston Cup race I ever ran. The chassis is the car's skeleton—an assortment of roll bars and structural components that you hang everything else on. Some teams give them names after a big race or a big win. But we don't. Tony Jr. says, "They gotta do something pretty special for us to name 'em."

So this is just chassis number one. Actually double-zero-one. Whatever it's called, it's real fast in morning practice. We run the fourth-fastest lap. That's good, but I'm not satisfied. In racing, you do so much with the latest technology, but you also do a lot by feel. The seat-of-the-pants feel. We're quick, but the car feels sluggish. Without hesitating, the crew yanks the engine out of the car and drops another one in. It's a risky move immediately before qualifying, but sometimes you have to go with your instincts.

Our instincts are right. The new engine is great, and I'm able to turn a blistering lap that wins the Bud Pole—for a while, anyway. There are still some cars that have to qualify, and Dale Jarrett rips off a faster lap than mine. But he's the only one. We have our first front-row starting position in Winston Cup, and for the fourth consecutive race we have set a new career-best starting position.

When Ricky Rudd struggles on his qualifying run, it makes us the only team to qualify in the top ten every race so far this season.

Everyone from Budweiser is happy, but they're also nervous because we're late, very late, for a scheduled photo shoot outside the track. It's a series of photos that will eventually become large Budweiser billboards. The photographer, the models, and the crew have been waiting all afternoon. There were rain and heavy clouds over the track all day, and the qualifying was pushed back two hours. You can't worry about things out of your control, and thankfully it works out beautifully when the sun suddenly breaks through in a brilliant, golden rush. I sit with some beautiful models in front of one of my race cars and act like we're having a great time over a beer at the end of the day. This is the fun part of the job, especially since it seems as if the models have forgotten their bras, which is all right with me.

It's been such a good day that when Denny Darnell of Winston comes by the coach to ask me if I'll be the featured guest at the media breakfast the next morning, I tell him yes, even though I'm not much of a morning person.

And sure enough, it turns heads when I arrive at the media center in the morning, not just on time, but early. The questions start immediately. You can spend a lot of time answering stupid questions, but if you're running good, it's a pleasure to answer the racing questions.

"How'd you feel about the top-ten finish at Las Vegas?" one guy hollers.

"I felt like we really had a good car last week. We're finding the equation that will put us in place to win. It's not just a case of hanging around in the top ten and then *pow*! there ya' go . . . It's something where we gotta be consistently at the front every week to get a win."

"How did it feel to lead the race at Vegas?"

"It was kick ass. That was the theme of our weekend—kick ass. [*Big laughs.*] We hung with the dude from *Rolling Stone* all week and then we ran well and led the race. It was great to get out there into the lead. The guys wanted me to be patient. I told them, 'The hell with savin' our tires, *we're leading*!' "

The next question is about a change in the car that NASCAR had allowed in the last week. A little tweak that gave us a two-inch addition to the front of the Monte Carlos to correct an aerodynamic disadvantage we'd had against the Fords and Pontiacs. Those things are always going on, little adjustments to keep the races competitive. They might not seem like much, especially to the naked eye, but they can make a difference on the track. Any change always creates an uproar from rival manufacturers and competitors.

"Yeah," I say, "I suppose it helped . . . somewhat."

The politics of a rules change is something I choose to stay out of. That's for experienced guys like my dad and Dale Jarrett to argue about. This is one area where it's good to be a rookie. Plus, I want all the credit for our speed to go directly to my crew—they prepared a great car with or without a rules change.

On Sunday morning, everyone on the team feels the growing confidence. We have a great car and a good chance to run up front again. The media has picked up on it and a lot of the prerace coverage is aimed our way, including a piece by ABC-TV, which is covering the race. We are racing with an in-car camera over my right shoulder (so that ABC can watch as I cruise around at more than 190 miles per hour), another camera on the roof, and a special sensor mounted on a rear wheel assembly that will show the speed of the car and other technical data during the race.

The wind is blowing hard at the start of the race. It blows right down the front straight, which puts additional air on the nose of the car as we dive into Turn 1. Since I know I have a fast car, I decide not to push it right into the lead but to wait and get a feel for how it handles in the wind—especially as it pushes us hard down the backstraight and into Turn 3.

We drop back to fifth, while Matt Kenseth is in the

lead. No sweat—I'm hanging back like a cat waiting to move in for the kill. After I'm comfortable with how the car handles, I start moving up, picking cars off one by one. I get by Kevin Lepage on the sixteenth lap, I'm leading the field, for the second consecutive week.

The car is running so good, and I'm so confident, that when Jerry Nadeau makes a move on me in Lap 20, I let him go by. I know I can get it back when I need to.

Then everybody in the pits and up in the stands sees the yellow flag come out. A car has clipped the wall in Turn 2.

"It's me," I say on the radio and the crew hears the disappointment in my voice. A car capable of winning is now junk.

The car had broken loose and I thought I had it saved. I went for the brakes, but the pedal went limp and the car slid into the wall.

As I come around to pit road, I let the guys know our problems are bigger than just some sheet metal damage.

"No brakes," I yell into the radio. "I have no brakes."

I can't stop at my pit stall and the car goes coasting by. I have to make another agonizingly slow lap before I head into pit lane again. This time, it's full of all the other cars and I can't stop without slamming into at least one of them, so I have to go around one more time. This all seems to take an hour, but the car finally stops with the help of a few brave Bud crew guys who leap out to help stop the coasting heap.

"What happened?" Tony Eury yells from the top of the pit box.

"I don't know. I went into the turn and it just snapped sideways. No brakes. The pedal just went to the floor."

"There's fluid all over the right rear," Randy Cox, the rear-tire changer, says.

Tony Jr. checks the damage on the right side.

"Looks like a brake line," he says. "There's a hole rubbed in it."

The green comes out again and the rest of the field races by while Tony Jr. crawls underneath to check the cut brake line. He finds that the sensor mounted for the TV data had worn a hole in the hose, causing fluid to leak onto the rear tires. When you get fluid on a racing slick, it's like a banana peel on a freshly waxed floor. That's what put me into the wall.

ABC reports this sheepishly and Budweiser executives (who had paid for the added exposure offered by the on-board cameras) are already on the phone saying there will never be sensors like that on the car again. Tony Eury is livid. He looks like he's ready to leap off his perch and tear the ass out of somebody, but who?

We get a new line on the car and I pump the pedal.

"The brakes are coming back," I tell Tony.

"Let's get gas and four tires on this son of a bitch," he says. His fast, gorgeous car has been reduced to a piece of junk by a strange piece mounted by someone who is not even on his crew. I know it must just drive him out of his mind, because he hates to put any camera gear on his cars. If he didn't build it or his crew didn't build it, get it the hell out of his car.

Meanwhile, back in Charlotte, DEI employee Billy Sutphin is watching the race on television. Billy is responsible for preparing that area of the car, and he's an example of the team spirit of DEI, because it is not just the men at the racetrack that have a sense of ownership, a piece of their lives riding every lap and every inch of the way with me. Every employee feels a connection. Sutphin is in agony, he feels like he might be responsible. Did he forget something or cause the failed brake line somehow?

"That was horseshit," he says later, relieved to learn it was not something he had done. "I'm watching the race on TV and worried about my job. It's a big relief to find out what caused it because I didn't know if I had a job Monday morning. But that didn't get those laps back."

We lose a lot of laps and any chance at winning. When I finally get back on the track I am forty-third, dead last, fifteen laps behind the leaders. The only thing left to do is just drive hard, finish as many laps as I can, and salvage some championship points from the day. Consistency pays off over the season and you don't gain many points for a DNF—Did Not Finish.

As I go by the crash location, lap after lap, the evidence of what happened is real plain.

"Where I hit the wall," I say on the radio to the guys in the pits, "there is only one tire mark. I had no rear brakes. So let's look at this as a long practice session and learn what we can for next time."

I try to keep my head, and the crew's head, in the race. It's one of the toughest things to do in a race car. Trying to stay pumped about pushing hard when I'm racing for fortieth or thirty-fifth sucks.

And the bad news keeps coming. The car has lost something. It just feels slow.

"I feel like an ol' lady in the fast lane," I bitch. It's good for a couple of laughs from the crew, at least.

But we keep working during every pit stop, and we

aren't the only team that's having problems. Other cars drop out or spend a long time in the pits. I keep picking up spots, and late in the race the car is running fast again. I go by sixteen cars in just twelve laps. I might be down a lap—or more—to these cars, but it still feels good to pass 'em so easily.

On Lap 261, Todd Bodine crashes and I barely miss getting into him because of some sloppy spotter work.

"Spotter," I spit, "just tell me when there's a fucking wreck, all right?"

I always try to be upbeat and supportive of the guys while I'm in the car, but I'm in no mood for jokes when I have to make a drastic move to avoid slamming into another car at 190 miles per hour.

By the end of the race, I'm only cruising, just trying to make up positions, while Dad is locked in a battle with Bobby Labonte for the lead. It is the kind of close, side-by-side, lap-after-lap racing that makes people love NASCAR.

There had been some complaining, especially in the media, that the races this season were boring—without enough lead changes and no close, exciting finishes. But they can't complain today. There are seventeen lead changes in all, and my father grabs the lead for the last time on Lap 306, with nineteen laps to go. Labonte, who had won four of the last seven races at Atlanta, waits for what he believes is the right moment to make his move. As the two cars come off Turn 4 on the last lap, Big E and Bobby are side by side, and stay that way to the finish line. The cars are so close at the line, no one knows who wins until the scoring computer spits out the details: the No. 3 by the tip of a nose (ironically, a nose lengthened by the NASCAR rule change this week).

Dad won it by 0.010 seconds in one of the closest finishes in NASCAR history.

Me? I'm twenty-ninth. For the first time this year, we finish out of the top twenty. Kenseth blew an engine and did not finish, so I'm still ahead in the rookie standings.

I try to put the best face I can on a disappointing day.

"We showed we can run up front with these guys," I tell the boys. "I'm more and more confident that we'll be able to stay there this year."

Somebody asks if I'll ever allow a sensor on my car again.

"Hell yeah. I'd have it on there next week if they asked."

# Darlington, South Carolina
## Mall.com 400

## We Need a Driver . . .

To those who follow NASCAR, the track at Darlington is something special. It is a legendary part of the sport, sort of like Fenway Park is for baseball fans. Darlington is where NASCAR held its first sanctioned race on a paved speedway, way back in 1950, when races were still run on dirt and sand. The track was built by Harold Brasington, who wanted a track that was paved and banked and faster than any other. But once he started building it, he ran into a problem. His neighbor had a minnow pond on the next property and refused to move it. The track had to be squeezed in next to the pond, and as a result the track came out egg-shaped rather than an oval. It looks bizarre—but just imagine trying to drive on it. You can't just find a comfortable groove that you can stay in all day long. The people who run Darlington call it "the track too tough to tame" or "the lady in black."

What do I call it? How about "an old track with not many improvements since it was wedged into place fifty years ago." The surface is awful. When the asphalt was mixed and laid down, small rocks and seashells were added into the mix. Now all that seems to be left are the same rocks and shells. This makes it a very rough track on tires. And cars. And drivers. The surface shreds tires like warm cheese across a grater. The surface is so abrasive that you feel like Superman when you have new tires, but that only lasts for a short time. Then the tires go away and you struggle to hang on for however long you can. When you're sliding around, you feel like you're gonna crash every lap. It is a helpless feeling. You just hope that a yellow flag comes out and you can dive into the pits to get four more new tires.

When you hit the wall, that's when you earn what people like to call a Darlington Stripe. The old guardrails used to wear a stripe into the side of the car as you slid into the rails lap after lap, scraping paint off the car. Today it's a safer concrete wall, but it's still tough to avoid hitting the wall here. They say you really haven't run Darlington until you've gained a stripe or two.

My father has won nine times at Darlington, so he obviously must know something about how to run there. But the track has reached out and bitten him too. He told a reporter one time that there "is no victory so sweet, so memorable, as whipping Darlington Raceway." He called it his "first love." But he can also tell you how you can lose focus and get into the wall before you know it.

The secret to driving Darlington, according to Big E and others who have won here, is to race the track and not the other drivers. At any point in the race, you could be on the track with tires that are shredded, and then you see some guy coming up from behind you looking like he's twice as fast. You have to know he has new tires, and you need to keep your own pace rather than try to keep up with him. Besides, you'll pass him in the same way when it's your turn to get new tires.

Tires. Tires. Tires. Keith Mansch, the guy who is in charge of the tires for our team, tells me they "lose grip just rolling across the garage area." And he isn't exaggerating. Not much, anyway. It wasn't as critical when we ran here in the Busch Series with lighter and less powerful cars, but now, as a team, we have to learn how to take care of the tires and make them last. We spend a lot of time in practice working on that goal, and our plan is to change 'em as often as possible during the race.

While we're here at NASCAR's oldest track, somebody asks me to answer some questions for a promotion called "NASCAR 2000." I guess they're promoting what racing will be like in the future, which is ridiculous because the racing right now is great and better than ever.

They ask, "What is the one thing you would add to your car in the future?"

"Music! Music!" I tell them quickly. "Someone get me some music."


The whole team is nervous about the race, but damn, we are fast in the first practice session and we qualify tenth best. I think I scared my dad (and the team) because I really let it hang out and the car slid sideways in Turn 2 on the qualifying lap. I was down on the apron of the banking, but somehow I never lifted my right foot. The fans really get off on shit like that. Total commitment to the lap. Of course, I can say that now because I managed to save the car. . . .

We've qualified in the top ten for every race in this season, and that's something nobody else can say. But I'm more relieved than excited. By Saturday's morning practice session, we make some more changes and somehow I run the quickest lap of the session. But one lap is deceiving, so we run a lot of laps on old worn tires so we'll know what to expect tomorrow.

The toughest thing will be to pace myself during the race and not go out and hurt the tires early on. I know I'll have to change my line on every lap to make up for the tires, so I have to be patient.

When the race finally starts on Sunday afternoon, I remember why it's important to qualify near the front of the field. On the second lap, several cars near the middle of the pack get into each other and the caution comes out. There are two more yellow flags before we've even run twenty laps. Tony brings me in on Lap 19 for fresh tires.

This ain't so bad! We're hanging in there and Matt Kenseth and I are both running in the top ten until just after Lap 100, when something happens to the way the car is handling.

"It's getting really loose, guys," I say into the radio. "It is loose as hell off the corners."

When a driver says a car is "loose," it means the rear tires start sliding before the front tires. It can be fun sometimes, and fast sometimes, but *not* at Darlington. And not *this* loose.

The lap times get slower and slower and the crew believes it is only because of worn tires, but there's also a bad vibration starting to come in.

When the problem gets worse, Tony decides to bring the car into the pits while the race is under the green flag.

You don't like to do this at any track, but especially not at Darlington, where you hope and hope there will be a yellow eventually so you can make a pit stop without losing a lap. The stop is good, though, and the other cars in the top ten also have to pit under green a couple of laps later. So we're still on the lead lap.

But the car is still not handling like it had been. There's something wrong. I keep losing ground on the leaders. On Lap 157, Tony Stewart puts me down a lap because the car just wants to throw my ass into the wall in each corner. I'm driving with everything I can give, but I can't keep up.

Once we are a lap behind, we decide to try something drastic in the pits on Lap 158. Tony Jr. puts a "rubber" into the right front spring. This is a pliable rubber wedge that stiffens the corner of the car. It's like changing springs or shocks, and if it works, it will help the handling.

But it doesn't work. At all. This car is evil and I'm all elbows and assholes in every corner.

"It's just so loose," I yell. "Feels like I'm gonna spin out every fucking lap. I don't understand it . . . it feels like the right front shock is completely off of it. . . ."

It's so bad that it only takes thirty laps before I'm down another lap when Dale Jarrett goes by on Lap 189. I'm just trying to hang on to this evil beast.

Finally, on Lap 200, the car wins the battle. It gets away from me and goes into the wall. Hard. First into the outside wall, and then it slides down to the inside wall and hits again. I'm just a helpless passenger, and I now have not one, but two massive Darlington stripes. The car is junk. I'm OK, but out of breath from the impacts.

I make the required trip to the infield medical center. The car is ready for the scrap heap, but as soon as it is towed back to the garage, the guys begin to hammer and beat and grind away to try and get it back out on the track to gain precious Winston Cup points. Ah yes, points. Every position is key because the dollar differences between each position at the end of the year are huge. Every lap and every position counts. NASCAR's point system rewards consistent finishes much more than winning finishes, so you try your best to get back out there and finish the race.

I'm more embarrassed than hurt, so I get out of the med center to get back to the car and the crew as quickly as I can. I'm definitely not excited about it, but I climb back into the trash heap. The leaders have covered forty laps since the crash, but our car is as good as it can be for now. This old track is hard enough with a shiny new car, but now I have to go out and try to finish in this ugly, ill-tempered thing.

They give me four new tires, but as soon as I get out there, the car isn't handling any better and I radio the crew. "I can't drive this son of a bitch."

"Just hang in there and get some laps," Tony says. The crew is worn out and probably pissed off, so I try to drive it.

"It's bad," I yell. "*Really* bad."

After twenty laps of trying to save my own ass and avoid taking out any of the other cars, I have had enough. I don't mind taking risks, but right now I'm a danger to all of the other guys out there. I feel like I have no choice but to bring the car back into the garage. There just isn't any sense in it. What if I take out the leaders and lose all the respect I have earned so far? How will the fans feel? They'd laugh my ass outta here if I wrecked somebody like that.

I pull the car into the pits and drive right into the garage. The car is broken. I'm done.

"Goddamnit!" Tony screams. "We need a driver that will get in this car. Go find Park. He'll drive it."

Steve Park, who drives the other DEI car, dropped out earlier. Now my uncle Tony and cousin Tony Jr. think that I've quit on them, and they want another driver to get in the car. My car. Their car. *Our* car.

I argue with both of them, but they don't wanna hear any of it. They want to win so badly that they just don't listen. Park has already left, so they just load the car into the hauler. We finish fortieth. There is one helluva lot of angry silence among all of us as the gear is loaded into the trailer.

Ward Burton wins the race and my father is third. Matt comes home sixth, an awesome result for his first Cup race here, and he takes over the rookie lead by a few points, but I really don't give a damn about that right now.

We don't have a long way to go to get back home to Mooresville, but for me it seems like an endless journey to the moon. It is a long, silent, gruesome trip. For the first time this season, I doubt myself. Worst of all, my team doubts me. Were they right? Was it me? Had I quit? The car was awful, but could Dad or Steve Park have been able to drive it? How could the team not believe me? Were they right? Had I simply given up late in the race, rather than make a few slow laps for a few measly points? Everybody told me there would be down times, but this is the lowest that I can imagine. What if my dad says he's had enough of my shit and looks for another driver?

I don't sleep much when I finally do get home.

Early Monday morning the team meets in the shop and the mood is grim. We are supposed to be the new hotshot golden boys of the sport, with the coolest sponsor, and now none of us can look each other in the eye. This sucks.

Just about everyone knows I hate to get up early, but I'm there with 'em at the shop to find out the same thing they want to know: Was it the car or was it the driver? Will I keep my job or will I be changing oil again at Dad's dealership like the good ol' days?

The crew begins to tear down the mashed car, searching for the cause of the problem. The answer becomes clear when they disassemble the drive train. One of the rear axles is broken. It was intact, of course, when we started the race, so it must have come apart while we were running. As it did come apart, the car continued to get looser and looser. No matter what minor changes we made to the tires or springs, it was undrivable. With only one rear wheel providing power to the racetrack, there was just no way . . . I was lucky to have lasted as long as I did before I finally got into the wall.

So, I was right. The car was *not* drivable.

Relieved, I grab the broken part and start showing it around. I want to show my dad. I want to show *everyone* at DEI. I want everyone to see it and understand exactly what happened. I did not quit, but still I feel like my guys are kicking me right in the nuts. How could they not believe me?

# Bristol, Tennessee
## *Food City 500*

## Living Up to Our Fathers' Legacies

There is no time to deal with this gnawing in my gut, because I have to jump on a plane right away to fly to Atlanta for an appearance at the National Sales Convention for Anheuser-Busch. Last year I gave a short speech that went over real well (I promised them I'd win races) but today I'm still down about the race and I have to work to get myself up. When you're running well and winning, these things are fun and it's easy to get into it. But when you're crashing and not winning, it's hard. An hour of autographs feels like three days in hell. Your mind is on other things, you just don't feel like joking and smiling, and it's especially hard to face your biggest sponsor when things are going badly.

We're running way late and that doesn't help my mood, but when I arrive at the convention there's a long line of Budweiser employees and wholesalers still waiting for autographs. I sign for everyone.

That evening, I'm invited to have dinner with a bunch of Budweiser-sponsored stars, including Super

Bowl–winning coach Dick Vermeil, NFL all-pro Orlando Pace, NHRA's "King of Speed" Kenny Bernstein, rodeo star Tuff Hedemann, Julie Foudy and Brandi Chastain of the U.S. women's soccer team, and NHL Hall of Famer Wayne Gretzky, who has just been named commissioner of the "Bud Light Bubble Boy hockey league." Great company, and I'm flattered to be included, but I can't get my mind off Darlington. The frustration just keeps seeping in and coloring everything. My confidence is shot.

Before the dinner, there is what most folks call a cocktail hour, but in Bud's world, it is "beertail hour." I share a cold one with August Busch IV and Yusef Jackson, Reverend Jesse's son. Busch offers a toast:

"Here's to living up to our fathers' legacies."

I can drink to that.

After dinner the Bud execs hand out wristbands that will get you into a series of events in the Buckhead section of Atlanta, where Budweiser has bought out a number of bars and nightspots. Faith Hill and Tim McGraw will be performing, and the "Whassup Guys" are among the folks that will be wandering from bar to bar. It seems like it ought to be pretty cool. But when we get there, we realize that huge chunks of the people who make the rounds are guys. Like 95 percent. They have literally bought out the neighborhood: if you don't work for Bud, even if you're an awesome babe, go home! My friends and I check out a few of the spots and then call it a night. C'mon, man! All I ask for is to hang out with a few Bud Girls, but we can't find any tonight. Just my luck lately.

In the morning I pull myself out of bed to attend another meeting and do another autograph session. Then I'm on the plane, heading for home as soon as I can.

Before we head to Bristol, there is a photo shoot scheduled in Charlotte for *Rolling Stone*. The magazine has sent Guy Aroch, a top New York fashion photographer, to take the pictures. This is cool as hell, because most of the time I'm being shot by guys who shoot race cars for a living. Not that they're bad, but Aroch pulls out his recent scrapbook with Polaroid after Polaroid of supermodels and naked women. Damn! This guy is good.

He uses a brightly colored section of the new grandstands at Lowe's Motor Speedway as the backdrop, and he wants me in my racing uniform. I drive my 1969 Camaro to the shoot, and Aroch loves the look of the deep blue car and says he wants me to pose with it when we're done in the grandstands.

I'm still brooding about the race but psyched to be working with somebody like Aroch.

He shoots me in the stands. Sunglasses on. Sunglasses off. Standing. Then sitting. Smiling. Serious.

"This is great," he says. "Just great. You look a lot like Sting."

So I guess he likes what he sees. I'm not sure about Sting, but I *am* having a damn good hair day. . . .

Then, to show more action and color, he has me pose against the catch fence on the wall outside of Turn 2. There are cars from the Richard Petty Driving Experience out on the track, and they zoom past in the background, just a few inches below the fence.

When Aroch has had enough of the red Bud uniform, I change back into my jeans and white T-shirt. He blurts something about James Dean and runs out near the car. He shoots some black-and-whites of the Camaro and me. Just trying to look badass and cool. Then we finish up with me and the race car in the DEI showroom.

The next day, I travel to Tennessee to the half-mile track at Bristol. I *need* a good run. It seems like we have had no luck since the rain started falling in Las Vegas.

NASCAR tracks are like people—they all have different personalities. And some of them have stronger personalities than others. Bristol is in a class by itself. It is a short track, only half a mile around. There are only three tracks on the Winston Cup tour that are less than one mile, and Bristol is one of them. It is also the highest-banked track. One driver said it looks like somebody just dug a big hole in the ground and poured a racetrack in it. Because it is so steeply banked, Bristol is fast. When you're running around Bristol at top speed, you feel like the rock tied to the end of a long string that's being spun around by an ornery little brat. You just hope the string doesn't break. When something happens at Bristol—and something always does—you don't have a lot of time, or room, to get out of the way. Like another driver said, "Bristol is the reason race cars have fenders."

This is a track where there is a lot of beating and banging during a race. If the high-speed, delicate maneuvering at Daytona looks like a graceful ballet, then Bristol is like slam dancing. Driving here is like flying a jet fighter in a cereal bowl. And the fans just love it. It is one of the toughest tickets to get on the whole schedule. Most fans wouldn't give up their seats for anything, especially because so many of them are so close to the track. I remember sitting outside of the track when I was young and being thrilled that I could look right into the car and see my dad steering the hell outta the thing. It was a great view.

Bristol is a track with a personality that fits my dad just about perfectly. He won his first Winston Cup race here, in 1979 when he was Rookie of the Year.

But the race he won that everyone remembers was last August. It was one of the most exciting—and controversial—races at Bristol or anyplace else for that matter. People are still talking about it. In fact, there is a big photograph in the media center of the No. 3 car going down the backstretch to the finish line with Terry Labonte's car spinning off the wall.

Labonte and my father had been chasing each other for almost two hundred laps and they were down to the last ten laps. Labonte spun after Darrell Waltrip hit him and he went into the pits. My father was in the lead when they went back to green, but when the white flag came out for the last lap, Labonte (and his fresh tires) went past him. Coming out of Turn 2, my father came up to try to get Labonte loose coming off the corner, but he hit him pretty hard and spun him. Labonte hit the wall then got into several other cars while Dad was making it through and heading to the finish. There were 150,000 people in that bowl and all of them were standing. Half of them were cheering my father, and the other half were booing him. Love him or hate him, right or wrong, my dad could always get the crowd excited.

After the race he said, "I didn't mean to wreck him, I was just trying to rattle his cage."

It was all that old "Intimidator" stuff, but like my father said, he got turned over at Talladega twice and nobody meant to do it. "Racing," he says, "is going and doing. Things happen."

And they happen a lot here. Bristol is wild. You have to be ready for just about anything.

In qualifying, our string of top-ten starts is broken, but we're twelfth, which isn't too bad. Dad qualifies eleventh, so he will be just to my left when the race starts. The big excitement of the day is for Steve Park, who takes the Bud Pole position. It's his first one, and it's also the first Winston Cup pole for DEI. My dad is really happy, and it makes all of us who are a part of DEI pretty excited.

Race drivers are tough guys. We like to act like nothing bothers us or gets us worked up. But you have to be totally crazy not to get goose bumps during the introductions before the race with the fans all standing and cheering. One hundred and fifty thousand of them, like a crazed college basketball crowd, cheering their team in a small, echoing gym. The little bowl holds the noise of all those people, and when the command "Gentlemen, start your engines" blasts over the loudspeakers, the noise gets even louder. I love rock and roll, and this track is the racing equivalent of a huge power chord. Everything reverberates on top of itself, building and building into an unbelievable rush of audio. In the stands and in the pits, earplugs are a must. The start at Bristol is truly hair-standing-up-on-the-back-of-your-neck stuff.

Five hundred laps here is one of the most grueling physical challenges in racing. I'm ready for it but I don't get much of a chance. On the second lap, with the field just beginning to settle into a rhythm, my dad slams into

Elliott Sadler and sends him into a wicked spin. I'm trying to get out of Sadler's way when Joe Nemechek, who is also trying to get clear, runs into me hard from behind.

Two laps. *Two laps.* And my car is a mess. Big E is the instigator. I was minding my own damn business, and I'm crashed. As usual, Dad escapes unscathed.

I grind into the pit, where the crew starts cutting away the bent bodywork and hammering on the suspension pieces that had been bent in the crash.

"Get me a Sawzall," Tony Jr. yells and starts hacking away at the twisted sheet metal with a small buzzing electrical saw, trying to somehow get us back into action. How can this be happening? *Another* crash! I can't even begin to think about it.

The crew does its work in twenty-second bursts during the yellow, so I can get back out on the tiny track in time to catch the tail end of the field and not lose a lap. Every caution lap, I'm in for twenty seconds and then back out. The spotter has to be sharp here and let us know the position of the pace car. He does his job and so does the rest of the crew, so when the race goes green again, I'm still on the lead lap but at the back of the field.

But it doesn't take Park, who is leading, very long to catch me and lap me. Less than thirty laps into the race, actually. We get another caution flag on Lap 38 and I'm back in the pits, making short stops, like before, trying to align the wheels so they will roll somewhat straight again.

When we're racing again, the car is a little better, but still not handling right.

"It's balky," I yell. "Steering really bad . . ."

To make matters worse, when the black No. 3 comes

by to lap me, he bumps me hard. I hold my ground, trying not to let him through. I think he's just messing with
me, and I'm not gonna back down and let him go by so
easily. He slides outside of me and we go down the front
stretch, father and son, banging wheels and fenders,
with tire smoke and brake dust flying into the air. Hell
yeah, I turned into him. The crowd loves it. They're
standing and cheering until my father is past me and I'm
dropping back.

"That son of a bitch," Tony yells after the smoke
clears.

After a few laps, I calm down enough to radio the
crew. "I hit him there! I turned into him so he wouldn't
fuck with me. He just races me so damn hard. . . ."

I'm not sure I understand it, but I know I have to stand
up to it.

Anyway, right now I've got other things to think about.
The accident has damaged a crush panel inside the car
and that's a big problem. The cars are built with "crush
zones," or areas that crumple in a crash to withstand impacts and protect the driver. This one is bent so bad that
fumes and debris from the track and from my engine are
flowing into the cockpit. It's as if I'm slowly being poisoned, lap after lap, five hundred times around.

I manage to keep the crippled car going straight, but
the fumes increase.

"It's getting worse," I say to the crew when I make my
sixteenth pit stop of the day.

Nothing you can do but keep racing. Sometimes
drivers will ask for a relief driver, but after the bullshit at
Darlington last week, I am not going to leave this seat

until the day is done. I return to the track on Lap 384. The end is in sight.

Unfortunately, Joe Nemechek is also in sight, and he's spinning out in front of me.

I'm light-headed from the fumes and tired of fighting the balky steering, and as I try to get the hell out of Nemechek's way, the car spins and hits the outside wall in Turn 4, then it rolls back across the track and hits the inside wall. I try to steer and correct and gas it and brake all at the same time, but it's just like last week: I'm only a passenger at this point.

I make it out of the car on my own and walk to the infield hospital. There is no chance the guys will get the car fixed today. I check out OK at the care center, and as I leave, an ESPN pit reporter asks me if I'm a little sore. Did he just ask me if I'm a little sore? The fumes were bad enough, but now he's asking if I'm a little sore. "Hell yeah, I'm sore!" I snap. "*You* try hitting something that hard and see how it feels." I walk off quickly, thinking, *Get these guys outta my face.*

I want to hide in the transporters and clear my head. Jade is in there with me for a few minutes, and I guess the fumes had really gotten to me, because he says I went into this wild, long tirade of obscenities. I guess he just turned around and got his ass out of the lounge.

Later on, my head is a little clearer and I've calmed down. Sorta. I still feel like I have a black cloud hanging over me. I'm pissed off because we've wrecked three great race cars in three weeks.

Rusty Wallace wins the race. It's his fiftieth career Winston Cup victory. Matt finishes twelfth and he's even further ahead of me in rookie points. We end up thirty-eighth, which sucks, but strangely, we're one spot ahead of Dad, who couldn't get around Kenny Irwin when Irwin was spinning down the banking. We drop all the way down to twenty-third in total points. This is embarrassing. I think we're better than most of these teams ahead of us, but now I'm just not so sure.

It is a bad day for the Earnhardts on one of NASCAR's toughest tracks. And a really bad month for the team and me. I wonder if there is ever going to be any other kind of day for me and the Bud car. How long can things continue to go bad? Either they're going to get better or I'll be looking for a new job. . . .

# Fort Worth, Texas
## *DirecTV 500*

# Victory!

> *I came, I saw, I conquered.*
> —JULIUS CAESAR

Three days before we get to the Texas Motor Speedway near Fort Worth, a tornado ripped through the downtown area, causing severe damage. The speedway, located about twenty miles from there, was not damaged, but many of the volunteers and off-duty law enforcement officers that usually provide security at the track are elsewhere helping with the clean-up duties. Not a huge problem until qualifying time, when Jade and I stride from the garage area. As we walk toward pit lane, an autograph-seeking crowd mobs us. Without any security officers to help, Jade (who, as usual, is screaming to no avail, "Let him walk! Don't stand in front of him!") is overwhelmed. His spindly body is knocked over by the mob, and he falls to a knee along pit lane. I find it pretty amusing and I can't wait to tell the crew the tale of the tumbled media dude. You just had to be there.

The next day, I am as happy as I have been all season. The rain is coming down hard and it is cold, which makes me even happier as I hop out of the coach to do an interview. I know things have hit rock bottom the last few weeks, but I have a feeling about this place.

I tell a soggy ESPN video crew (who have been struggling to find a story, *any* story, on a day when so little is happening) that this is the most comfortable car I've ever driven. I also tell them I think we have a real good shot at this one. I'm still a punk rookie that my own team has lost faith in, preparing to start only my twelfth Winston Cup race, so that is as close to bragging as I can get.

Throughout the interview, Kenseth yells from inside his own motor coach, *"Dale Jr.! Dale Jr.! I wanna autograph, Dale Jr.! I wannaaaaaaaaaautograph!"* He sounds like a squealing young female. With a chuckle and a quick flip of my middle finger to Matt, I leap back inside to enjoy some quality chillin.' Happy hour—the final practice session before tomorrow's race—has been canceled.

So why am I so damn happy?

We qualified fourth, a great starting spot (it's the fifth top-ten start of the season for us). Plus, the wickedly fast 1.5-mile Texas track has been good to me before. In 1998, in only my sixteenth career start in the NASCAR Busch Series, I scored my first major victory here. The win launched us to six more wins that year and our first Busch Series championship.

Before the rains came, the morning practice went really well for us. Our car was easily the quickest among those who were working on race-day setups—faster even than most of the teams trying to gain that last ounce of pure speed for only one lap in second-round qualifying. Plus, the red No. 8 is consistent on long runs—a good sign for Sunday's five-hundred-miler. It's like the "Tortoise and the Hare" scenario. The win does not always go to the car that is fastest initially but to the team that can make subtle tweaks to the car throughout the day, and remain at or near the front of the pack until the checkered flag waves. You need to be fastest when it counts most—in the last fifty miles.

Today's rain is great because our car is already awesome. Without a happy-hour session, the others guys have no time on the track to improve their cars. We seem to have discovered an edge on the experienced teams, and the rain means our advantage will continue into the race the following day.

It is chilly and dark, but at least it isn't raining when the green flag flies in front of nearly 200,000 crazed Texans. Most cold-weather race days produce a quiet, muffled fan response during prerace activities—maybe because it's hard to clap loudly with gloves on—but the reaction when I'm introduced is enthusiastic and vocal.

This makes me feel really good, because I think they are cheering because of what I have done here in the past. I'm sure some fans are probably cheering for me just because I'm an Earnhardt. I feel like that's the case at most all of the tracks we go to, especially when I get a big fan response even though I've never raced there before. But here, it's different. I really feel like they are cheering for *me*. I like Texas, and Texas seems to like me.

The guy from Budweiser who oversees the Winston

Cup program is Tim Schuler, the senior sports marketing manager. I notice that Tim looks a little pale as he watches the prerace activities.

"What's up, man?" I ask.

"I just ran into Tony Furr," Schuler says. Furr is the crew chief of the No. 25 car driven by Jerry Nadeau, the same Hendrick team that was sponsored by Budweiser for a number of struggling, winless seasons. "Furr said they were running great and that they had a chance to win the race. If that 25 team wins before the 8 team does, we may as well quit our jobs. . . ."

How's that for pressure? Damn. He's probably joking, but he's not smiling.

When the race begins, I run cautiously, making sure to take care of the tires. After seventeen laps I decide to let the car stretch its legs, and it easily bolts into the lead. One lap later the yellow flag flies, bringing the team to full attention for our first pit stop of the day. We chose the pit box at the far end of pit lane, so it's a long, slow drive to our stall. Once I get there, the crew leaps into service, sending me back out with four fresh tires and a full fuel tank in less than sixteen seconds.

Even though we had a good stop, we restart eighth, behind teams that have chosen to take only two new tires. Still, I effortlessly maneuver into the top four after only six laps. By the hundredth lap, I'm joined at the front of the field by my buddy Kenseth. We streak away from the field, and I radio to the team, "This thing is on a rail!"

Matt and I duel back and forth until Lap 170, when the crew makes another sparkling four-tire stop under yellow flag conditions. Each time I pull into pit lane, I have a strange, confident feeling that the pit stops are gonna be great. As we return to the track, I look for Matt's car, but he is penalized one lap for a pit lane violation. Just like before, we are shuffled back into the field for the restart when other teams choose to only change two tires.

When you are leading a race, things seem easier. You can usually set your own pace, and you run out in clean air, giving the car maximum aerodynamic benefit while the guys behind you fight the turbulence. But even if you have a rocket-fast car, it is really nerve-racking to have to start back in the pack. Not only do you have to deal with the cars in front of you, you have to worry about the lapped cars that line up on the inside for restarts. Even if you're ten miles per hour faster, you can easily get caught by someone else's mistake.

"This is a chill-out restart," Tony Jr. tells me, reminding me of the more than 160 laps left. "Just hang in there and take 'em out one by one."

We restart eleventh, and just like I had worried, the guys around me act like it's the last lap. They're racing like crazy, and I survive some close calls around slower cars that are already one or more laps behind. It takes more than fifty laps to retake the lead, and as soon as we do, Tony decides that we will pit on the next lap.

As we complete our stop, the yellow flag comes out, which really hurts our track position. Once again, things beyond our control hurt us. We return to the track, but there are two cars that have chosen not to make a pit stop and they are now ahead of us by a full lap.

It looks bleak as Kevin Lepage and Chad Little—two drivers from the Jack Roush stable—gain the lead through fuel conservation and lucky timing. They are the only cars on the lead lap.

With less than one hundred laps remaining and a complete lap to make up, the time to chill out passes, and I feel calm and confident that we have the speed to do it. I manage to make some aggressive, hold-your-breath moves, sliding past Jeff Burton and a lapped car in a three-wide duel. The break we need comes on Lap 246, when Dale Jarrett, the defending champion, crashes. This yellow flag allows me and several other cars to make up the lap, and it sets up a final sprint to the checkered flag. Lepage and Little lose their advantage when they make their pit stops.

By Lap 261, I retake the lead for the fifth time, and it is apparent that the race for the win is between me, Bobby Labonte, and Jeff Burton. Two proven veterans with top-notch, veteran pit crews against us—the new kids in the garage, the brash brats from the Busch Series.

Conventional wisdom within the racing community is that most young teams and/or drivers will have several of these golden opportunities to win races, only to let them slip through their grasp with faulty strategy, a bad pit stop, or simply being overwhelmed by a more experienced team that had been holding back until the end of the race. Only after you have learned from these hard knocks will you be fully prepared to take a victory. However, there is little conventional about this team, and we steel ourselves for the final sprint. I'm prepared to drive my ass off.

I think about Tim Schuler from Budweiser, who was so worried earlier about the No. 25 car. That car is nowhere to be found, but for us, this could be the day. I know everyone on the team is thinking about it, but like a superstitious baseball team avoiding a pitcher who is throwing a no-hitter, no one says anything. Budweiser hasn't sponsored a winning car since Bill Elliott won at Darlington in September 1994. Could the King of Beers return to the Victory Circle today? I had promised them that we were gonna win, but this soon? Can we do this? Have Burton and Labonte been toying with us—waiting until the end to show all of their speed?

The answer comes on Lap 275.

"This one here is for all the marbles," says Tony Jr. on the radio as all of the leaders head toward the pit area for the final stop of the day.

Again, I feel calm and confident that the guys are gonna give me a kick-ass stop.

When I arrive, the over-the-wall gang goes ballistic, led by Tony Jr., who is changing the two front tires as always. The jack drops the car to the ground, and we're rolling after being stopped for only 14.7 seconds. Less than 15 seconds to change four tires and fill the tank with fuel. Like a perfectly timed offensive play in the NFL or a brilliant double play in baseball, the crew executes their loud ballet with dazzling speed.

It's time to pull out all the stops, and other teams gamble by taking only two fresh tires. It's their only hope to get out ahead of our car. Thankfully, they don't succeed. As good as our car is, I worry about passing them if we come out behind too many cars.

The green flag flies again on Lap 278, and it takes me only four laps to retake the lead. The car is unbelievable. The remaining laps are merely a formality as the red Bud machine streaks away from the rest of the field. I am able to stretch the margin to more than six seconds (an eternity in NASCAR terms) over Labonte, who is in second place.

It's hard for me to contain my emotions as it becomes apparent that we are going to win the race. On the last lap, I'm so excited, and I can see the fans are excited as well. When I drive through Turn 4, I see all of the flashbulbs flashing. I can't believe it—the people are screaming and cheering and waving their arms and hats and . . . I can't believe it! We have won a Winston Cup race! I'm screaming into the radio after I cross the line, and then I realize that this means I will probably be able to keep a job driving race cars . . . at least for a few more years. Forget Darlington—we just won a Winston Cup race!

*"Hellllllllllllllllllllllllllll yeeeaaaaahhhhhhhhhhhhhh!"* I scream.

I do a slow victory lap and many of the other guys come up beside me and wave or give a thumbs-up. . . . I can hear the crowd, and when I come around the fourth turn, I can see the Bud pit area is a mass of red and black uniforms in one big, joyous monkey pile. Everyone is embracing each other like a rugby scrum, and I'm sure they are in disbelief just like I am. It was as if everyone had stopped breathing for the final forty laps, and then suddenly we were allowed to take a deep breath of victory as if it were pure oxygen.

Only when you understand how hard each of these crewmen works can you appreciate the joy and elation when *their* creation—a living, breathing, grumbling race car built with love one piece at a time—defeats the other cars on the track. Our crew had worked nonstop since early January—seriously nonstop, no days off, no vacations—to build the fleet of cars that I get to drive week after week. For all of us, to see our hard work, our sweat, *our car* cross the line first in front of 200,000 fans and a network television audience is truly mind-blowing.

I pull down along the front straightaway and start doing some tire-smoking, celebratory donuts. The fans love it (even though the guys that build my engines hate it). I get a little too aggressive and I completely fry the clutch. The crew guys that built and prepared the car now have to run down pit lane to push it themselves for the final hundred yards to the hallowed ground. How appropriate.

Once we arrive in the winner's circle, Jade inches toward the car to hand me a Budweiser hat and towel for the postrace TV interviews. As he is within reach of the cockpit, a huge hand grabs him by the shoulder, throwing him backwards like an empty can of Bud. (For the second time this weekend, he is felled in one swoop!) The team owner has arrived, and nothing and no one is standing between Dale Earnhardt Sr. and me.

The seven-time Winston Cup champion ducks his head inside the cockpit for a private moment with me.

"I love you," he says. "I want to make sure you take the time to enjoy this and enjoy what you accomplished today. You can get so swept up with what's going on around you that you really don't enjoy it yourself, so I want you to take a minute and celebrate how you want to celebrate."

Just like always, he is right to the heart with common sense. He is so happy that it makes me even more excited. He's the car owner, and the team is a product of his. He's proud of his son too, but he put this team together and now it has gone out and won a race. No matter who's driving, he's happy about that. Dale Earnhardt Inc. is a winning team in Winston Cup. Just like it had been in the Busch and the Craftsman Truck series.

My proud papa hoists me out of the car with one mighty heave by the shoulder straps on my uniform. We embrace before I take my place on top of the car, where I am best able to drink in the adulation of the team, the media, and most of all, the fans. Confetti shoots into the gray sky, flashbulbs pop, and the team empties the first of many cases of Budweiser. Arms aloft, I feel like the conquering victor.

The excitement of the first win has me speaking in clipped, short sentences, almost as if each thought is trying to get out ahead of all of the other thoughts racing through my mind.

"I'm so tired, man—I drove my heart out. I need a breath!" I gasp for the television audience. "Well done by my guys—they did super. This is pretty special. This is crazy. Tony and Tony Jr. built a good car, and I pretty much did what I wanted to. It did what I asked it to do. We didn't change anything all day. I'd just point and shoot and that thing went! I adjusted my driving style to fit each set of tires. When we made the race at Charlotte [my first-ever Cup race in 1999], it was a success for us. It was a pat on the back for us, but not even close to this. This here is awesome. It's incredible!"

This victory is not just the first in Winston Cup for DEI, but for me and my team as well. We have become winners in only our twelfth Cup start. (Ron Bouchard won in his eleventh start in 1981, the earliest in the "modern era" of Winston Cup.) Dad won his first in his sixteenth career start twenty-one years and one day earlier (April 1, 1979) at Bristol.

"Whaaaaaassssssssssuppppppppp?" is the joyous cry from my crew. The Bud catch phrase is seemingly everywhere, and now it is coming from a cell phone pressed to my ear in the midst of the victory mayhem. August Busch IV is calling. The fourth-generation Budweiser executive is calling to congratulate the team and me and to revel in the victory with us.

Dad pushes Lori Bailey, my guest this weekend, into the photo with me. She is a Miami Dolphins cheerleader, and the photographers perk up when she joins the team photo to stand next to me.

No one can stop smiling. This makes it all worthwhile.

The checkered flag had signaled the end of the race, but it also marked the beginning of a whirlwind week. Only two months before, I had the thrill of joining an exclusive fraternity when I raced in the Daytona 500, but now I have joined a much smaller, much more exclusive club as a Winston Cup *winner.* This newest club comes with a long list of responsibilities, and they begin immediately.

A typical winner's circle is controlled mayhem, as the winning team and driver do what is known as "the hat dance" in front of a gaggle of photographers and video cameras. Each sponsor, from the major sponsor, Budweiser, through the associates like Remington Arms, Nabisco, and the Outlaw (an oil additive from Pennzoil), down to the small contingency sponsors that dot the fenders behind each front wheel, provides hats for the winning driver and crew. In order of importance, the sponsor hats are placed on my head one at a time for photos with the trophy and without the trophy, look this way, look that way, hold up one finger, stand up, kneel down, now with the entire crew, now everybody wave, now look this way . . . Over and over again for as many sponsors as there are hats. Each photo will make its way into an ad (called a "win ad" as companies proclaim their role in helping us secure the victory) or back to me to be autographed before being presented to a corporate executive at that company.

Once the seemingly endless dance is done, I just want to celebrate with all of my guys, but before any of that can begin, the track staff insists that I be escorted to the media center to speak with the large assortment of journalists on hand.

"I'm not going anywhere without Tony Jr.," I yell. I want to publicly recognize the effort my cousin has put into providing a perfect car for the race.

"Get Tony Jr., damn it! He's coming with me to the media center. I'm not going without him!"

When Tony Jr. and I are on stage in the theater-style media room of the Texas track, I decide to admit the relief that I feel after struggling so much with my confidence.

"You can beat yourself up only so much before you take a lot of confidence away from yourself," I explain. "I talked to my buddy Hank Parker Jr. I talked to people who have had more adversity than me to hear what they say about it and how they got over it. Hank has been through some crap in his racing career. There was a time he thought he was never going to drive again, but talking to him makes you chill out and get ready to go again."

Someone asks if my dad had offered advice, but I explain that the most impactful advice had come not from my father or even my buddy Hank, but from another familiar face in the NASCAR garage. Gary Nelson, NASCAR's chief technical guy, who works closely with the rookie drivers throughout the year, pulled me aside following the mandatory rookie meeting Friday morning.

Gary sat down with me and he told me some things that nobody else had said before. Even though a lot of good things have happened to me in my career, I sometimes need to be told that I'm a good race car driver. Just like being in a marriage. Even though your wife knows you love her, you've still got to tell her sometimes. That was kind of the situation I was in. It was like it'd be nice to get patted on the back sometimes even though we had a bad weekend. Gary sat down with me and told me he knew I was going to be able to make it and be a good race car driver, that I just needed to calm down. It was good to hear. I haven't heard that from anybody else.

When we crash out of a race or something, I go to the house and the phone doesn't ring. You sit there and wonder if anybody gives a shit. Race car drivers are choked in and out of the series. It's kind of hard sometimes. I really wondered if Dad was going to fire me. To hear from somebody like Gary Nelson, who can't play favorites and has nothing to gain by telling me that I'm going to make it, that sounds pretty good to me. It had put my mind more at ease for the weekend, and it especially makes sense now.

In the past few weeks, I didn't know what to think. We went to Atlanta and had the problem with the brake line and the telemetry from the TV guys. Every time you find a part failure on a car, you speculate why it happened and how it happened. We'll never know if there was actually brake fluid on the tire. We'll never know that. The next week we stripped an axle, but how long had it been stripped? Did it just do that when I wrecked or had I been driving the car like crap all day long? We went to Bristol, and I didn't know if that was in my hands or out of my hands. You put yourself in position to win. You put yourself in position to lose. You put yourself in position to wreck. Even though it's not your fault, if you qualify bad and get back in a mess, you're going to get in a wreck that happens even though it's not your fault. You're still going to be in it.

In addition to all of that, I'm relieved to know that I'll be able to keep a job as a Winston Cup race driver in the coming years. I have been validated as a winning driver. I also feel relieved because I earned some respect today from the other drivers. It was fun racing Bobby Labonte because I admire him a lot—how he carries himself around the garage area and stuff. He's a really cool guy, real quiet, and he doesn't ruffle anybody's feathers. After the last three weeks, it was fun to get out front and show these guys I could use my head and make smart decisions. Even when I've got a real fast car and I'm not up front, I can be patient and I can pick my way up through there. It was fun to prove that to them and prove my status as far as drivers go.

While the media session winds down, a van backs up to the side door of the media center to whisk me upstairs to the Speedway Club, where track VIPs are waiting to see and hear from me. Again, I insist that Tony Jr. come along. Also in the van with us is Eddie Gossage, track president, who never misses a photo or media opportunity.

We are driven outside the track to a secure entrance to the track's massive tower of suites and escorted upstairs to the Speedway Club. I was just expecting a restaurant or a typical corporate suite, but they say everything is bigger in Texas, so I shouldn't have been so surprised as we trailed Gossage into the room. It is a gigantic ballroom as gaudy as any hotel anywhere—filled with close to six hundred VIPS that erupt into an ovation as Gossage introduces me.

Everyone is given a champagne glass to salute the win, but Tony Jr. and I grab a bottle of Bud instead. (My contract insists that I cannot drink any alcoholic beverage other than Anheuser-Busch products!) I sign a few autographs for several kids that have run to the front of the stage, and we are whisked away to another corporate suite.

It is nearing darkness outside, and the chilly day is getting colder as the sun disappears. It is another quick sprint to the van for the trip back to the garage. All of the hoopla has died down, and I really want to hang with the guys in the crew. Savor this one awhile.

Once inside the quiet of the van, the impact of the victory begins to hit Tony Jr. and me. It all sinks in.

"We're in the Winston!" I spurt. The Winston is NASCAR's version of an all-star game. Only past champions and winning drivers are invited into the Winston—and it is one of the richest and most prestigious races each season. It is an unexpected bonus race for the team and for all of the sponsors.

"We're in the Winner's Circle program too!" I say. "Winner's Circle" is a program administered by NASCAR that brings winning drivers to race markets in an effort to sell tickets and gain publicity for the events. It means more public and media appearances for me, but it means extra prize money for the team each week.

"How much does that pay?" is Tony Jr.'s question. No one in the van knows for sure, but we're happy no matter what the amount.

As we arrive back at the transporter, the car is being rolled through the final stages of postrace inspection. Tim Schuler, who was so worried earlier about the 25 car, jokes about the riot that would erupt if NASCAR disqualified us now. No need to worry, though, because the car is legal. NASCAR gives the OK, and the crew begins to load it into the hauler for the long ride back to North Carolina.

I slip away briefly to the motor coach to change out of my uniform—still smelling like it has soaked in sweat, beer, and champagne for several days. When I arrive, I find Lori, the Dolphins cheerleader (who has missed her flight home), and a note from Matt, who had run very well, but crashed late in the race. I was worried that he might have been hurt, but he managed to walk away. The note congratulates me on a job well done. For Kenseth, it must have been bittersweet to see me—the man who won the championship in the Busch Series the last two years—to again beat him to the punch and gain my first victory in Winston Cup. But as a friend, I know he's happy for me.

Clothes changed, I head back to the transporter to wait for the team van that will take us to the airport for the trip back home. I bring Lori, with the promise that I'll arrange somehow to get her to Miami from Charlotte.

The race has been over for several hours, but we struggle to fight through the mess of traffic that still clogs the few roads outside of the track. By the time we make it to the airport, it is late in the evening, and my special guest puts us over the plane's capacity. Ty Norris, the DEI man in charge, takes one for the team, and says he will give up his seat for her. (He will fly back commercial the next morning.) The joyous mood on board is soon replaced by a full load of sleeping crew members.

The plane lands at the airstrip near Statesville, North Carolina, at 3:00 A.M., and the expected party-of-the-century turns into a sleepy drive home for everyone.

The crew will be back in the shop within several hours—practice for the next race begins in four days.

# Martinsville, Virginia
## Goody's 500

# The Greatest Two Hours
# of My Life

There are three flagpoles in front of DEI. One for the American flag, one for the flag of North Carolina, and the third for a DEI flag, which has the logo with Dad's signature. When I show up Monday morning, there is also a checkered flag flying from the third pole. It will be there all week. This happens any time a DEI team wins a race. This time it's flying for everyone who helped us win at Texas. If a DEI car wins a championship, a checkered flag will fly from that pole all winter long.

The flag is great to see, but inside the building it's back to work. Even after a win—or maybe *especially* after a win—it's business as usual. The joy of winning only prods you to work harder so that you might be lucky enough to feel that same thing next week. You keep racing because you know the forty-two other teams are going to work harder to beat your ass next time around.

A couple of things are a little out of the ordinary, though. The first delivery of the day is one hundred cases of sixteen-ounce Budweiser cans with the special Texas Motor Speedway graphics and the No. 8 car. The cases are delivered direct to DEI for the employees, who will also enjoy a free lunch in the trophy room while a tape of the race is shown on the television.

We're also bombarded with media requests. Right in Victory Lane, NASCAR and Winston had handed us a list of radio stations and syndicated shows that a winner should call a day or two after a victory. Some of them are no-brainers but we cherry-pick the list for the best shows and make the calls.

On Tuesday, I'm scheduled to do ESPN2's *RPM2Night.* Meanwhile, Budweiser and NASCAR are working together to book a satellite media tour for the following day. These are great because I sit in one place, and then we hook up with networks and stations across the country.

The producers of *Inside NASCAR,* a Sunday morning program on the Nashville Network, also call to arrange an appearance. I'm going to be busy but I'm not complaining. It comes with winning, plus I did a lot of this same stuff when we won races in the Busch Series. I'm a little disappointed that it feels the same. I expected a Winston Cup win to produce some new media opportunities.

Jade and I have arranged to travel together to the new regional ESPN studios about forty-five minutes from DEI. He shows up at the house, but I'm at the mall, and I don't realize what time it is. When I do see a clock, I hop in the pickup and speed off. I don't have time to go home first, so I head straight to the television studio. Jade finds my house empty, so he drives over to DEI.

Nope, nobody has seen me today. Most everyone just gives him a shrug. So he calls my cell phone. It's turned off. He pages me, but I don't have my pager.

First he gets nervous. Then irritated. Then pissed off. Finally, after an hour of pacing, he decides there isn't anything to do but call ESPN.

"Dale Jr. will be running a little . . . ah, *late,*" he says tentatively.

"What?" the producer says, sounding confused.

"We'll be late. . . . Junior is running behind."

"No he's not. He just finished here and right now he's doing an ESPN radio interview next door."

"What?" Jade says, confused but also relieved. He calls *Inside NASCAR* to confirm the details of tomorrow's interview.

"Yeah, Dale was just here a little while ago. He thought these were the ESPN studios, so we gave him directions."

"Oh . . . uh . . . yeah, thanks. . . ."

When I see Jade the next day, he's still kind of pissed.

"Why didn't you call?"

"I didn't have my cell phone."

A Winston Cup winner, but some things never change.

The next day, I'm in a garage at DEI, with a camera in my face and an earpiece in one ear, doing interviews with networks and stations across the country. A satellite media tour can be drudgery. I speak with stations in five-minute segments so their anchor can speak with me directly. Then each station I speak with can air it that evening as if they had an exclusive interview. But I have to do that for two hours, five minutes per interview, answering the questions over and over and over. One of the challenges of keeping this interesting is to come up with a different way to answer a question each time I'm asked. But believe me, I'm so glad that I can go back home when it's done rather than fly from city to city.

One topic that comes up is the death of Lee Petty, who died this morning at the age of eighty-six. Petty was the NASCAR champion three times and the head of the Petty clan that includes his son Richard, his grandson Kyle, and his great-grandson Adam, who made his first Winston Cup start at Texas last weekend. I'm a third-generation racer myself, so I have some feelings about this one.

Everyone in racing knows about the Pettys of Level Cross, North Carolina, just like they know about the Earnhardts. This is a sport where you have family dynasties, and those families are strong and loyal in the old southern way. Lee Petty was a strong man who drove hard and didn't say much. He worked hard and he put his family first.

"My thoughts are with his family," I say, over and over, but I mean it every time. "He meant a lot to NASCAR but he meant so much more to his family. They're a great family and I'm thinking of them today."

After a week of answering questions and speaking with what seems like every media outlet known to man, Friday morning finally arrives, and I head to the race-track.

When I arrive at the tiny old track in Martinsville, Virginia, it might be the best two hours of my life. A lot of drivers, team members, and NASCAR officials make a point of coming by to congratulate me. I get back-slapped and hand-shaked and "attaboyed" everywhere I turn. I have been trying so hard to earn the respect of these folks, and I finally begin to feel like I'm starting to get there.

But just so I don't get too full of shit, my father doesn't miss a chance to give me the needle. "You're a rookie all over again this week," he says. "Don't let it go to your head." Maybe, but it still feels good when somebody like Dave Marcis, the oldest driver in NASCAR and a veteran if ever there was one, stops by to say congratulations to a rookie.

Even if I did get a little bigheaded, the track here at Martinsville, where I have never raced, will quickly take care of any ego. This track is older than NASCAR, and it is a brutal mother. I know that even without driving it.

Martinsville started out as a dirt track, and then, without doing much else, they paved it. It is a half mile and barely banked—just enough to drain it, the drivers say. The track is small, the grandstands are small, and the pits are small. It seems odd that we're racing at a track where the average speed is less than one hundred miles per hour. But that's plenty fast enough when you are racing so close together.

Martinsville is a place where the brakes are just as important as the gas pedal. You want to brake hard going into the turns so you can get back on the gas before you come out of the corners, fighting for traction and position. But the thing is, as much as you have to use the brakes, you don't want to use them too much or you'll burn them up. A 500-lap race here is only 250 miles, but it's 1,000 left turns. You can boil the brakes if you lean on them too much. This happens when the brake fluid gets so hot it literally boils and you get air in the lines. You have to run smart at Martinsville and you have to drive strong. You steer so much you use a lot of pure, brute strength. I'm a wiry guy, not weak, but I'm not a bodybuilder. Martinsville will be a workout.

No matter where you qualify, once the race starts, it gets crowded and chaotic and bad things happen that you can't help or avoid. But you still want to be near the front, so I'm concerned when we come up with our worst qualifying effort of the year. We'll start twenty-second.

Still, the mood is good. Upbeat. Confident.

I have been wearing the same style of Bud hat most of the season, but the souvenir people tell me that they are overstocked on a particular style of hat, so would I wear it for a day or so? Just so the fans see me wearing it and go out to buy one for themselves.

It's a khaki hat with a "distressed" bill that makes it look about ten years old, with tattered holes and frayed seams. It's a real cool look—especially with college kids—but it's something entirely new in NASCAR. Grunge took over the world of music and fashion in the early nineties, but it hasn't made an appearance here in the garage yet. Until today. A lot of people in the garage laugh and joke and ask where I got such a ratty ol' hat, and they look in disbelief when I tell 'em it's a new hat. Within days, the souvenir rigs have sold out of the tattered hats that no one had wanted before. The next weekend, a crew member from another team comes up to tell me he caught his son raking a new ball cap across the asphalt in his driveway trying to make it look like a Dale Jr. original.

On Sunday, before the introductions, I sit quietly on the pit wall. I'm worried about taking care of the car for the whole distance on a new track where I know the racing is going to be close and tough. Expectations have been so high all season and now, after the win in Texas, it feels like they are even higher. And here I am, racing on a track where I've never seen a green flag before. I don't want to go out and make an ass of myself and disappoint all of the people that now expect me to win every week.

Patience, I tell myself. Just be patient.

When the race starts, I run with the pack. Not passing and not falling back either. The traffic is so tight, there's no sense in tearing up the car now. For a while I'm in line with two other rookies, Dave Blaney and Stacy Compton. Maybe we're looking for safety in numbers.

I make a little contact with other cars—no way to avoid it on this track—and each time I ask Dale Cagle to check for damage. Dale is an employee of Jeremy Mayfield who joined our team as a raceday spotter because of his long-time experience and cool demeanor. Each time, he tells me it's "only cosmetic." The sheet metal is bent and tattered like my new hat, but this doesn't affect the performance of the car.

Then, on Lap 138, the patient Sunday drive is suddenly over. The engine merely quits running.

"It's blown up," I say into the radio. "I'm coming in."

I roll into the pit and the team is all over the car. They have an idea that it isn't a blown engine, but a problem in the electrical system. We had an electrical gremlin all week long and were never able to find it, and now the battery in the car is dead.

For weight distribution and balance, the battery is located immediately in front of the left rear wheel, which makes it a tough thing to change quickly, but Tony Jr. changes it deftly. The rest of the field keeps racing under green, and by the time I'm back out, we are four laps down and in fortieth position. I start to pick up spots and actually gain ten positions when we get a yellow flag on Lap 308. I get a lap back on the restart and I'm getting a real workout, manhandling this beast through traffic.

"This is the hardest track as far as beatin' my ass goes," I say into the radio. "How many more laps?" I ask, hoping to hear that the race is nearly over and I can rest my aching arms and feet and body.

"One hundred and fifty to go," they tell me.

But the car is fast and I'm having fun until the needle on the voltage meter drops again.

I pit for my second battery change, and lose a lot of what I'd worked so hard to get back in the last two hundred laps.

In spite of some body damage, the car is essentially in one piece when the race ends, a major accomplishment at Martinsville. I finish twenty-sixth. Mark Martin becomes the eighth winner in eight Winston Cup races this season. Dad, who later tells me this was a pretty tough race, "even for Martinsville," is ninth. He's now second in Cup points and I'm sixteenth; I'm ahead of Matt by four points in the rookie standings.

After the race, I'm drained. I feel like I've been in a twelve-round fight with a car that outweighs me by more than 3,200 pounds. My entire body is sore.

I may need some of those Goody's Body Pain tablets, but otherwise I'm feeling OK. (Goody's sponsored the race and sometimes you just can't help but mention a sponsor, even if sometimes it's someone else's.) This little track is the hardest I've ever driven as far as beating me up in the car. My foot is sore from mashing that brake pedal almost a thousand times. That's hard work now!

I'm ready to get home and rest up, as much as I can, for next week at Talladega. From the slowest track in NASCAR to the fastest. Never a dull moment.

## Talladega, Alabama
## DieHard 500

## Over before It Began

The Talladega Superspeedway is in the middle of rural Alabama. It is the biggest, fastest, longest, and widest track that we race on. When it opened, back in 1969, most of the drivers boycotted the race because they thought the track was unsafe. Too fast. NASCAR plowed ahead with replacement drivers, so the regulars who sat out soon came back. As the speeds continued to increase, Bill Elliott set a NASCAR record with a lap just slightly over 214 miles per hour. That's an awesome number, and I'd love a chance to be able to go that fast here. *But* there are some very scary consequences of going that fast. The worst is that the car can spin around and slide backwards, which allows air to get underneath the car and actually send it flying high into the air. That happened to Bobby Allison in 1987, and his car nearly flew into the grandstand.

So NASCAR made some rules changes for this track—and Daytona—to slow the cars down. The principal change was the addition of restrictor plates, which cut down on the air flow to the carburetor so the engine can't produce so much power. But that causes problems too. When nobody is any faster than anybody else, cars tend to bunch up, and at Talladega you see guys racing three-, four- and even five-wide. Guys will be just inches from each other, or the wall, and if something happens, the cars behind them don't have the extra burst of speed to get out of the way. So you can get some big crashes involving most of the cars in the field. *Big* crashes.

The way to race Talladega is to use the draft, be patient, and drive smart. I think of it like a chess match because you always have to outthink the opponent and plan one or two moves beyond your current position. Although I am new to this type of restricted racing, I like to think I'm pretty smart and I may have an advantage over the next guy. Especially if he didn't grow up watching every move made by the greatest restrictor-plate driver of all—Big E.

Dad claims he doesn't like restrictor-plate racing and he isn't shy about saying so. He hates anything that slows the cars down. "It ain't real racin'" he grouses.

But Dad's the smartest driver out there—there is a lot more to him than that "Intimidator" stuff—and he knows how to get himself in position on the track. He knows how to use the draft, how to use the air around his car to help himself or hamper the cars around him. When the time comes to make his move, he does it and he wins more often than not. He's won more "plate" races than anyone.

I've got a ways to go but I'm learning fast. I've only raced twice here in the Busch Series, and we'll be running within inches (or less) of the other cars while traveling more than the length of a football field every second. Think about your local high school or college football field: now imagine going that distance in one second with other cars hammering away at you. It makes Martinsville seem like we were coasting.

We're eleventh fastest in practice and I'm pretty happy with the car. But the truth is, I could probably teach just about anybody with a driver's license to go that fast on a track this wide with no traffic around.

Before we go out to qualify, NASCAR inspectors tell us our rear spoiler (the tall flap at the back of the trunk that keeps the rear of the car glued to the road) was set too low in practice, and that pisses me off. I'm worried that when we correct it to the higher angle, we'll lose a lot of speed.

Before we can find out, rain holds up qualifying. With the restrictor plates, it takes each car at least two laps to get to top speed, so the qualifying seems endless once it begins. Some of the last cars to go out have to qualify in the dark, with only a few lights along the front straightaway. At those speeds it can be scary in broad daylight—but in the dark?

When the long day is finally over, we're sixth best. We've qualified in the top twenty-five in fourteen consecutive races now (that's every race in the Bud team's short Cup history), and it's the longest current streak in Winston Cup. So I guess the spoiler thing didn't hurt us too bad.

Saturday we run the second IROC race of the season. The cars are supposed to be set up equally, but some cars are much more equal than others. My car is one of the others. I'm struggling right from the start with an engine that is barely able to pull the car around the banking. When I lose the draft of the cars ahead of me, I'm already half a lap behind. Or so I'm told, because I can't see the rest of the field. Each time I cross the finish line, the engine sounds more and more like an out-of-tune tuba.

"Just embarrassing," is all I can say after the race. I climb out and walk off.

During happy hour in the Winston Cup cars, Bobby Hamilton comes up from behind and gets his nose into me pretty hard. I'm out of shape for a split second, but manage to save the car. My crew gets pretty pissed off about it. I'd given him a bump at Martinsville and they figure this is payback. But we were running much slower last week.

The car is a little banged up, but it will be ready for the race.

After we go to the garage, Ryan McGee, a producer with *RPM2Night,* comes by to talk about a story he is working on for *ESPN* magazine. The magazine had done a cover story about me and Matt earlier in the year. Another writer wrote it, and he really made Matt and me look like crap in the story. He described me as the off-spring of "an unholy alliance between Jed Clampett and Courtney Love."

I thought it was a shitty, personal attack at the time, and I haven't changed my mind. I mean, I might even think it's kinda funny and, hell, I like Jed Clampett and Courtney Love. But that's a nasty description. In response, I take the side door and ditch McGee at the transporter. I know it's not his fault, but you have to make your point somehow. He waits for another half hour or so before he figures out I'm long gone.

With the high speeds and the potential for major crashes, there is a lot of tension before the race. You can feel it among the drivers, the crews, and the fans. It just lays there like a fog until they scream, "Gentlemen, start your engines."

While I'm pulling onto the track for the first pace lap, I tell the team, "I never thought I'd start in the third row in this race. Thanks. You guys did a good job!"

Just ahead of me in the outside lane, starting fourth, is the black No. 3 Goodwrench car. At Daytona, the only other time I'd raced against him in a restrictor-plate event, we smashed and beat on each other all day and it hurt us both. Today, Dad will be strong every lap like he always is here. So I plan to stick with him and try to learn as much as I can. Soak it all in, and then at the end, just hope I'll be racing with him for the win.

After several parade laps, the field lumbers through Talladega's big tri-oval and begins to build up speed as we head for the starting line and the green flag. One thing about plate racing—it takes the cars forever to get up to speed. It looks like we're being held back by giant elastic bands attached to the rear bumpers.

While coming up to speed, Bill Elliott, who is in the car starting in front of Dad in the outside row, lifts off the throttle or misses a shift. When he slows down radically, Dad backs off to keep from slamming into him. But I'm not so lucky. I'm concentrating on shifting and accelerating when I see what's happening. I slam on the brakes to avoid smashing into Dad's rear bumper, but we still make contact.

It happens right in front of my pit area. The whole team is watching closely and they can't believe what they see—huge plumes of smoke pouring out of the right front corner of their car after the contact. The race is over for us before it has even begun.

They scramble to prepare to fix the car, no matter what the damage is. Tires? Brakes? Engine? Radiator? Bodywork?

In the meantime, the rest of the field passes me. I need to make it 2.6 miles back around to the pit area without damaging the car worse. The track is so big it seems like this takes about an hour. Once the right front tire goes flat, the car scrapes the ground, grinding suspension pieces across the rough pavement. And there is nothing I can do but keep going and get it into the pit.

I come grating down pit lane and get on the radio. "No brakes, no brakes!"

With the help of all of the crew, we get it stopped and take the car behind the pit wall so they can go right to work. They may have to replace most of the right front corner of the car. The right front wheel is ground down almost in half. It looks like a crescent moon. The team replaces it. And many of the suspension pieces. Tony Jr. discovers that the front brake caliper is locked closed. Most likely, it failed when I stomped on the brakes to avoid Dad. It stopped the right front tire from rolling, which caused it to go flat and then get ground to a pulp. So new brakes are installed.

The repairs take twenty-nine long minutes, and I'm twenty-five laps down when I finally get back on the track.

As I'm leaving pit lane, Tony Jr. gets on the radio.

"They say this builds character." Long, dramatic pause. "But it still sucks."

The rest of the race is like a very intense test session for both me and the team. We have a lot to learn about restrictor-plate racing, and this is as good a way as any to learn some of it.

But the fun ends in one of those big, chain-reaction crashes that seem to happen at Talladega at least once per race. I almost make it through unscathed. Seventeen cars are sliding across the front stretch, and I see the light at the end of the melee. But before I can reach the light, Robby Gordon's spinning car slams into me. I'm okay but the car definitely isn't. Somehow I roll long enough to get it behind the pit wall again.

"That was pretty wide-ass open," I say with a grin when I crawl out of the car while Tony and Tony Jr. leap to see if they can make it fit to race again. I hope they aren't able to fix it, but they do, and I go back out. After a few laps limping around like a one-legged man, I bring it back in for good.

"I can smell the water burning," I tell the crew. We damaged the radiator in the crash, and it has hurt the engine.

Jeff Gordon, who had been struggling so far this year with a new crew chief, Robbie Loomis (Gordon's former crew chief, Ray Evernham, left to start the Dodge NASCAR program that will hit the track in 2001), wins his fiftieth career Winston Cup race and is the ninth different winner in nine races this season. Many of the fans who cheer for my dad boo and hiss Gordon wherever he goes. Maybe they think he's a little too slick, too clean, too damn *perfect* for their taste. Now that he's won, the crowd seems to be divided in half: those that are cheering him and those that are booing him. It's a weird sound. No matter what anyone thinks of Jeff, I can tell you that he is one helluva race driver. He is always driving hard, yet he rarely crashes and he just seems to be able to do things with the car that I'm still trying to figure out. He's awesome.

Dad doesn't win but he finishes third and he's still second in the points race. After all of our work, we finish forty-second.

We are about a quarter of the way through the season, and we get the next weekend off. It seems like we've been racing for two or three years without a break since Daytona back in February. We can all use some time to relax, especially after a day like today.

# Fontana, California
## NAPA 500

## I Have to Deliver Beer

The season has been flat-out since Speedweeks at Daytona, so nobody is complaining about the one-week break we get between races in mid-April. Least of all me. I've been practicing, testing, doing media and sponsor appearances, signing autographs, and even driving the occasional race, so I've been left with little time to kick back. I'm ready to sit on the couch and just chill.

But my sponsor has other ideas.

I have to deliver beer.

Instead of a week off, Budweiser is making me do a promotional appearance for a day and a half. Delivering beer.

Oh, did I forget to mention it's in Hawaii? Here's the deal: If I make appearances and promote Bud at a couple of key military locations for a day or so, then I can have the rest of the weekend to myself and a few close friends in a resort hotel. Not bad, eh?

The promotions are fun. The military service people are enthusiastic and I feel good about doing something they appreciate. We tour the battleship *Missouri* and it is one awesome machine. The ship fought in three wars and it is where they signed the surrender documents that ended World War II. I am kind of a history buff, and it gives me chills walking those decks and thinking about everything this ship has been through.

When we're finished delivering Bud to the troops, I check into a private suite on the beach and barely leave the hotel for the rest of the time off.

I'm back at work in the middle of the next week, testing on the road course at Sears Point in Sonoma, California, where we'll be racing in a couple of months. We don't do much road-course racing in NASCAR. Mostly it's ovals, so I need the practice turning right and left. I have my problems and spin the car a couple of times and run off into the gravel pits a few more times. My father warned me that it's a difficult course to get around, and he was right about that. But I'm not too worried. We spun out a helluva lot testing for the road-course race at Watkins Glen last year in Busch Series. Then we went out and won the race.

Anyway, right now I need to think about the California Speedway in Fontana, outside of Los Angeles, where we'll be racing on Sunday in the NAPA Auto Parts 500.

This is probably the nicest track we will see all year. Roger Penske—owner of Rusty Wallace's team, but a man most famous for his successful Indy 500 teams— built the course in the 1990s on the site of an old steel mill. The site had been condemned by the EPA as an environmental hazard, but the Penske people moved all the old scrap metal and junk—thousands of tons of it—and then relandscaped the site and put in all the amenities you could want. There are convenience stores in the infield and you can even get pizza delivered. There are ninety-thousand seats and you can see the entire two-mile track from all of them. The track is beautiful and it certainly improved the neighborhood. The France family's International Speedway Corporation now owns the Fontana track, and it is unquestionably the standard that other tracks will be measured against.

I arrive confident, if not tanned, from my Hawaii visit. I explain to the envious team that I spent more time inside the suite, hanging out with friends, than outside on the beach soaking up sun. With my complexion, too much sun would make me look like a lobster. But I'm refreshed and ready.

In the two Busch races we ran in California, I won and finished third, leading a combined 221 out of 300 total laps. The track has been good to me and I hope to keep this momentum going.

During practice it looks like we can continue our streak, but for some reason, when we go to qualify, the car feels extremely loose. It won't stick and I have to drive it hard down in the corner. I felt like I'm driving over my head and we only qualify twentieth.

On Saturday we celebrate my father's forty-ninth birthday. I wish him happy birthday and he says something about how he'll be doing his real celebrating tomorrow, after the race.

Meanwhile, our part of the garage looks like it has been taken over by a big-time movie crew. Fox Sports, which will be televising the first half of next season, has sent a crew to shoot promos and get some footage to promote their coverage in 2001. I'm doing the usual lines—"This is Dale Earnhardt Jr. and you're watching Fox"—when Riki Rachtman, the former MTV VJ, stops by. He's wearing a Dale Earnhardt Jr. T-shirt and sporting some broken fingers from a skateboard accident. He's hard to miss, with his tattoos and spiked hair that's as black as one of the Goodyear tires. Hard to say who is more surprised—me because he's a fan, or him because I'm a fan. Some people have trouble with the idea of a rock-and-roll racer because NASCAR has been seen as a country-and-western–type crowd. Now, I like a lot of country music, but I gotta have rock and roll, and it's cool to meet someone else who is into both like I am.

The next morning, the race starts earlier than I'm used to, because we're on the West Coast. I'm not a morning person and today the Chevrolet is not what you'd call a morning car. We start falling back right away. By Lap 30, I'm in twenty-seventh place.

But we make some adjustments during the first pit stop, and back out on the track, the car is responding a lot better. I kick it up a little, match the lap times of the leader, and start picking them off. By Lap 86, I'm running ninth while my rookie buddy Matt is leading.

With less than one hundred laps to go, I'm more or less stuck around tenth. Then the car starts going to hell. It's getting loose again and I'm getting pissed.

Kenseth is running away from the field and everyone is trying to remember the last time two rookies won races in the same season—1981 when Morgan Shepherd and Ron Bouchard each won a race.

It's no time for history lessons now, because I have all I can handle with the car. On the final pit stop, at Lap 220, I tell the crew, "When I hit the brakes, it pulls hard to the left." The power steering has failed.

I'm not the only one with mechanical problems. Jeremy Mayfield, who is running near the front, has a problem that causes the oil temperature to climb to more than 300 degrees Fahrenheit. The oil tank on a Winston Cup car is located right behind the driver's seat, and Jeremy's butt is frying. It sounds funny, but it isn't. Inside the car, the air temperature can reach up to 140 degrees, but this is much worse. His crew is trying to help him all they can, but there's only so much they can do. Cold water may feel good initially, but it drains into the bottom of the seat where it soon begins to boil. Still, Mayfield and his charred ass beat Bobby Labonte and Matt to the checkered flag. Matt could have won, but a late pit stop dropped him back and he was only able to make it back to third. He'll get one soon, the way they're running.

To add insult to Mayfield's hot seat, NASCAR inspects the car and says the roof is too low—but only because Jeremy climbed on the roof to celebrate the win.

Still, he gets the victory and a lot of drivers would trade those kinds of problems to come in first. We come home twelfth in spite of the steering problems, which just about wore my ass out. Without power steering, you feel like you are fighting that car. After I hoist myself out of the car, I sit on the back of the transporter for a while, saying nothing, exhausted.

We had a good car today, but not a great car. It was good to finish the race strong. We've been in too many crashes lately and had so much bad luck. We were very fast, but then the steering began to go away and there was nothing we could do.

After a little while, I go looking for Dad. He finished seventeenth, so I guess there won't be any big combination victory/birthday celebration. But maybe he'll let me hitch a ride with him on the jet. It's a long flight home and his jet is fast and can make it on one fuel load. I'll be home in a few hours instead of the next morning if I were to fly back home with the crew. There are some perks that come with being the team owner's kid, and today, as whipped as I am, I'm going to take advantage of them.

## Richmond, Virginia
### *Pontiac Excitement 400*

## I Love You . . . Now Find Your Own Way Home

It wasn't that long ago that New York and NASCAR were two things you just wouldn't put together in the same sentence. New York was supposed to mean big-city sophistication, and NASCAR was supposed to be redneck racing. But New York recognizes one thing: money. The more successful NASCAR gets, the more New York likes it. It's a slow process, but we're getting there. A few years back, NASCAR began holding the year-end awards banquet at the Waldorf-Astoria Hotel on Park Avenue. Slowly, we're invading the consciousness of Wall Street. And this year, a few days before the Richmond race, I'm in New York City to make an appearance at the New York Stock Exchange.

I'm here for Anheuser-Busch Day, signing autographs and meeting with the media in front of the famous NYSE Wall Street façade. The Budweiser Clydesdales are on hand along with some very nice looking women who are not dressed in the usual scanty Bud Girl outfits for this one. Today they are wearing big hair, short skirts, and sharp blue blazers, and instead of calling themselves Bud Girls, they are "Bud Ambassadors."

NHRA Top Fuel driver Kenny Bernstein is here too, and after the interviews and autograph session we get the VIP tour of the trading room floor from Dick Grasso, chairman of the Exchange and a big racing fan. He even climbs in the seat of my car that is here on display and gets Kenny and me to sign his autograph book. It is full of names that everyone would recognize and some they wouldn't. Everyone from Muhammad Ali to the lil' Taco Bell Chihuahua.

I wasn't looking forward to today, but I'm surprised that there are so many people in line for autographs. The stock exchange workers who are wearing ugly trading vests over their high-dollar suits line up just like the fans at Darlington or Daytona. One of the New Yorkers invites me to join him with some of the Bud Ambassadors: "Yo, Jooon-yah," he shouts, "why don'tchoo an' me grab some o' dem girls and take 'em in da back dere? Ba-da-bing." It's *Mayberry Meets the Sopranos.*

Touré, my buddy from *Rolling Stone,* has taken a cab from his apartment down to Wall Street to get in on things. He hangs out and watches all the suits, and when we're done, he says, "Come on, Jann wants to meet you."

"Jann" is Jann Wenner, publisher and founder of *Rolling Stone.*

So we take the car uptown to the *Rolling Stone* offices, which are like a museum of rock and roll. There are murals on the walls—cover shots from the magazine's past—that include the biggest names in music and show business. Madonna. Steve Martin. Pete Town-shend. These are some of the most memorable and high-impact images of the last thirty years, and they really grab your eye.

The staff is exactly what you'd expect: young, hip, attractive and relaxed in a sort of I-am-so-damn-cool-I-can-wear-these-leather-pants-to-work-because-it-just-comes-naturally kind of way. I'm still in the suit and tie I wore to the stock exchange—not exactly my usual threads—and some of the laid-back staffers get on me about my "formal wear." It's unusual for me to be the most conservatively dressed guy in the room.

Jann Wenner's big office is on a corner with views in two directions of the busy New York streets below. A very cool place. He welcomes me in like he's honestly happy for the chance and says, "We might have sold more copies if we'd put you on the cover." Sarah Michelle Gellar, the actress, was the cover model, sitting spread legged on the hood of a car.

"Nah, you did great with the blonde," I tell him. "Everyone wants to see her."

We chat awhile about cars and motorcycles and music and he asks me who I've been listening to lately.

"My favorites right now," I tell him, "are Third Eye Blind and a Canadian group, the Matthew Good Band."

"Matthew Good?" Wenner says.

"Yeah. They're big in Canada. They sound a lot like Our Lady Peace. They may have a record come out in the U.S. next year."

He shakes his head. I guess I've stumped him.

Even if he doesn't know my fave Canadian bands, he is charming and gracious and says that sometime in the future one of his other magazines, *Men's Journal,* should do a feature on me.

Sounds good to me.

From New York, it is back south on the jet, to Richmond, Virginia, where I've had some of my best racing success. It started life as a half-mile dirt track but has been constantly improved. Now it is D-shaped and longer—three quarters of a mile—and is one of the most modern tracks on the tour, combining superspeedway-style driving and short-track intimacy. The track is wide and smooth so you have room to race, and there are seats for ninety-five thousand people. Fans like Richmond and so do I. In my two Busch seasons, I won twice here. And I ran one of the five Winston Cup races we entered last year here. We cooked the brakes early in the race and were never able to push hard again, but we were still fast. I was a ball of fire before that and I still got a top ten. My first in Winston Cup. So it's good to be back.

When we start practice, the car isn't handling right and I'm down in the middle on the timing charts. We need time to work on it, and we also need some help from the qualifying draw. Each week, NASCAR holds a random drawing to determine the order cars will go out to run qualifying laps. At Richmond, qualifying starts late in the afternoon when the track is still hot from the sun. As the suns starts to set and the shadows get longer, the track cools down and it gets faster and faster. It's a big relief when the drawing is complete—we'll be one of the last cars out.

We take advantage of the break and I rip off a great lap to qualify fifth for my eighth top-ten start in eleven races. My average starting position is the best in Winston Cup, and although we struggled in practice, I'm happy to start so close to the front.

After qualifying, I'm escorted off to a special hospitality function, a Busch-sponsored beer-garden party where the fans have been enjoying themselves, and the cold beer, since early in the day. The crowd yells and cheers and it is pretty raucous. Really raucous in fact.

The floor is opened for questions and the first guy to speak sounds like he's been drinking a little too much of the cold Busch brew.

"Why is Rusty Wallace still such a badass driver?" he says, kind of belligerent.

The crowd boos and moans and I kind of write that one off.

After few more questions, though, the mood turns bizarre and another guy challenges me. There is a controversy going on about the Confederate flag flying over the South Carolina capitol, and that's what this guy wants me to talk about.

He makes a little speech that ends up with the question, "What do you think of the rebel flag?" This is followed by a chorus of redneck yelps and cheers.

The guy has put me in a bind. As much as I brag about being a no-bullshit-tell-it-like-it-is-here's-how-I-see-it kinda guy, I know that these are the fans that pay my salary, so I'm hesitant to tell him the rebel flag represents closed-minded, racist views that have no place in today's society. Give 'em a straight answer and I may piss off the "rebels" in the crowd, and I'm not in the business of trying to make an escape from this drunken crowd. But I have my opinions and I don't want to give a dishonest answer, either. I feel like the weight of the Civil War is resting on my shoulders.

I take a couple of breaths and say, "I think it means something different to me than it does to y'all. . . ."

That gets mixed reactions. Some hoot and yell, some kind of snicker.

But time is up and I'm not going to stick around and argue the point. I'm ready to split and the promoters have been telling the crowd that I do not have time for autographs. But there is this kid, about ten years old, with a Dale Jr. die-cast car, and he's holding it up for me to sign. I have a hard time passing up a kid and hardly ever do. But when I reach out to sign for him, the stampede is on. Fans of all ages, shapes, and sizes are leaping on the stage with all kinds of stuff for me to sign.

Whoa, man. The crush is on. The dam has broken. I'm being pushed and the kids are being pushed and it gets real frantic real quick. I'm off the stage as fast as I can jump, running for the golf cart that will carry me back to the garage area. But other fans have staked out the cart and they're crowding it too, so I'm signing as much as I can while Joe Glynn, the Bud guy driving the cart, is trying to get rolling and get out of there.

When we're finally moving and leaving the crowd behind, I take a breath and mutter to Joe, "That was pretty shitty. I'm never doing that again. . . ."

Most Winston Cup races are run on Sunday afternoon, but at Richmond they race on Saturday night. It's a nod to the traditions of NASCAR, and the old Saturday night short-track days when most of the biggest names in the sport got their start. I get extra pumped up, racing under the lights. And it's exciting for the fans. The stadium lights give the illusion that the cars are going a lot faster than they actually are. I can't explain it, but it's true. You see exhaust flames coming out of the pipes and sparks flying from underneath the cars when they dive into the corners and make contact with the asphalt. I think we should race at night much more often!

But night racing is hard on the drivers and crews because you're doing in two days what you usually do in three. The days start early in the morning with practice and qualifying sessions, and you're working all day in the sun even before you spend several more hours under the lights. It's really hell on the crew guys.

After the final practice session, I decide to head back to the motor coach to get something to eat and catch a nap.

Shane Mueller, who drives my coach, is my unofficial chef. He usually grills outside the coach, and he makes my usual favorite—grilled marinated chicken. As a bonus of sorts, he also has some spicy cheese dip with chips for me. I dig in and fill up.


When the race starts, I take it easy until a yellow on Lap 8. I'm already worried. The brakes feel like I only have half a pedal.

You need good brakes at Richmond, same as any short track. You have to get on them hard to slow down before you come into Turn 1 and again in Turn 3. I remember the brake failure here last year, and so do Tony Jr. and the rest of the guys.

But the crew has done some things—like adding extra air ducts for cooling the front brakes—and when we get back up to speed it looks like they are paying off. As it gets darker outside, most of the cars show a bright red glow from superhot brakes. This is usually not a good sign. In contrast, the only red you see on the No. 8 car is the paint.

Even so, after one hundred laps I'm dropping back in the field. The car is tight in the corners. The front tires aren't gripping enough and the nose is sliding toward the wall. I have to let off on the throttle in the middle of the corner, and I'm slow coming out. This hurts my straightaway speed, but if I stomp on the throttle too hard, or too soon, the tires go chattering across the asphalt.

The tight handling has me down to twelfth by Lap 117. I get a few spots back after some adjustments in the pits and then start falling back again. Maybe we have a bad set of tires.

When we pit again on Lap 173, they give me new rubber, and I start passing cars like a madman. I go by my father and I'm up to sixth before the tires hit the limit and I fall back four positions in three laps.

We get a yellow flag on Lap 240, and the guys make a great stop. I came in tenth but I go out in sixth place. After only a few laps, I'm running third.

I'm starting to feel it. We may have a shot here.

Another yellow comes out on Lap 263, so with 137 laps to go, pit strategy is the name of the game. Tony Sr. decides not to stop.

"You guys are the reason we're up here [in second place]," I radio. "This ain't no second-place car but I feel like we're in the second-best spot to win this thing because you guys are making the right decisions."

The continuous adjustments the crew made to the car tonight—tire pressure changes and chassis adjustments—are really paying off. I'm not just fast for a few laps anymore. I gain ground on the long green-flag runs. With less than seventy laps to go, I'm content to ride in second place, and it looks like it will come down to a fight between me and Tony Stewart, who has the fastest car on the track.

When you're racing, you are also calculating. From Lap 1, you need a strategy so you are ready when you make that final run to the finish. Saving the tires and brakes or saving fuel is critical. Going all out on Lap 350 may look good to the fans, but it's bad strategy if you don't have anything left when you need it on Lap 400. Leading is fun, but they only pay you for the final lap.

"Tell me when there's twenty-five laps to go," I tell the spotter. If it's green flag all the way to the end, that's when I want to make my move.

Then we get a yellow flag on Lap 362 and that's the end of *that* plan. Go to plan B.

Because Richmond is a short track, the pit lane is even tighter and more congested than usual. More than twenty cars that are still running on the lead lap shoehorn into their stall for the last stop of the night. We're in the second pit stall, near Turn 1. The Bud crew knows that this one really counts, and they do a brilliant job. In and out in 15.88 seconds.

And then . . . chaos.

I make a hard right turn to avoid Todd Bodine's crew

members in the stall just ahead of us. (Todd is in the car that his brother Geoffrey "don't call me Geoff" had started the race in.) Their tire carrier was out beyond the back bumper of the car, right in my path. When I turn to avoid him, the right front bumper of my car catches Tony Stewart's left front bumper as he's coming quickly out of his own stall from behind me.

In the confusion, noise, and commotion, we all know I've hit something. But for a few seconds we aren't sure what—or *whom*—we hit.

"Did you hit a tire?" somebody from the crew says.

"I didn't hit them boys, did I?" I shout. One of my biggest fears is hitting a crewman, and I wonder if I clipped one of Bodine's guys.

Turns out I didn't. But I sure hit something.

"I think I hit the No. 20 car getting around the No. 60 car," I say. "I don't think the right side is rubbing. But check it, please."

In rapid order I try to check everything: brakes, tires, steering, suspension. Is it all still intact? Things soon settle down and it's clear what happened. Stewart has a flat left front tire that was cut or damaged when we hit. He had the dominant car, no question, but now he's going to have to make an extra stop and he's almost certainly out of contention with so few laps to go.

The spotter looks my car over and calls down, "The right side is OK. Doesn't look like the tire is rubbing."

It may look all right at slow speeds, but the tire or the suspension piece may have been damaged. We'll know when we get up to speed. There are thirty-two laps left, and when the smoke and confusion clear, I see that Big E and I are running first and second. Dad was buried deep in the field before the caution flag, but he and his team have decided to gamble. They don't take new tires during their stop, hoping that Dad can hold off the field. If anyone can, it's him. But I have four fresh tires, and I think I will be much faster.

Now we go to plan C.

The fans are on their feet. This is what they've been waiting for and what the media has been building up and hyping for years now, ever since I started winning in the Busch Series—father and son dueling to the finish.

How many times have I been asked the question, "What would you do if you were behind your dad on the last lap?"

How many times have I tried to come up with an answer? How many times have I wanted to hear another question—anything new, anything different than "What would you do if you were behind your dad on the last lap?"

Well, now we'll find out. I have to make a move quickly—strike while my tires are much fresher. If I wait until the last lap, it might be too late.

The green flag drops and I see the strobes of flashbulbs popping all over the grandstands. It looks like fireflies on a summer night. But the suspense doesn't last long. About fifty seconds, to be exact, just a little less than it takes to run two laps. I get beside Dad on the first lap and then blow by him on the second circuit. I take the car so hard into Turn 1 that sparks fly from underneath. It's awesome that we're in the lead for the first time tonight, but new worries arise. Are the sparks flying just because I'm driving hard or because there is damage to the car from the pit lane incident?

My only option: run flat out. If it breaks, it breaks.

With twenty-five laps to go, there are no signs of trouble and I'm pulling away, trying to open as much of a lead as I can on the cars that are now passing Dad and trying to catch me.

Terry Labonte gets past the black No. 3 and moves into second place. His car seems slightly better than mine, and he keeps closing, lap by lap, a tenth of a second at a time. He is a few car lengths behind me with ten laps to go. No question he can catch me. But can he pass me?

Many people are wondering if he might try to come through me rather than around me, kind of like the way my dad did to him in the famous finish at Bristol last year. Like some sort of family revenge. Payback.

I don't know and I don't want to let him get close enough to try. So I'm driving my ass off and the sparks are flying on every lap. (From the car—*not* my ass.)

Two laps from the finish, Labonte pulls to the inside. He's on my back bumper and if he wants to boot me, this is the perfect time. I hold my line—and my breath. But he can't keep up and he races me clean. No contact. I've got just enough tires and brakes left to hold him off on the final lap, and we win by .159. Less than two tenths of a second. Can you believe it?

Tony Stewart, who got back on the track after our collision in the pits, finishes eighth. Dad's gamble with old tires drops him to tenth at the finish, but that's probably better than he would have finished if he had changed four tires and dropped back into the field. And I head to Victory Lane with our second win in eleven races. We are the first team to take two races this season. Rookie team. Rookie driver. Winners, not just once, but twice.

The race analysts on TV are asking how it could happen. They'll have to wait to ask me until I finish turning a few donuts and tire-smoking burnouts. I create so much tire smoke it looks like the place has been sprayed for bugs, and I damn near blow up the engine. (Dad pulled me aside later and said, "The engine shop says, 'No more burnouts!'")

The crew is leaping and hugging, screaming and laughing, and running for Victory Lane for the second time in five weeks. And they should be celebrating. They did great work. Bring on the Bud.

When I get the smoking car to Victory Lane, I get out, climb on top, and then do a big swan dive into the arms of the crew. We are all just so damn happy.

The ESPN crew fights its way in for a live interview before they go off the air. I was supposed to stay on one side of the car, but after my swan dive, I'm buried in red shirts thirty feet away.

After the interview, we all hug and yell some more. The ESPN and NASCAR guys tell me I have to put on a microphone and a headset for a live *SportsCenter* interview coming up in a few moments. And then . . . I wait. And everyone else waits.

The crew is bathing in Bud but all I want is some water. I'm exhausted, leaning against the car, waiting for the live interview to start, when Dad comes barreling into Victory Lane. He kneels down to where I'm resting, puts a big hand around the back of my neck and tells me he loves me . . . *but* I'm going to have to find my own way home. Big E waits for no one. Not for his son. Not even for the race winner. The helicopter is leaving.

Just like at Texas, "Whassssssup" is the cry. People are hollering it into the sky. And tonight it is a real question. "What's up with the interview, man? C'mon! Hurry it up!" We wait on ESPN for what seems like forever. Five minutes . . . six . . . seven . . . and finally we're on live. . . .

Once that's done, I get a chance to hug my mother, who lives near Richmond with her husband, and always comes to see me race here. Maybe that's why I do so well here.

But I don't feel so hot. One of the crew guys says I look like Casper the Friendly Ghost and asks me if I need more water before we pose for all of the endless photographs and interviews.

"No, man," I groan. "I need to take a shit."

It must be the spicy cheese dip. My insides are about to boil over like an overheating radiator.

The hats and the media are going to have to wait.

Joe Glynn, Budweiser's jack-of-all-trades, leaps into action and finds the nearest restroom and some security people to escort me there. That's something you don't ordinarily experience—a security escort on the way to the bathroom.

I return feeling a whole lot better and ready to do the hat dance. When that's finished and I've done some more television interviews, I go to the press box, which is located in a very public area outside of Turn 1. The fans have figured this out and have the route staked out, so it's a madhouse as soon as we get out of the tunnel under the track.

I've got four big state troopers surrounding me, and

they push and pull their way through the crowd, carrying me along as they go. We move through the masses like a big ocean liner cutting through water, and in our wake, some of the other guys like Tony Sr. get smashed and submerged when the crowd closes back in behind me. One fan rips the hat off my head. Bad move, dude. The troopers get the hat back . . . instantly. Another fan, who is standing on top of his beer cooler to get a better view, takes a header when the Styrofoam cooler collapses and the crowd overwhelms him. Ice, water, and generic-brand beer go flying everywhere. But thankfully, no one is hurt, and eventually we make it to the press box.

I start out by thanking the crew. I'm proud to make it to Victory Lane for them, because they deserve it. We did not have the best car out there—but they were great on the pit stops, plus they made the right choices to make the car better every time we made a pit stop.

It seems like it was a lifetime ago back in Darlington when the team was wondering if I'd quit on them.

We've got a lot of celebrating to do and we have a weekend off and the Budweiser is going to taste real good.

Now I need to find a way home.

# Charlotte, North Carolina
## *The Winston*

## Here Comes This Red Thing

After Richmond, the tour takes a break for a weekend, and it couldn't come at a better time. Our schedule is the longest of any professional sports season in the world, so to say it is a real grind is an understatement. After a win, you feel like you've earned a chance to relax and celebrate. Most of the time, there is little opportunity to enjoy it, because there are so many media and sponsor commitments and everyone is right back at the next track in only a few days. But having a week off right now is awesome. We can savor the elation that comes with a win for as long as possible.

But the feeling goes away immediately the following Friday, when I learn that Adam Petty has been killed in a crash in New Hampshire. He was practicing for the Busch Series race when he crashed into the wall head-on in Turn 3. Adam was only nineteen years old, and he was the first fourth-generation American professional athlete, following his father, Kyle, his grandfather Richard, and his great-grandfather Lee Petty.

I can't believe it—I looked at him almost like a class-
mate. We grew up together, playing in the infield at racetracks with other kids like Jason Jarrett while our dads
were busy racing. We shared a lot of interests and we
shared a lot of laughs. He had his grandpa's electric
smile that looked like it was always lit by some sort of
hidden spotlight. The fans loved him, and he had the
same kind of easygoing, friendly-to-everyone tempera-
ment that the entire Petty family seems to carry. He and
I also shared the same sort of pressure of trying to live
up to the legacy of more than one generation of great
race drivers.

One of my most prized possessions is a pair of red
driving shoes that he gave me. I had shown up at a race
and realized I'd forgotten my racing shoes. These shoes
are custom-made. They're heat-shielded and fireproof,
with thin soles providing a direct feel of the throttle and
brake pedals. It's not as if you can just race with ordinary boots or your coolest pair of Adidas. I was screwed
until Adam was nice enough to loan me a pair of his.
Then I went out and won the race. It was so cool when
he said I could keep the shoes to remember the win.

My dad always said he didn't want to attend any more
funerals after he went to his dad's service, so even
though many other drivers go to the memorial services,
he and I stay home.

I feel bad. I feel like I have something to say to Kyle,
Adam's dad, because I was a friend. I just don't know
how to say it. I guess I'm a coward. I feel like Kyle
knows I miss Adam, so I don't have to tell him. If I were
in his position, I wouldn't want people to come up and
remind me that my son had died. I don't wanna bother

him. I'm scared, I guess, and I don't know how to say it or admit it.

The news hits the whole NASCAR family hard, especially since it comes so soon after his great-grandfather Lee Petty passed away a day after the Texas race. That race had also been Adam's first—and only—Winston Cup start. The entire family, especially Kyle, had built the future of Petty Enterprises on Adam, and now he was gone. I know he was going to be a huge star, and I had lost the chance to race against him for many years to come.

Everyone knew it would feel empty to go back to the track without him. But that's what we do. We race, so we have to go forward. Like Richard Petty said, if we were farmers, we would have to go ahead and harvest the fields even if someone had died. It's our job. It's our life.

Earlier in the week, I had decided to throw a pool party for the team on Saturday night. The news about Adam was horrible, but I thought it would still feel good to get everyone together. You know, good food, good brew, and a relaxing time at the pool on a rare weekend away from the track. When party time arrives, Tony Jr. is there, but the rest of the guys don't show. I guess their idea of relaxing is staying home with friends and family, making up for lost time. I can't blame 'em, but the crappy turnout doesn't make me happy. I'll have to find some way to get even.

The next weekend is the Winston—our all-star bash— at Lowe's Motor Speedway (although it will always be known as the Charlotte Motor Speedway to me 'cause that's what it was called from before I was born up until a few years ago). It's about thirty minutes from the DEI shop, so it's like being able to race in your own backyard. After the Winston, the Coca-Cola 600 is held the following week at this same track. Everyone will be sleeping in his or her own bed for a while longer. As much as we travel, that bonus feels like it's worth a ton of gold.

When we get to the track on Friday afternoon, everyone is up—relaxed after winning and getting a little more rest than usual. The pain of losing Adam is actually lessened by being at the track around the NASCAR family. I miss Adam, but it feels good to be at the track. And it doesn't hurt that we have a car that is as fast, or faster, than anything in the garage. Lightning fast.

I make a short practice run and then bring the car back into the garage area. I stop the car about ten feet short of our stall. I motion for the crew to come over and push me in. The guys get on the car and start pushing. But it doesn't move. They push harder, but still nothing because I've got my foot on the brake pedal.

"That'll teach you guys not to come to my party," I say.

"Didn't teach us nothing," someone says, laughing.

"OK then," I snap back. "It'll be like third grade. One person mouthed off, but the whole class has to be punished."

We all share a big laugh.

After the next practice run, I pull back into pit lane and roll to a stop about a hundred yards from the garage. I radio in that I had to stop for another car and I need a push. The guys see I'm blocking several other race cars from coming into the garage area, so they begin to jog toward the car. I am already unbuckled, and before they can get to the car, I detach the steering wheel, climb out, and walk off. It leaves them fumbling and juggling to get the steering wheel back on and then push the car out of the way and back into the garage while I laugh my ass off. Next time maybe they'll come to my party. All is forgiven, and we're pumped up for tomorrow night's race.

"Let's raise the roof on this thing," Tony Jr. is shouting as the team pushes the car, red and gleaming, through the entrance to the pit lane for the Winston. The crew is pumping their fists in the air, whipping the crowd into a frenzy. "All Star" by Smash Mouth—a band I'm buddies with—is blaring through the PA system like some kind of anthem, and with the fireworks, the smoke, and the lights, it's like a huge rock concert with 150,000 screaming fans. It could be Springsteen and the E Street Band, but instead of "Bruuuuuce," the crowd is screaming, "Juuuuuuun-yeeeer." Damn, it gives me the chills.

I have to ride around in the back of a pickup so I can wave at the throng of people surrounding the entire track. When I get back to the car, it's sitting with the other nineteen cars on the front straightaway, only a few feet from the crazed fans in the stands. The energy and anticipation is enough to make the hair on the back of my neck stand up. This is how all the races should be!

This is the NASCAR version of the all-star game, and there isn't anything else like it in racing. It's the show of shows in NASCAR and that makes sense since it's at Humpy Wheeler's track. Humpy is one of the biggest characters in racing, a guy who is the promoter's promoter. People call him racing's answer to P. T. Barnum. Humpy just loves to put on a spectacle. He's had school buses jumping through the air like Evel Knievel, and one Memorial Day, he put on a reenactment of the invasion of Grenada with helicopters and firepower. Blowing shit up and everything! Humpy said it was more exciting than the actual war. You might say Humpy is colorful, but he is also a smart businessman and he's had a lot to do with NASCAR's growth.

The Winston is like the best of the new and the old about the sport. It's all of the best drivers and teams racing at the most innovative track under high-tech lights in a race that is just like an old-time Saturday-night short-track shoot-out. There are no points on the line, and a winner's purse of more than $500,000. Half a million is great, but I think we'd all race just as hard if there were only $10 to win. As Grandpa Ralph used to say, it's "blow or go!"

No one is conservative in this race. It's always balls-out action, with a lot of crashes and a lot of one-time-only paint schemes that will soon be showing up as die-cast collector's items in a catalog or hobby shop near you. I remember sitting in our family's condo, located just outside of Turn 1, watching my dad win the Winston and seeing some amazing races. The Winston will always produce enough sparks and on-track fireworks to fill one of those chills-'n'-spills-and-they-walked-away crash-and-burn videos.

Because only winning race teams are allowed in the field, we're lucky to be here. We got in when we won at Texas. That made us just the second rookie team to ever qualify for the race. The first since Davey Allison, another son of a famous driver, did it in 1987. The Richmond win was like icing on the cake—not necessary for the invitation, but it did make us the hottest team out here.

The race is seventy laps that are broken into three segments. Thirty, thirty, and a final ten-lap shoot-out for bucketloads of Winston's dough. That works out to a little less than five thousand dollars a mile. If there was ever a race designed for me and the way this team likes to race, then this is it.

Up to now, we've been on a steep Winston Cup learning curve, figuring out how to make the car handle the long runs. We've won a couple of times, but in the other races, conserving the car and the tires has been a challenge for us. We'd be doing really well after a pit stop and then, after thirty or forty laps, we'd start dropping back.

But tonight you throw all that out. The car has to go *now*! It has to be fast immediately. None of this waiting around for the car to "come in" in long runs. It doesn't matter how it does on long runs. It only has to go for short stints and then, in the final ten laps, you just haul ass.

My kind of a race.

Wheeler has a tradition of predicting the winner of the race and he's almost always right. This year he picks me.

My dad found Humpy a few days later and chewed his ass. "Why are you putting so much pressure on my boy?" he said. "He doesn't need that kind of pressure!"

Humpy is one of the last guys to stick his head in the cockpit and wish me good luck before the race starts. I've been telling people all week I hope he's right, picking me to win, but I'm just glad to be here, racing with all this talent. That's bullshit. The truth is, I think we've got a great car and a great shot to win. I can't wait to start this thing. As we start the engines and start the pace laps, I can still hear the crowd above the engines.

We start the first segment in the fifth position. Then, on the first lap, almost like it was scripted, two cars crash hard. When we get back to green, I'm the fastest car on the track. I'm in third, motoring along easily, until I come up on Rusty Wallace.

Nobody, including my dad, races me harder than Rusty. I like to beat Rusty, and I know he likes to beat me. Maybe it's because a rival beer company sponsors him, or maybe it's because I'm a punk rookie. All I know is, when the race results are passed around the Budweiser headquarters on Monday mornings, the "beer cars" are highlighted. If the Miller and the Coors cars both finish behind us, we get a thumbs-up from the boys in St. Louis. I'm sure it's the exact same thing for Rusty. We race each other as hard as we can and when we get close, you can expect fireworks. I tail him for a lap or so, and when I pass him, on Lap 23, we get *real* close.

I'm running third at the end of the first segment.

While the teams get a ten-minute break to work on the cars, the track and Winston have a drawing to see if the top twelve finishers will reverse positions for the restart. The drawing is supposed to be random, but this is Humpy's show and everybody expects the answer to be yes. Which is exactly the way it turns out. I'll be outside on the fifth row for the restart.

When the second segment begins, it takes me less than a lap to blow past three cars. I'm sailing, and there's no better feeling in the world. I'm in fifth place on the fourth lap when something happens. Something bad. It feels like the fillings are being shaken outta my teeth. I head for the pits.

But we luck out big time and get a yellow flag when there's a crash a few seconds later. We don't lose a lap! We change left-side tires, go back out to catch the slow-moving pack, then come back in for right-side rubber. Everyone's kind of nervous about the vibration, but the crew discovers what they believe was the problem. The left rear wheel hadn't been tightened all the way when we changed tires between segments. It took a lap or two to come loose and cause a wicked vibration. We had ten minutes to do it and maybe that was too much time for a crew that is used to doing it all in fifteen seconds or less. They lost their rhythm.

It takes me only five laps to get back up to fourth, with the three front-running cars in my sights. NASCAR's computer timing and scoring system shows that the Bud car is running half a second faster than any car on the track. But I don't need the computer. I know it. I can feel it. I can see it.

*"Woooooooooohoooooooo! Hellllllllllll yeahhhhhhhh!"* I'm screaming, coming up on Rusty in that "other beer" car. When the car is this good, I feel like a he-man. Totally macho—like I can bench-press five hundred pounds. Look out Superman, here I come.

Maybe I got a little carried away, because when I swing wide on Turn 4 to pass him, I catch the wall. The entire right side of the car hits hard and is flattened like a pancake. Sometimes you can just barely touch the wall with your right rear tire and it pulls the car into the wall like a big magnet.

*Slam!*

I'm sure I've damaged the car and I'm sure the raised yellow Goodyear lettering has been rubbed right off the tires. I just hope nothing falls off or goes flat.

I keep my right foot mashed to the floor. I'm sick I hit the wall, but damn, until then that was fun! I think we bent the rear end, but I know we gotta run the last ten laps as hard as we can.

My lap times fall off until I'm running the same as the rest of the field. On Lap 54, there is a multicar pileup and I duck into the pits to change tires and check out the damage. Before I hit the wall, the car was haulin' ass. After, it wasn't haulin' as much.

We finish the second segment in third place, again. We pit and take two new tires just to be certain and to check out the car again. Some cars choose not to stop, so that puts us in eighth for the restart. Unlike normal races, the Winston restarts are double file instead of single file. So instead of having a line of seven cars in front of us, the field is bunched together two-by-two and we start on the outside on the fourth row.

On the second lap of the last segment, Steve Park and Joe Nemechek get into one of those deals that seem to happen every year at the Winston.

Steve got into the back of Nemechek and nearly spun him along the backstraight. But Nemechek got it gathered up, and when he came back up behind Steve on the front straightaway, he just punted him hard and both cars wrecked hard going into Turn 1. It's a big-time crash, and I'm worried that somebody might be hurt. It looks like four or five cars are in the crash and unable to continue.

With eight laps left, we have to make an agonizing decision. The unscheduled stops for loose or smashed wheels have used up all of our new tires. A couple of the Bud crew guys race down pit lane to borrow four new tires and wheels from Jeremy Mayfield's team. (Jeremy had dropped out earlier.)

So we have four new tires if we choose to make a pit stop. We'll go to the back of the pack if we stop, or we can just sit tight and hope that we can move up a few positions. It's a huge gamble if we stop, but we're not gonna win if we don't. After all the crashes, there aren't that many cars left. But coming from the back will be tough with just eight laps left.

"I'll drive the shit out of the car, no matter what," I urge, "but you guys need to make the call."

"Hang on," Tony Sr. answers. "We're voting over here."

It seems like forever as I creep slowly around Turns 3 and 4. The pit lane entrance is approaching.

"We're going for the gusto," Tony says at the last possible second. "Pit that son of a bitch."

I yank the wheel to the left and roll down pit lane. We change the tires in 15.9 seconds and I'm tenth on the restart.

I pass four cars real quick and get to sixth. It's easier to pass several cars at once when they're bunched up on restarts.

Seven laps to go. Dale Jarrett, who is leading, starts to show smoke out of the back of his car. Tony is begging the NASCAR officials to bring him in, and we keep racing.

Six laps to go and one more car down. I'm running fifth.

Four to go and I'm running behind a car with the gaudiest Peter Max paint job you've ever seen. It looks like it ran through a car wash that's spraying Day-Glo paint rather than soap. My dad is driving the car. The Man in Black is in neon tonight. It just seems weird. But he was the first one to do a special paint scheme in the Winston, in 1995, when he drove a gorgeous silver Goodwrench car. Everyone involved saw that the special scheme meant tons of extra sales of collectibles for this one-time-only car.

I get by Dad and his pastel monster pretty easily. Only Jerry Nadeau and a still-smoking Dale Jarrett are ahead of me.

Three to go: I sweep past Nadeau and only one more is left. Tony Jr. is so excited that I see him leap onto pit lane as I go past, giving a wave of his hand almost as if he can will the car into the lead.

Two to go and I'm closing on Jarrett quickly as the smoke continues from behind his car.

I am told later that, at the very same time, a bizarre and hilarious scene begins between Jarrett's pit area and our pit. Nabisco is a sponsor of several NASCAR teams, including mine. On the side of Jarrett's car is a Planters Peanuts logo. Every time Jarrett wins, a marketing person from Nabisco dresses as Mr. Peanut to attend the winner's-circle festivities. On the side of the red Bud car, an Oreo cookie logo rests ahead of the rear window. Oreo is represented in the winner's circle by a funny, round Mr. Oreo contraption. While Jarrett was leading, the Nabisco guy got much of the Mr. Peanut costume fitted. But when he sees that the Bud car is coming fast, the guy is confused—unsure of whether to leave the Mr. Peanut suit on or grab the Oreo suit.

On Lap 69, Jarrett knows I'm a lot faster, but he makes it as hard as possible to pass by hugging the lower, faster groove. I feel bulletproof as I swing the car high and pull beside him. The key tonight is that my car works really well in the higher, second groove. When they expect me to go low, I go high and easily blast past.

The crowd goes wild. I sense the flashbulbs and the screams. It's like the old footage of the Beatles at Shea Stadium where you can barely hear 'em playing. The sound of the crowd drowns out the sounds of the cars.

The television audience watching on The Nashville Network hears the announcing crew of Eli Gold, Buddy Baker, and Dick Berggren go wild as well. I can watch the video of these final laps over and over again, and it's just as exciting as when it was happening.

"I've seen a lot of things in my life," Baker, a former racer, yells, "but I don't know if I've ever seen the determination of this young man here. And he's *passing on the outside!*"

"He's kicked those Clydesdales into high gear," says Gold.

"Look at him go! What a driver! What a team!" yells Berggren.

"What a future!" interjects Gold.

"The ovation this crowd is giving him is monumental," screams Berggren. "They love this kid!"

Once I am past Jarrett in Turn 3, I have clear track for

the first time tonight, and I try to drive even harder on the last lap. I drive it nearly flat out just so they know they got a good butt-whoopin'! When the car is this good, it's hard to describe the feeling of power and strength. The team and I joke about it, but it's like you're invincible and you just need to tell the other guys to get the hell outta our way or be crushed by our superior strength.

The top three spots at the finish are all Dales: me, then Jarrett and Dad across the line. All non-Dales need not apply.

I imagine Mr. Peanut must be nearly naked as he rips off the nut suit and reaches for the Oreo costume. Will he make it in time to the winner's circle to meet me, or will he be left alone in pit lane in nothing but a pair of black tights?

The feeling is great—and I wanna do some tire-smokin' hell-raisin' donuts along the front straight. The fans are going wild, and so am I. The car spins around with a ton of tire smoke, and then I kinda creep along near the wall, going the wrong direction so my driver's-side window is closer to the fans. They all crush against the fence and scream and shake their fists back at me.

In memory of Adam, the usual winner's circle at the speedway is closed. The new, makeshift circle is a huge flatbed trailer with an elaborate raised platform. The trailer is pulled onto the front straightaway, only thirty feet or so from the grandstands. I drive around waving to everyone for so long, NASCAR has to send some officials in a pace car to guide me back to the finish line.

It's crowded with team members high-fiving and pouring beer on each other, and I pull in slowly. Confetti and fireworks are flying all over the place as I climb out of the car and onto the roof in one swooping motion. Someone hands me a can of Bud with confetti all over it, and I decide to do my best imitation of the WWF's Stone Cold Steve Austin, guzzling the beer in record fashion. The crowd is so close to the temporary stage, I stand on the car pumping my arm in the air and cupping a hand to my ear like a lead singer, daring the crowd to get louder! "Lemme hear ya! Lemme hear ya!" It is pandemonium.

Out of nowhere, Dad swoops in and puts a huge bear hug on me. *That* was what all the commotion was about! Maybe the neon paint job got to him, but I have never seen his smile so wide. He rips the Winston winner's hat off of me and hugs me again. At that moment, for maybe the first time in my life, I feel almost like I'm on the same level as my dad. I had watched him win the Winston before, and now I had done it as well.

"I love you," he tells me when we hug.

"I couldn't believe it," he says to the TV audience. "I thought I could get up there to give Jarrett some trouble and I looked in the mirror and here this red thing comes! It looked like he adjusted it there on the wall and got it running better. . . ."

Following the live interviews for television and radio, we are all asked to climb to the top of the elevated platform. When we get up there, I feel like a king on the throne addressing thousands of my friends and neighbors.

"Earnhardt! Earnhardt! Earnhardt! Earnhardt!" is the chant from the stands. I start to look around for my father until I realize that this time, this night, the chants are for me.

The trophy presentation is made, and then the big winner's check is brought out. *Yeah!* It says $516,000! Not too bad! We all pose for photograph after photograph. I pose with Dad and then with Tony Sr. and Jr., and then guys from the team. While we're up there, everyone keeps dousing each other with Budweiser, champagne, and any other liquid we can find. It is the ritual of victory, but can you imagine the smell of beer, sweat, champagne, and motor oil?

But wait! With all of this joy and celebration, something is missing. Where is Mr. Oreo?

The stairs up to the elevated platform are not really designed for a costumed mascot, but with some help, he is able to make his way up to the upper level. But his short, round shape means no one—especially the photographers—can see him behind the railing on the platform.

Some of the quick-thinking crew guys decide to stack empty Budweiser coolers at the front of the stage so Mr. Oreo can be propped up for his photo opportunity. I come over and offer the large, fake cookie a cold Budweiser. He waves his stubby little arms, saying "No thanks!" in cookie-style body language. (Later I hear rumors that the Nabisco folks were not amused by me offering their cookie a cold brew. . . . I guess ya can't please everyone all the time.)

The celebration seems endless and surreal, as if it almost isn't really happening to this group of happy and hardworking people. Then a horrible dose of reality invades our party. Jade is pulled aside by Winston and

Lowe's track officials who explain to him that there has been a terrible accident outside of the speedway, and that the media interviews need to be rushed along. He pulls me into the corner of the stage and tells me a spectator bridge spanning the highway outside of the racetrack has collapsed. Yes, there are injuries, yes, it is serious, but that is all that is known at this time.

I am slammed out of the victory buzz almost immediately. A group of security guards surround me as we slip through a small gate and into the grandstand area. No one here knows what has happened outside, and many fans push and crush forward to touch or even get a glimpse as we run up the stairs. The security guards push and pull and bring me straight up the aisle to the very top of the huge grandstands and then to the top level of suites, where the press box is located.

Before we enter the media center, we spot the flashing lights outside through a thin opening in the stairs. We see a huge section of the pedestrian bridge rests on ground level and there are flashing lights and chaos as fans are blocked from leaving the track via the main highway. The gravity of what has happened hits home even harder and someone says up to one hundred people are injured.

Seeing all that, I'm pretty sober walking into the press box for the postrace interviews.

"The highlight of my life is seeing the smile on my daddy's face tonight," I tell them. "I mean, that's what this is all about—making people happy. It does my heart good to know how happy he is, how happy my team is. . . ."

My thoughts turn to Adam, who had been parked in the garage across from me at the test session here only a couple of days before his accident.

"I'm missing my buddy Adam. I've just been thinking of him all week, and I just wanted to dedicate this one to him. I know if he's watching us he's happy because it was a great race, but I really do miss him."

In the background, Jade is on the phone trying to piece together news of the tragedy outside the track. The bridge collapse has closed the main highway adjacent to the track, so no one is able to leave through the tunnel that connects the infield to the outside world. The night that looked like it would be an endless party turns into a long wait in the garage, followed by a weary, less-than-wild stop at the Waffle House for breakfast. So much for the victory party of the millennium.

I wait nervously for my turn to qualify for the 2000 Daytona 500. As a rookie, the pressure to make the starting lineup is almost unbearable. (*Harold Hinson*)

Nothing could prepare me for the media crush I experienced during my rookie year. (*Harold Hinson*)

Matt Kenseth and I became close friends during the two years we spent competing against each other in the Busch Series. Although I won the Busch championship in 1998 and 1999, Matt whipped our ass and won the 2000 Winston Cup rookie of the year. (*Harold Hinson*)

The DEI headquarters sprang from my dad's visionary imagination. It's often called "the Garage Mahal." (*Dale Earnhardt, Inc.*)

Victory! We are one
big happy team after
we win our first
Winston Cup race,
the DirecTV 500
at Texas Motor
Speedway, in only
our twelfth start.
(*Harold Hinson*)

Basking in the
glow of victory at
Martinsville Raceway
one week after my
first Winston Cup
win. (*Harold Hinson*)

I share the spotlight with Mr. Oreo. Nabisco, the company that makes Oreo cookies, is one of my longtime sponsors. (*Harold Hinson*)

A truly great moment as Dad joins me for a wild celebration after I become the first rookie driver to win the Winston. This is one of my favorite photos of Dad, and I'm happy that my stepmom, Teresa, was there to enjoy it as well. She's the one right behind me on the left, looking immaculate. (*Harold Hinson*)

I guzzle a cold Bud, just like the wrestler Stone Cold Steve Austin, after winning the Winston. (*Harold Hinson*)

Dad sits in Kenny Bernstein's 320 mph NHRA Top Fuel dragster while Kenny and I flank him on each side. (*Harold Hinson*)

Fans line up to see the special Olympic-themed Budweiser Chevy in front of the DEI museum, showroom, and gift shop. (*Harold Hinson*)

Hello, Bristol! The Bristol racetrack is like the Rose Bowl on steroids—the grandstands seem like they go on forever all the way around the half-mile track. (*Harold Hinson*)

What does a hard-working race team do during a rain delay? We eat, of course. Brandon Blake digs into another slice of pizza while we wait for the race to restart. (*Harold Hinson*)

Dad and I are introduced to the crowd before the start of the Winston No Bull 5 held at Richmond. Five teams are eligible for a million-dollar prize (and another million for a lucky fan) if they win the race. (*Harold Hinson*)

Dad gives me advice after I experience some trouble during a
practice run at the New Hampshire International Speedway. I was
pretty spooked, because this was same track where Kenny Irwin
and Adam Petty both crashed and died. (*Harold Hinson*)

A video crew from MTV, led by Bill Richmond holding the camera,
shoots footage of me signing autographs for a documentary called
"True Life: I'm a Racecar Driver." (*Harold Hinson*)

Every member of the over-the-wall gang wears a Budweiser do-rag during the World Pit Crew competition. In clockwise order: my uncle Danny Earnhardt is in front of the car; my cousin Tony Eury, Jr., changes the front tire; Jeff Clark is the jack man; Steve Wolfe changes the rear tire; and Keith Mansch is behind the car. David Lippard, the catch man, and gasman Kevin Eagle are on the right side of the car. (*Harold Hinson*)

Kerry and me with Dad at the 2000 Kmart 400 in Brooklyn, Michigan. It was the first time in 40 years that two brothers and their father started in a NASCAR Winston Cup race. (*Harold Hinson*)

I'm dejected after a wheels-off-the-ground-banzai-headfirst slam straight into the wall at Martinsville Speedway knocked us out of the NAPA Auto Care 500. (*Harold Hinson*)

Tony Eury, Jr. (*left*), Tony Eury, Sr., and I in the garage at Homestead Speedway. (*Harold Hinson*)

The end is here, finally. I look pale and tired as my rookie season comes to a close on a Monday morning at the Atlanta Motor Speedway. (*Harold Hinson*)

The view from the driver's seat of my car. The steering wheel pops off, allowing for a quick exit out of the driver's-side window. (*Harold Hinson*)

I strap myself in for a qualifying run at Bristol Motor Speedway.
(*Harold Hinson*)

I lead the field during the Budweiser Shootout, held one week
before the 2001 Daytona 500. (*Harold Hinson*)

What a difference a year makes! The nerves are gone and now I'm all smiles before qualifying for the 2001 Daytona 500. The T-shirt was a gift from Chevrolet for racing with Dad in the 24 Hours of Daytona one week earlier. (*Harold Hinson*)

The three DEI drivers (*left to right*): Steve Park, me, and Michael Waltrip sit on the pit wall before the start of the race at Rockingham one week after my father's death. Steve Park went on to win the race. (*Harold Hinson*)

Tony Eury, Jr., and I often feuded during the 2000 season, but we both matured and were able to put all that behind us the following year. (*Harold Hinson*)

The victory in the Pepsi 400 at Daytona was like lifting the weight of the world off my shoulders. (*Harold Hinson*)

Tony Eury, Sr., the crew chief for the No. 8 Budweiser car, has a right to kick my ass when I'm outta line. After winning the Pepsi 400, we pose with the trophy
(*Harold Hinson*)

A fan comes out of the bushes at Pocono Raceway to take a picture of Sterling Martin and me.
(*Harold Hinson*)

Going home is always one of the favorite times of a race weekend. (*Harold Hinson*)

Co-author Jade Gurss. (*Harold Hinson*)

# Charlotte, North Carolina
## Coca-Cola 600

## A Hottie

After the accident outside the track and in light of Adam Petty's death, nobody is in the mood for celebrating at DEI. We put the winning car out in front of the main entrance to the museum and gift shop. It's still covered with confetti and drenched in beer and champagne, just as it was when it was loaded into the transporter after the race. There are a lot of fans—thousands of them—that stay in the area for two weeks of racing—the Winston and the 600—and a lot of them travel to DEI just to stand in front of the car, gazing at it like religious tourists at a special cathedral.

Winning the Winston has pumped up me and the team, and it has also increased the number of media requests. So has the *Rolling Stone* story, which is out on the newsstands. We're getting calls from just about every media outlet you can imagine. Everyone wants to ask questions about the *Rolling Stone* interview, as if they now seem embarrassed that they didn't know such things about me. No one had ever bothered to ask be-

fore. It was always "If you and your dad were racing together on the last lap, going for the win . . . blah blah
blah . . ." Now they all wanna do their own version of
the story.

CBS and WTBS call, one right after the other, wanting to do a video version of the *Rolling Stone* article.
They both want to follow me around and do one of those
day-in-the-life *Real World* deals. Because they called
first by a hair, we work it out for CBS cameras to tail me
and some of my buddies, like MTV's *Real World,* on a
typical day away from the track. WTBS will focus on
my love of music and some of the slick street cars I own.
Then we spend a day knocking out as many interviews
as we can.

I meet with a guy from the *Charlotte Observer,* the
biggest paper in the heart of NASCAR land. But colum-
nist C. Jamal Horton doesn't normally do motor sports
and what he wants to talk about is . . . me as a sex sym-
bol. He was at the Winston and was stunned by the
general female population's reaction to my win. He
manages to ask questions that aren't raunchy, but it's
still uncomfortable. He seems like a cool guy though,
and we chat about everything from music to what I was
like in high school.

For the WTBS thing, I'm wired up to talk music. I
chat with Marty Snider while I'm leaning against my
race car, flipping through a few of the hundreds of CDs
in my collection. Then I climb into my '99 Corvette and
do some tire-squealing burnouts in the parking lot. I talk
seriously about how music is my own personal psychiatrist that helps me get in the right mood before a race. I
like to talk about music because the subject is important

to me. If I listen to something hard, like Limp Bizkit, I'm gonna go out there and race everybody as hard as I can race 'em. But, let's say, if I listen to Otis Redding, I'll go out there and I'll be patient, waving everyone past, knowing that there is a long way to go in a five-hundred-mile race.

I talk about trying to share some of my music with my father. He's got this hardcore image but the stuff he likes is not really that hard, and it includes a lot of female artists like Alison Krause, Sarah McLachlan, and Sheryl Crow. I tell them about trying to get my dad to listen to Limp Bizkit and how he just wanted me to get that thing the hell outta the CD player as soon as possible. Immediately would not be soon enough.

I wanted him to hear a kick-ass Metallica song, and he got about halfway through it and I thought, *This is going OK*. But nope. Song over. He was reaching for the Eject button.

I finish up by introducing the racing world to the music of Eminem. This was before he became the number-one-selling artist in the world. His CD *The Marshall Mathers LP* makes sense to me because of the way he talks about the crazed fans, and the way he uses humor to offset his anger.

Before I know it, it's time to suit up and start practicing for Sunday's race. The car is as strong—maybe stronger—than the one we won with last week. It's the same chassis we drove at Texas and at Las Vegas, and I'm second quickest in my first lap on the track. I'm as confident now as when I was tearing up the Busch Series.

Finally it is our turn to qualify. The crowd cheers and then I'm out on the track, going for the fastest possible lap time. And I get it, breaking a track record that had stood for six years. Before today, no one had ever driven a stock car around this track at more than 185 miles per hour. I do better than 186 and get my first career Bud Pole and a thirty-six-thousand-dollar check that goes with it.

Is this team on a roll, or what?

I'm happy to be on the pole, naturally, but the thing is, I'm not happy with the lap. It could have been faster. I made a couple of mistakes and lost a little time in Turns 3 and 4. But we're in the Bud Shootout next year—a race held at Daytona, during Speedweeks, featuring the pole winners from the previous season. But right now I'm thinking Sunday. If we can keep it in one piece, I guarantee we'll finish in the top five.

On Friday the media barrage continues with a color shot of the Budweiser Monte Carlo on the front page of *USA Today*. There is no on-track action, but I head out to the speedway to sign autographs at one of the tractor-trailer rigs that goes from track to track, selling Dale Earnhardt Jr. merchandise. People have been waiting in line since 2 A.M. for a session that starts at 11 A.M. The fans get tickets that allow them one autograph each. There are four hundred tickets and that isn't enough.

After the signing, I head into town for Charlotte Speed Street, a festival that pretty much closes the center of the city for most of the week. There, I do a live appearance on *Who Wants to Be a Millionaire?* I'm supposed to help the contestants answer racing trivia questions, and I get a lot of good-natured ribbing from Regis Philbin. No one wins the million.

In the evening, I go back to Speed Street to see my buddies in the band Bridge. There are a lot of young women in the crowd who, to put it mildly, are fans. A few of them manage to get backstage for autographs. And, big surprise, I sign them.


On Saturday morning there's the *Charlotte Observer,* with a color shot of Regis and me, walking on the stage with my fist in the air. Seems like I'm seeing myself—and him—everywhere.

We do two practice sessions at the track and not much happens, except crew member Randy Cox (a.k.a. "Fabio") has to get some stitches in his forehead. During the Busch race, Randy leaned up against the huge toolbox for a quick nap. He fell asleep until he felt a searing pain in his forehead. He woke up and immediately suspected that one of the other guys had played a cruel joke on him. Not so. A wrench that had been resting precariously on top of the toolbox rolled off, fell six feet, and slammed him above the eye. He tried to be macho, but he was finally convinced to go to the infield medical center for stitches.

When happy hour is done, I get word that Tony Stewart, who is doing some guest hosting for WTBS, would like to interview me. We haven't spoken since that bump in the pits at Richmond, and I'm wondering if he's still mad. Maybe, I say to someone, I'll need some stitches too.

But Tony and I talk and laugh like best buddies.


On race morning, page one of the *Observer* sports section has the interview I did earlier in the week, with lots of stuff about "Club E," and the way the women fans call me a "hottie." A *hottie!*

I can see it so clearly, it's like the opening scenes of a movie. The music in the background would be "Addicted to Love," by Robert Palmer. You see a short and skinny twelve-year-old, who rides along with his dad to an old race shop behind his grandmother's house. The youngster likes to go with his dad to the shop because he can see one of his best friends who lives nearby, but mostly because he can also see a girl. This is the first girl that he really likes. The camera pans to show the girl's twin sister handing a note to the kid's chubby buddy. He brings it to the skinny kid, who reads the note and is heartbroken.

"I don't want to see you anymore" is the basic message. Harsh. Cold. Blown off. Damn!

While his dad drives him home, the skinny kid sits in the passenger seat, crying.

Then you would see the chubby kid and the skinny kid sneaking around the neighborhood for the next few days, looking for the girl. They hang out behind bushes, trash cans—they even check the local public swimming pool just to look for the cold-hearted girl. No luck at all.

Now the young skinny kid, grown now, imagines her

face as he walks through the grass toward a huge stage on the racetrack. The crowd in the grandstands goes crazy—especially the women, who like his tight-fittin', lady-pleasin' firesuit. He is introduced on the PA system as the Bud Pole winner, and he relishes the screams from the crowd as he walks across the stage. He wonders, "Where is she now?"

But enough of that stuff. Now it's time to race.

The Coca-Cola 600 is the longest race in NASCAR and one of the best events in all of racing. The TV ratings for this race are closing in on the Indy 500, once the most famous race in the country. The 600 is the first race I ever ran in Winston Cup, so this is sort of a first anniversary for me and the guys. The twelve months have been more successful than I could have imagined, and a win tonight would make it even better. I feel like I'm ready and I know the car is ready. So, of course, I pull away at the start and lead the race.

It's great to be so fast so early, but this is not only the longest race, it is also the only one that starts in the late afternoon and finishes under the lights at night. The ever-changing shadows and temperatures play havoc with this track, so we need to be prepared to make adjustments to the car throughout twilight and into darkness.

After a few laps, I drop back a position or two. But I can get it back again, any time I want to. The car is a little loose but no problem. You can be both fast and loose, especially on a clean track. And as the race goes on, the groove will gain grip as more and more rubber gets ground down into the asphalt.

We pit a couple of times and we drop as far as seventh, but I am able to get back into the lead. When we go past the one-hundred-lap mark, I'm laughing into the radio.

"I *am* the man."

Three of us—me, Jerry Nadeau, and Dad—pull away from the pack, and pretty soon we're racing each other for the lead. It's like the other cars aren't even on the same track as the three of us trade positions like cards being shuffled. Dad and I run side by side for a few laps, and I can see the flashbulbs going off like crazy in the grandstands. I'm smiling and I'm sure Dad is too. This is about as fun as it gets.

Halfway through the race, I'm in third but then I make a single, swooping pass that puts both Nadeau and Dad behind me.

There are huge storm clouds hanging in every direction, and it is sure to start raining soon. With lightning flashing in the background, things get a bit more aggressive. Nadeau and I bump a little, and I come out of it in the lead. If I can win this thing, it will be a great racing day for Budweiser. Juan Montoya won the Indy 500 earlier, and he was sponsored by Bud for that race.

The wind picks up and the temperature drops. Weather plays games with you at Charlotte, and the colder temperature does not agree with the Bud car. The game between the top three cars changes into a dogfight among the top six or seven cars. Bobby Labonte passes me like I'm standing still.

The rain starts falling on Lap 242, and five laps later it's coming down so hard that NASCAR throws the yellow flag to slow the field.

The race is past the halfway mark, so if the rain comes

really hard, they might call it an official race. But it's still early in the evening and NASCAR will probably try to wait out the storm and finish the race, so staying out and betting the race will be called seems too risky.

We pit.

I get back out on the track and join the slow parade of caution laps. The rain keeps falling. Soon it's falling so hard that the red flag comes out and everybody makes it into pit lane. I climb out of the car to wait out the delay.

The media wants to ask questions about the dominant car, but I want to talk about racing with my father.

"'S'cool, man," I say. "We were having fun. One time, he must have been right up on me because I got *real* loose. I passed him back and then he went by again. It was fun."

During the rain delay I hang out with Dad, and the media is all over us. They sense that he and I may battle all night for the win.

After almost an hour the rain stops and the track is dry enough for a restart. I check the scoreboard and see that Matt's No. 17 car is in the top ten.

"Watch out for that 17 car coming up," I tell a reporter. "If he and I could battle it out, it would be so great. It'd be just like the good old Busch Series days."

When the action starts again, Nadeau's engine blows up, so it's the Earnhardt family out front with Rusty Wallace and Kenseth chasing. I'm in the lead after three hundred laps, but Matt is turning faster lap times. We both make a pit stop on Lap 309, and Matt's crew gets him out first. He gets the lead and I'm right behind

him. We race side by side and the crowd is on its feet
again.

But all of a sudden, this black No. 3 rocket comes out
of nowhere and we're three-wide. Dad pulls alongside
and I can almost hear the fans over the engine noise.
Somehow I keep the lead, and twenty laps later I'm in
front by three seconds, and stretching it out to five seconds by Lap 360. This is looking like Texas all over
again.

A yellow flag comes up on Lap 362 for oil on the
track. We have less than forty laps to run, and a final pit
stop to set up for the finish. We've gone more than five
hundred miles already, so this distance is new territory
for teams, drivers, and cars. Some teams take two tires
and get back out quick. We take four and are in sixth
place on the restart, but this isn't a problem if I keep running the way I have been.

But right after the green flag, I can't believe what I'm
feeling. I think a tire is flat.

"We gotta have a loose right front! Is it flat?"

The spotter takes a close look and tells me it looks
like it's still inflated.

Somehow I make it past Jeff Gordon but there is still
something very wrong. The tire isn't flat but the car isn't
handling any better and it takes all of what's left of my
strength to keep from crashing in every corner.

When you get used to four-hundred- or five-hundred-
mile races, you think you're in pretty good shape, but
these extra hundred miles really take a toll. I can barely
hold my head upright from all of the G-forces lap after
lap after lap. Luckily I have a headrest that I can lean
on. My arms and hands are sore from gripping the

wheel, and even my eyes start to trouble me. My vision gets fuzzy, and it seems like I've been out here in this hot, dirty, loud car for twelve hours. With the rain delay, it's actually closer to six hours. Right now this is *not* fun.

The guys in the pits are helpless. Unless we get lucky and get another caution period, we've made our last pit stop of the night.

My lap times start falling off badly and I'm struggling with the car. The only thing we changed was the tires, so that has to be it. We've got a set that is just . . . evil. Goodyear has been great to me, and especially to my dad for years, but this is ridiculous. They have a monopoly—there's no other tire company to challenge them—so why is it that they can't make a batch of tires that are consistent from one set to the next? This is bullshit. The tires are like a roll of the dice: sometimes you get the perfect roll, and sometimes you get snake eyes and lose all of your money. We've been dominant all night, and now, when it counts, we're screwed.

Meanwhile, Matt is flying. He takes the lead with twenty-five to go, and I'm just holding on, chasing Dale Jarrett just like the Winston. But the car is handling so badly that when I get the inside line to pass him we touch. I keep my foot planted and somehow, someway, I make it past him into fourth place. But there are only a couple of laps to go.

Matt's car is great when he needs it, and he wins. It's his first Winston Cup win and I know how he feels as he slides his car across the wet grass, doing a new free-form style of high-speed spins and donuts across the infield grass.

We finish fourth, right behind Dad in third. We roll slowly into pit lane and we both climb out of our cars.

Dad walks back, throws up his hands, and says, "What happened, man?"

He knew as well as I did that I had the car that should have won.

It feels strange to finish a six-hundred-mile race in the top five and still be so disappointed. Normally, we'd be happy with fourth place. But we were running so well . . .

I led the most laps of anyone (175 laps—more than 260 miles) and had a five-second lead before that last pit stop. Then the tires just went away.

I'm exhausted, and without the adrenaline of winning, I have little to say to the media. Before leaving the track, I go and see Matt. He and his crew are having their own moment in the spotlight, so I pour what I've got left in my bottle of water down his neck. We shake hands, hug, and I congratulate him on a great run. But it's his moment, so I try to get the hell out of the way as quick as I can.

We should be drinking cold Bud in that victory circle. But after I calm down and think about the last few weeks, things feel a little bit sweeter. We had a helluva month. A win in Richmond. A win at the Winston. The Bud Pole here and fourth place tonight. And we have won more than $745,000 in prize money during May. Not bad for a rookie team.

But we can't rest on it. It's well past midnight, and after some sleep, we're off to Pocono for testing on Tuesday morning.

# Dover, Delaware
## MBNA 400

## Juniormania

We raced at most of the Winston Cup tracks when we were in the Busch Series, but we never ran at Pocono. To make sure we're ready for the race there in a couple of weeks, we go to the strange triangle-shaped track for two days of practice. It goes well until the second day, when I total the car after running into the wall. I'm fine, but it sets the whole team back when you suddenly have to repair or rebuild a car. If it's totaled, you need to build a new one. It hurts the budget and it hurts the guys who are already working too many hours, too many days in a row.

After regrouping from the crash, we load two more cars into the transporter and move to Dover, Delaware. Dover is called the "Monster Mile" or "White Lightning." It is like a larger, faster Bristol with high concrete banking that suits my style. I'd be lying if I said I wasn't expecting to continue the hot streak we've been on.

After our month of May with two wins and another top five, the newspapers are having fun with it all, calling it "Juniormania!" I have to laugh when I see they're calling me the "golden boy," and "a folk hero," and even a "revolutionary." The thing about that stuff is, you can't help but like it—I mean, you're racing to win and winning gets people talking about you—but you can't let it get into your head. Hell, in a few weeks the same people will be writing that I'm a fraud, a jackass, or something like that.

But the other guys sure as hell aren't going to let me pass just because of what the papers are saying. Anybody who has been around racing knows it can go away just as fast as it comes. I've seen Dad, one of the greatest drivers in history, go through dry spells. It wasn't that long ago when everyone was asking if he'd ever win again, wondering if he was washed up. Dad never forgot how to drive that car—and he continued to learn things and get smarter all the time. The combinations just didn't add up for him for a couple of seasons.

Winning is great, but what I want to do here at Dover is to just keep the momentum going and aim for consistency.

And it looks good when after changing an engine we qualify in sixth place. It's the tenth time in thirteen races we've been in the top ten. We also won here twice in the Busch Series, so I take that as a good omen.

But the car is tight in happy hour and that makes me nervous.

Luckily, because a couple of cars ahead of me in qualifying crash during the final practice, they must move to the back of the field, and consequently I start the race in fourth position. I'm running second after a couple of laps and then take the lead after Steve Park and a couple of others wreck.

I'm in fourth after one hundred laps and motoring along. This shit is fun.

Then, just like our last run at Charlotte, we run into the tire problem. Normally Goodyears are great, especially on all my Corvettes at home, but these tires do *not* handle anything like the set we had on earlier. I start dropping back like I'm dragging an anchor. A yellow flag gets us into the pits, where the crew pulls a rubber from the springs while getting four new tires. When they check the old tires, the crew sees that the right front is really torn up. That means I was abusing that tire trying to get it to turn into the corners. Since the car doesn't want to run down in the bottom groove, I have to take a high line and this costs me. I go down a lap to Tony Stewart on Lap 221.

It's frustrating when the crew calls to tell me that the other cars are following the low line. I let them know I can't drive the bottom line and if I could I would.

I stop for a splash of fuel with a hundred laps to go and come out in seventeenth place. I slice through the traffic and get up to eighth before another yellow flag shuffles the field. I hang on to finish tenth for our third consecutive top ten. That's something but I'm almost too tired to enjoy it.

Tony Stewart wins, making him the twelfth driver to win in thirteen races. Kenseth, who always seems to do well here, runs an awesome race and takes second place. Good for him, but bad for us because he's now fourteen points ahead of me in the rookie standings.

We'll take a top ten and remain encouraged by this sign of consistency. But it's not the same as winning, and I don't imagine that I'll be in many newspapers this week when we go to Michigan.

## Brooklyn, Michigan
### *Kmart 400*

## Not Drinking Enough . . . Water

I've heard of "racing fever," but this is ridiculous.

I feel like death when we go out to qualify for the Kmart 400 at the Michigan Speedway in Brooklyn. I picked up a flu bug that is whipping my ass, and all I can do is run a couple of practice laps and sign a few autographs before going out for our qualifying lap.

I may not feel well, but the car is good and we earn the sixth position. This makes me the only driver to qualify in the first round (top twenty-five spots) for every race this season. That's a great stat, but they pay the money for Sunday, not Friday, so there's no cause for celebration.

Qualifying does me in. I don't have the strength to practice for the IROC race I'm running tomorrow. Just as soon as I'm done qualifying, I shuffle off to a Bud golf cart and ride back to the motor coach, where I climb in bed and stay there until morning. I hope fifteen or sixteen hours of sleep can cure me.

But I'm not feeling much better the next morning, and

when I walk out to the grid for the IROC race, my skin is just about as white as the T-shirt I'm wearing underneath my uniform. As bad as I'm feeling, I hope it doesn't hurt my driving. At first it doesn't. I move past guys in bunches, even slicing into the grass on Lap 20 to make a pass. By Lap 30, I'm in the lead. Then I make contact with Eddie Cheever, an Indy car driver, and fall back a few places.

Strangely enough, now that I'm not leading, I begin to sense the heat in the cockpit. Unlike my Bud car, which is designed for long runs and has proper ventilation for the driver, these cars are built for short races and have no such comforts. The heat starts to get to me, and in my weakened condition I start to fade—especially in the standings. This won't be a repeat of last year's IROC here, when my father and I raced so hard and crossed the finish line together. But I manage to keep it together long enough to finish seventh. Cheever wins his first IROC race, and when I get to the pits, it's an effort just to crawl out of the car. I manage to straggle back to the motor coach, where I lie down and someone runs to grab one of the doctors at the infield medical center. A whole team of doctors and nurses and helpers return and . . . damn, it looks like some kind of MASH unit inside my motor coach. They check me out and give me oxygen and an IV to replace the fluids I've lost. The bag drains so fast they decide to give me another. I'm that dehydrated.

Tony Eury keeps checking up on me, but I assure him I'm driving that car even if they have to wheel me to the grid on a stretcher. Just to be safe, we cancel all the media stuff and I spend the rest of the day resting.

I feel a lot better on race morning, but after getting

checked out again, the doctor gives me another IV bag. I tell the crew not to worry, that I can go the whole distance, but they're not taking any chances. They've added extra air ducts to the car so I'll get a good flow of fresh air into the cockpit. They've also made sure that there are plenty of fluids in the car. And they've got ice packs ready in the pit that they'll put inside my uniform if I need to be cooled down.

During the first pace lap, I radio the team, "Don't worry about me."

But once the race starts, they worry. I drop from sixth to twenty-third by the fourth lap, and I'm sure they're wondering, *Is it the driver or is it the car?*

"Fuckin'-A!" I yell into the radio. "This is one loose-ass race car! These tires may have worked in qualifying, but they're skating everywhere now."

So now they can stop worrying about me. It's the car.

The team makes some adjustments during the first two pit stops, but I'm still running nineteenth, halfway into the race, and worrying about going down a lap to Tony Stewart, who is leading and setting a hot pace. As fast as he's running, there is no way I can keep him from lapping me, so I'm thrilled when I see the first beads of rain on my windshield. I radio in and insist that NASCAR ought to stop the race or at least yellow-flag it to slow the field.

What I see as a downpour they see as a slight drizzle, and we keep racing.

So I try a different approach.

"I see debris out here," I say into the radio, hoping for a caution. That gets laughed off too, and on Lap 102, Stewart puts me down a lap.

I make a stop and the crew makes some good changes. I get nose-to-tail with Matt and start making up some spots through the field when the rain does get heavy and the yellow comes out. Then, when the rain really gets bad, they red-flag it and we stop for more than ninety minutes.

I get out of the car and I'm still not 100 percent. A reporter asks how I'm feeling. "Better, but I guess I haven't been drinking enough . . . water."

When we restart, I manage to run with the leaders even though I'm still down a lap. At one point I pull over so my dad, who is running well, can go by and race Stewart for the lead. The skies get darker as Dad runs three-wide for the lead and I sit in thirteenth. Dad has Stewart in his sights and it looks like he's going to make another one of his famous charges for the flag. But when the rain comes, it hits so hard the race is stopped on Lap 194, six laps short of completion. We wait it out awhile and then NASCAR calls the race official. Stewart wins his second in a row and now I'm not the only Cup driver to win two races this season. I finish thirteenth and Dad is second.

Even if he couldn't race for the win in the final laps, the second-place finish moves Dad only ninety-eight points behind Labonte for first place in the points standing. I may have been the big story in NASCAR the last few weeks, but it will be the story of the year if Dad can win another Winston Cup. It would be his eighth title and would put him up there on top in the record books. Right now he and Richard Petty each have seven titles. He's got a good shot and I figure I want it for him almost as much as he wants it for himself.

# Pocono, Pennsylvania
## Pocono 500

## I Guess I Was Just in Dad's Way

The Pocono track is somewhat of an odd-man-out on the NASCAR tour. It's an aging, outdated facility, located out of civilization's way in the Pocono Mountains. Its strange triangular shape is nothing like we see anywhere else. We've proven as a team that we are quick learners, but this place throws up a steep learning curve. Until the test session two weeks ago, I had never turned a lap here. Then I totaled a race car, so I wouldn't say our confidence is high coming in here. The long, long front straight also forces drivers to shift gears—a rarity on an oval track. Some drivers take years and years before they are comfortable on the three very distinct, very different corners. For the first time in a while, I feel like a rookie.

We do surprisingly well in qualifying, slotting into the thirteenth spot on the grid for Sunday's race. There are also other reasons to be pleased. "Juniormania" has died down to a whisper, but the latest edition of *ESPN* magazine has just hit the newsstands and includes two segments about me. The feature story by Ryan McGee (the writer that I stiffed at Talladega in April) has some good stuff about Dad and me, plus ESPN *SportsCenter* anchorwoman Linda Cohn spoke with me about the perks of being a famous athlete. It's a good magazine, and it's cool to see me alongside a lot of other big-time athletes.

Did I say "Sunday's race" in the previous paragraph? Well, scratch that and make it "Monday's race." Sunday is a complete washout: steady, chilling rain wipes out all activities for the day. While I relax all dry and cozy in my motor coach, a lot of the fans have to scramble through the mud to make arrangements to stay an extra day. I wonder how many of them have to call in sick to work Monday morning. A massive outbreak of "racing fever," I reckon.

We start the race with the goal of staying on the lead lap and learning all we can. Hopefully, we can hang in there and then run hard at the end. We tiptoe through the first few laps, acclimating ourselves to the track that has been washed clean by all the rain. All goes well until Lap 4. Dad must have run over some debris, because his right front tire blows in Turn 2. He manages to save it from crashing and then tries like hell to get to the inside lane to make it to the pit area.

I guess he figured since he owned my team and that he is my dad, I would back off and just let him slide across to the inside, but I'm in no mood to surrender any momentum and track position. I guess I was in his way, because he slams hard into the right side of the car.

*Wham!* He hits me and then slides into the pit lane.

Our car is damaged, but because we don't want to lose a lap, the team decides to stay out on track and hold on as best as we can. Dad makes his stop for a new tire, and manages to rejoin the field in last place but still on the lead lap.

Though we continue, the car is damaged and gradually slows down for the rest of the day. The damage isn't extensive, but it's enough to upset the aerodynamics of the car. We even make an extra pit stop on Lap 75 to try and correct some of the problems, but we drop as far back as thirty-sixth position. We manage to remain on the lead lap despite all these problems.

Meanwhile, Dad is kicking ass. It seems like he is leading the race in the blink of an eye. On a tricky track, his experience really pays off. He leads the race until the final turn of the final lap, when Jeremy Mayfield pulls close enough to give him a slight tap in the rear bumper. Dad's car slides out of the groove and toward the outside wall. He somehow manages to avoid crashing (just like when the tire blew), but Mayfield streaks past to take the win. Dad hangs on for fourth place.

It is quite a moment, because Mayfield did to Dad what Dad has done to so many other drivers throughout the years. Dad catches up to Mayfield on the cooldown lap and flips him the finger, but even he knows that he has gotten some of his own medicine.

We manage a top-twenty finish, sliding across in nineteenth. Considering we limped on home from Lap 4, it's not too bad. I tried to learn the track, so hopefully we'll be more competitive when we come back here in a few weeks.

It was Mayfield's second win this year, so he joins Tony Stewart and me at the top of the multi-win list. I liked that list a whole lot better when it was just my name at the top.

# I Am NOT Riding That Thing

It sounded good on paper.

For another of my special Budweiser appearances across the United States, I was asked to attempt a world record. You know, Guinness Book of Records stuff—set a mark that will live forever in history. The Salt Lake City Anheuser-Busch wholesaler, General Distributing, has secured what is believed to be the world's fastest motorized bar stool and has invited me to make the official land-speed attempt.

It conjures images of Utah's great Bonneville Salt Flats, where many land-speed records have been set. Visions of Craig Breedlove's *Spirit of America* jet-car topping six hundred miles per hour in the 1960s, and grizzled legends of speed like Sir Malcolm Campbell (who had also set records in the 1930s on the beaches of Daytona long before NASCAR was conceived). I can see myself rolling across the white sands where so many legends have made their mark. It seems like fun and a great way to gain some lighthearted publicity.

However, as the event approaches, more and more details trickle in. The attempt will actually not take place on the wide-open salt flats, but at a local oval track, the Rocky Mountain Raceway, a 0.4-mile paved oval similar to the small tracks where I began my racing career. Not a great setup for a sizzling land-speed record of more than . . . twenty miles per hour.

They requested that I arrive in Salt Lake early enough to test-drive (test-ride? test-pilot?—what the hell *do* you do with a motorized bar stool?) the bar stool at the headquarters of the Bud distributor. I think that's a great idea, because the more I think about it, the less I think this is a good idea. I can't see myself calling Dad to tell him I can't race this weekend because I broke my ass on a motorized bar stool.

When we arrive at the warehouse, I quickly look for the contraption, but it is not there. Not a good sign. I'm told they are doing some final preparations. With no bar stool to test, I sign autographs for some excited employees and family members. Then they let me know that the bar stool will be at the racetrack when I arrive.

We hop into the limo provided by the local distributor to travel to the track. A local cameraman hired to videotape the events of the day is already in the limo.

"Did they tell you about the crash?" he asks. "Some old guy was testing the bar stool and the throttle stuck open," he explains. "He jumped off and fell to the ground. Got all skinned up. The bar stool ran into that cement wall at full speed. It was bent up pretty bad, so they took it away to fix it."

"Damn, man," I tell my publicist, "I am *not* riding that thing!"

He assures me he will do all he can.

We are escorted into a special tent to sign autographs for several hundred fans that won a chance to meet me in a local radio station contest. I sign and sign some more while flirting with the two local Bud Girls, and all the while the behind-the-scene negotiations are ongoing.

Repair work continues and the stool has yet to arrive.

"He will *not* ride the bar stool," Jade insists. "Dale Jr. will do all he can for the fans, but we are not risking his health and the millions of dollars invested in him if this thing is not safe," Jade yells, while searching for any alternative, any solution.

Finally, a glimmer of hope: a Budweiser No. 8 show car is on display. Maybe I could drive that instead?

Most show cars are mere shells of the real thing: former race cars that look exactly like the ones that race each Sunday. These replicas travel to grocery stores and events across the country to give people a glimpse of what my car looks like. Mostly it's bodywork mounted on a chassis that was wrecked beyond repair in a race or practice session. Most do not have an engine, although this one does.

The man who hauls the show car across country from shopping mall to convenience store to nightclub is asked, "Will the engine run?"

He hesitates.

"Well, sort of. I wouldn't push it. It overheats in a big hurry," he says.

That's enough for me. Negotiation over. I will drive the show car on the track in addition to presenting the winner's trophy for tonight's feature race, the Budweiser 100 for hobby stock cars. Hobby stocks are like an inexpensive, beginner's version of Winston Cup cars, much like what I started with.

When the race ends, I'm shuttled to the start/finish line in the limo, making some sort of grand entrance in front of the grandstands. I hop out, rather embarrassed because—even though limos are nice—it just looks shitty to pull up at a racetrack in the back of a stretch limo. It may have worked for Elvis, but I'd be more comfortable in my Chevy pickup or something. Along for the short ride are the attractive, scantily clad Bud Girls that have not been far from my side since I arrived. We present the trophy to a gruff-looking, bearded winner. You can tell he's proud as hell of his win, and I would be too.

I speak to the crowd on the PA for a few moments as a van pulls onto the track. The stool has arrived. The silver, streamlined gizmo is rolled out of the back of the van and pushed toward me.

"They've had some mechanical problems with the bar stool," I tell the crowd on the microphone, not taking any chances that I will be forced to hop on the little death stool. I figure I'll get the crowd on my side if they try to force me on that thing. "So what I'm going to do is drive one of my race cars for a few laps. . . ."

The crowd cheers and the show car is rolled out to the start/finish line. I walk past the lil' bar stool, hop in the car, and start the old, fragile engine.

It sounds like some sort of high-speed popcorn popper, but I wheel it as hard as I can for nearly ten laps. The fans love it, but the smoldering engine can't stand it any longer, and I return to the infield.

I agree to pose for photos with the bar stool, but I look at it warily and refuse to sit on it. Then all hell breaks loose as a gaggle of NBA team mascots barrel onto the racetrack, creating mayhem—squirting Silly String and threatening to carry off the Bud Girls.

In a chivalrous attempt to save the Bud Girls from the grips of someone dressed as a bear or gorilla or some sort of cheesy medieval knight, I invite them to depart with me in the limo.

I wave to the crowd and hop into the back with the Girls.

"Damn, *that* was a rock-and-roll moment," I say, laughing. "We've come to your town and we're stealing your best-looking women!"

Once outside the track, I hop out to stroll through the pits, where the guys work on their own race cars. Like many local racetracks across America, most of the cars look as if they are held together with rubber bands and duct tape, prepared with love by regular Joes who work at the local garage or body shop in order to make enough bucks to buy fuel and tires for their race car each week. Unlike the high-pressure, high-stakes Winston Cup grind, this is where racing is truly fun, and it's where I was less than three years ago. It seems a long time ago now, but, unlike riding in a limo, I feel at home immediately here in the pit area.

I'm much more relaxed surrounded by the racers, who clamor for autographs and ask advice on how to correct an overheating race car.

"Let's take a look," I tell one of the drivers. "Bring your car over here."

I poke my head into the engine compartment. No need to raise the hood first, because there is no hood.

"See here, you have some cheap hoses," I point out. "They're old, and when they get hot they can contract or collapse, and then the engine can't get enough coolant. I used to have that problem, so I bought some better hoses and it took care of it.

"Plus," I continued, "you need to shorten these hoses. Make 'em only as long as you need to, and it'll work more efficiently. . . ."

This is fun, so I spend another hour shooting the shit, shaking hands, high-fivin', even autographing several race cars and driving a gigantic monster truck through the parking lot.

My extended visit in the pits has made me late for the last flight of the night to San Francisco. I will have to leave early the next morning, so the Bud Girls suggest a local pub in downtown Salt Lake City. The owners of the bar are race fans, and they treat me as if Brigham Young himself has set foot in their establishment. My cardboard stand-ups are everywhere, and fans come by one by one to politely say hello to the three-dimensional Dale Jr.

I am in for a rough weekend at the Sears Point road course. Just like Pocono, I have never raced here, and neither has the team. We'll be lucky, and happy, to finish the weekend with the car still intact.

When qualifying arrives Friday afternoon, the string is broken.

Statistically I had been NASCAR's best qualifier this

season, and I'm the only driver with an average starting position in single digits. Preparing to make our twentieth career Winston Cup start, the team and I have qualified in the first round (the top twenty-five positions) for every event. Until today.

This road course is considered the toughest on the tour, especially for first-timers. Though we had a productive two-day test session at the picturesque track a month or so earlier, our inexperience shows on the timing charts.

I am thirty-first best after round one of qualifying. For the first time, we must make a second qualifying attempt tomorrow. While everyone on the team is disappointed, it's not a total surprise.

The track requires technical driving skills. You have to know how to get the car to turn and you have to know what the weight of the car is doing to each tire in each corner. The run-off areas and gravel traps entice you to push harder and harder. You just want to go faster and faster through some of the corners.

I'm not saying I'm any good at it yet, but it's fun when you get into the rhythm and start going fast. Then it's like driving a go-kart! Of course, in the test session, I ran off into the gravel six or seven times.

We start the race from the ass end of the field. It looks different from back here. When the race starts, I'm still slowly working my way around the very slow final corner, a right-hand hairpin turn that seems to produce a lot of drama.

My dad has some very simple advice: Keep it on the pavement, because the way guys crash and screw up here, you can take it easy and get a top-twenty finish without even passing a car!

He was never known as a road racer, but I know he worked hard at it, and he was so proud to get a win here, further proving that he is one of the best drivers ever on every type of track that NASCAR visits.

I try to keep his advice in mind, but I manage to actually pass a few guys before my car starts getting ornery. Through an aggressive pit strategy, we even work our way as high as fourth place midway through the race, but mostly due to the other leaders stopping for fuel and tires. In the middle of the race, the car is actually handling better than ever, and I start to push a little harder than before, getting a better hang of it with each lap. But eventually it bites me and I have a quick, harmless spin in the tight hairpin turn. It isn't too bad, and I only lose one position.

At the end of the race, I manage to keep it on the asphalt (most of the day anyway), and we finish twenty-fourth in the SaveMart 350. Not bad for our first time on a road course.

It wasn't pretty, but hey, it was fun for me.

I am more relieved than anything to come out of this place without a wrecked car or a fortieth-place finish. Now I have to endure the long trip home . . . but Daytona is next on the calendar, so at least I have that to look forward to.

# Daytona Beach, Florida
## Pepsi 400

## I Want to Emphasize BIG Curves

Jim Fluharty, a photographer for *NASCAR Winston Cup Illustrated,* approaches me with a pretty neat proposal. He wants me to use a disposable Kodak camera to take pictures of myself during race weekend. This is a cool idea.

First I shoot some of my buddies who have come down from Mooresville ("Dirty Mo") to hang out for the weekend. They're all part of the Dirty MoPosse, a group of my friends.

I shoot pictures of the crew getting the car ready for practice. I hide the camera inside my Bud uniform, and once I'm out on the track, I grab the camera and start clicking away even as I move along at nearly two hundred miles per hour. Then I hold my left arm out and shoot a picture of myself at the wheel, winking at the camera.

When I use up the film, I give the camera to one of the guys in the Dirty MoPosse and he takes it to one of those one-hour processing joints. I want a set of these

pictures for myself. They will look good on the refrig-
erator at home.

After practice, a couple of people from CBS-TV stop
by with a copy of the finished story they're calling
"Junior's Real World." They'll run a long version before the race and a shorter version during a yellow flag
or if the race is hit with a rain delay. The Dirty MoPosse
cheers and slaps high-fives while the tape runs. It's cool
as hell, and my buddies love the part where I tell 'em
my vision of the perfect woman includes very big
curves. And I want to emphasize BIG curves.

It's been a good day and the mood is loose, right up
until I go out to qualify in the thirty-first spot.


There's another son of a famous guy at the track
tonight, but he's not racing. George W. Bush is the honorary grand marshal. He comes into the drivers' meeting for an introduction along with Hallie Einsenberg,
the curly-haired Pepsi girl.

Bush gets a big ovation from the drivers when he is
introduced. He's a racing fan and even came out to the
Texas Motor Speedway to check out the action when he
was governor. In a room full of NASCAR drivers who
have private jets, motor coaches, and run in big-money
races sponsored by Winston tobacco, you can bet he
feels right at home surrounded by all these white male
Republicans.

I go out to the driver introduction area early to shoot
some footage for NBC, which will join Fox in televising the races in 2001. I'm the first driver out near the
stage, and I run into Bush when I arrive. He's a politi-

cian, so he's not about to pass up a photo op. He positions us both perfectly for all the photographers to see. I quickly excuse myself and leave him talking with one of the Dirty MoPosse. I hope George W. ain't pissed.


I start near the back where bad things can happen. I want to get up front, so by the fourth lap I'm running three-wide in one of the fastest cars on the track. Other guys know a fast car when they see it, and I pull four cars in the draft and we pass car after car. Jimmy Spencer is right behind me and he is itching to get out and lead the group. If I can get him to work together, we can blow through the field.

Spencer isn't patient (as usual) and a few laps later he slips past me and now he's the one pulling the rest of us. But I'm still faster. By Lap 60, I blow by him and move into the top ten. The top six cars pull away from the field, and I work with Jeff Gordon to catch them. With all the drafting and maneuvering, cars make contact. Hard contact sometimes, like when I come up behind Gordon a little too fast and I run into his rear bumper.

A yellow comes out and I check my water temperature gauge. It's been creeping higher since I hit Gordon.

The crew gets a report from another driver who says the damage doesn't look too bad. Regardless, the radiator must have taken a hit. The temperature gauge is going up, past 255, and the engine won't last a full four hundred miles running that hot.

I start ducking the nose of the car out of the draft, trying to suck some cool air into the engine. It isn't pretty, but it works. Sort of. I can't imagine what the other drivers are thinking, though. The water temperature drops but I can tell the damage has been done.

I come in to make a pit stop on a yellow flag, and the crew pulls tape off the radiator vents in the nose of the car to increase the airflow to the engine. I try not to worry about it, but it's impossible, especially when a new twist begins to develop. Something is burning up and it stinks.

At about that time, all hell breaks loose on the track in front of me. Cars slide everywhere. I make an instinctive move that carries me down onto the apron at the end of the straightaway. The car slides sideways as it launches from the apron back up onto the steep banking. Somehow I manage to save the car and stay out of the wreck. Now that's what I call driving wide-ass open.

The crew calls me in during the caution, pulls the pins on the hood, then opens it and uses a pressurized tank to force some fresh cool water into the engine and get the temperature down a little. We try everything. We do this thing with the water three more times during the caution.

The fresh water cools the engine some, but the time it takes to get the temperature down puts us at the tail end of the lead lap. I'm thirty-third on the restart. But we move up to twenty-ninth after one lap and then eighteenth the next time I cross the start/finish line. I move up eleven spots in one lap. On the next lap, I reel off another seven cars and I move all the way up to eleventh. Damn, this is why restrictor-plate racing is fun—I got a good run up the middle and it was like parting the seas.

They say that engines run best just before they blow up. It's folk wisdom, I guess, but it's true today. The car is hot in more ways than one.

But it doesn't last. I lose power, slowly dropping back into the field.

The yellow comes out with ten laps to go. If the engine lasts until the final lap, I may be able to limp to the line. But when the green flag flies on Lap 156 with four to go, the strain is just too much. The engine expires, and I get it down off of the racing line as quick as I can so it doesn't leave any fluids on the racing groove.

We finish thirty-first while Jeff Burton barely beats Dale Jarrett to win the race. Even though we finish poorly, it's obvious we have a great superspeedway car. Passing eleven cars in one laps was unbelievable. I can't wait to get back here next year.

Following the race, I have a little fun with the Dirty MoPosse. We let off a little steam by racing golf carts around the Daytona infield and enjoying the fine taste of my sponsor's product. There's nothin' better than a cold Bud at the end of a long, hot day.

We're one golf cart short, so we borrow one from Michael Kranefuss, who owns the No. 12 car that Jeremy Mayfield drives. This is no normal golf cart though. It has fancy chrome, slick tires and wheels, and a paint scheme that looks like their race car.

We thrash and race and crash and slam the golf carts across the infield. When the night is done, it looks like I'll have to replace Kranefuss's cart. It looks nothing like it did an hour ago.

Damn, that's a five-thousand-dollar golf cart. I just hope he's not too mad.

Thankfully, when Kranefuss sees me at the track the next week, he says although he'll never let me borrow any of his shit again, he'll cover the bill.

Cool guy.

# Loudon, New Hampshire
## *New Hampshire 300*

## Tragedy . . . Again

On Wednesday morning, the day after the Fourth of July, there is a Winston media teleconference. I'm supposed to be the featured guest. But at eleven o'clock there's no word from me.

Jade, my publicist, gets a panicked call from the Winston rep and starts trying to track me down. He calls me at home. No answer. Cell: not turned on. Pager: no response. He calls DEI but nobody there has seen me.

Twenty journalists and several top Budweiser execs are waiting on the line, so he sends a DEI security guy around to knock on my door. No answer.

Twenty minutes after the teleconference is supposed to start, an incredibly pissed-off Winston media rep terminates the call on account of "no Junior." The phone calls are flying. One of the Winston guys says that in more than twenty years of doing these teleconferences, this is the first time one has ever been canceled.

I miss this whole scene since I don't wake up until late afternoon. I call in and apologize and agree to make up for my absence by doing a Friday morning news conference at the track. When the "make-good media conference" starts, I tell them why I missed the tele-conference.

Truth is, I was drunk and slept through it. I needed about twelve hours to recover from the night before. The Winston guy is on me and Jade pretty hard, and he particularly likes the fact that Mike Helton, NASCAR's head honcho, wants to talk to me on Sunday morning. It's no secret what Helton wants to talk about.

In the meantime, I need to practice and qualify for Sunday's race on the track where Adam Petty was killed. It's a short track with sharp turns where you can easily hit the wall head-on. That's what happened to Adam and it's on everyone's mind. There is a somber mood in the pits. This is already one of the worst places on the schedule anyway, so it is really bad this morning.

We go out to practice and before I finish two laps, my spotter gets on the radio and says, "C'mon in. Red flag. Looks like the 42 car is upside down."

Kenny Irwin crashed at almost exactly the same spot where Adam hit the wall. Practice comes to a stop. The gloom that already hangs over the speedway seems to get worse the longer we go without word on Kenny's condition.

After learning practice has been canceled, I turn to walk back to my motor coach. Jade grabs me and tells me Kenny is dead. I'm in disbelief. How can this happen?

Almost as fast as these thoughts flare up, I try to get hold of myself. If there is any trait that can help a racer in the heat of battle, it's being able to control his emotions, and I try hard to control whatever is bursting through my brain and my body.

Everyone in the garage area walks around with the same zombie gaze. How can this be? Twice on the same track? And so close together? It's numbing.

Although practice is canceled, NASCAR does not call off qualifying. This seems cold to some people, but there are fans who have bought tickets for today and Sunday, so the show must go on. Plus, it won't bring Kenny back if we don't race, so it almost feels better to get back on track rather than sit and ponder the horrible news. Nobody's got much heart for qualifying, but it goes on anyway.

Later I make it to the local mall, where I buy a kitten—a short-tailed, furry Manx breed. I wanted to get one for a while, but today just seemed like the right time to get a new pet. Animals are great—they are very soothing and I enjoy having them around.

Back at the motor coach, the cat is right at home. We name him Bud, after the sponsor, and he's a lot of fun. He's a great comfort to me and he entertains the people who drop by the coach.

After dinner, Dale Beaver, the newest pastor with Motor Racing Outreach (a traveling program that provides ministry for the racing community), stops by to see how I'm doing and to just sit and talk. He's thirty-something and a really good guy. He stays for more than an hour and describes the impromptu memorial service at the track that afternoon. I never enjoyed going to church because I could never identify with the sermons or the somber old people giving them, but he's different. I can identify with him.

On Sunday morning it's raining. Nobody feels much like racing but nobody wants to stay around here a minute more than we have to, either. Everyone is praying for the sky to clear so we can race at least 151 laps and then get out of here and go home.

My meeting with Helton is still on, in spite of the accident. I hike over to the NASCAR trailer with Ty Norris, DEI's top man at the track.

Helton is a big, imposing man. But I was raised by somebody who can give a lot worse than he can. Plus, I've known Mike for a long time—he and my dad are close, close friends.

"These teleconferences are very important to us, to Winston, and to the tracks," he says, coming on tough and very stern.

"I know," I say. "But you've got forty-three drivers out there. Of all of them, who do you expect will be the most hungover on the day after the Fourth of July? Just think about that when you schedule me for these things."

I catch the hint of a smile but Helton does his best to conceal it.

"This is *not* going to become a habit," he insists, regaining his tough-guy tone. "If this does become a habit, I will come get you myself after every race, and we'll go to the media center together. Every week."

I assure him that it won't be a recurring problem, and the meeting is over. I'm not the first hungover driver in the history of NASCAR, so it isn't that big of a deal. It's kind of a hand-slap. A first strike. It's his fatherly way of dealing with it, but I know if it ever gets out of hand or if it becomes a regular occurrence, Helton and Big E will both kick my ass.

The race is like an afterthought. It's boring and lifeless. Thankfully, the rain stays away long enough so that we won't have to come back the next day to finish. But it still shortens the race, which is fine with just about everyone.

Tony Stewart wins the race. This is appropriate, since he and Kenny Irwin were fierce competitors their entire careers. They raced each other hard and they had some angry moments. Most famously, last year at Martinsville, Tony threw his heel guards at Kenny's car after they had wrecked, and then he tried to go after him while Kenny was still in the car driving by under the yellow flag.

But they were friends. Tony dedicates the race to Kenny and gives a great tribute to him by saying, "He made me better as a race driver, every step of my career."

I finish twenty-first, and might have run higher if the race wasn't called with twenty-seven laps to go. It was just one of those days when nothing really fell in our favor.

My father finishes sixth and moves within forty-five points of Bobby Labonte in the Winston Cup standings. He's only won one race, but he has fifteen top-ten finishes in eighteen races. He is in position to win championship number eight. We gave up any illusion of a championship this year long ago, but now it's looking like we may not even win the Rookie of the Year award if we don't get our shit together.

# Pocono, Pennsylvania
## Pennsylvania 500

## Junior, Are You OK?

The mayor of Philadelphia proclaims July 20 Dale Earnhardt Jr. Day. I'm here to hang out with the Inner City Youth Racing League. It's one of my favorite charities. They take about one hundred inner-city kids and put them in vocational courses that are geared to teach them the mechanics of motor sports. The program is the only one of its kind, and I really believe in it. I make at least one trip a year to meet the kids and see how they're doing.

This year the kids are working on several Mini-Cup cars—high-speed karts with full bodies. They look like Winston Cup cars that have been left in the clothes dryer too long.

We're going to race these small cars on an oval track that is set up on some blocked-off roads in a city park. I am going to drive against a few local media people and some of the kids. When the green flag falls, I stand on the throttle. No mercy! I get the tires squealing in the corners, and the fiberglass body on that baby is shud-

dering like it's about to come apart. The kids watching
the race eat it up and scream and cheer whenever I go
by. It's a ten-lap race and I put all the other cars, except
one, down a lap. I can't let these kids see anyone beat
me! Everyone cheers when I get out of the car. It's almost as good as the Winston. The one kid I didn't lap
is about fourteen or fifteen years old. He reminds me
a lot of myself at that age: quiet and shy, but itching
to get into a race car. He might be good someday, and
it would be great for NASCAR to have more—hell,
*any*—talented black drivers in Winston Cup. It needs to
happen soon.

I hang around, signing some autographs and talking
to the kids. When the time comes to catch my flight to
Pocono, I've been here more than three hours, and I
hate to leave.

We qualify fifteenth because I overdrive the car. If I
was more patient, I would have easily been in the top
ten. That pisses me off, but I still feel pretty good about
the car for the race.

The next morning, we get the car set up for the race,
and I go out for a quick practice run. I don't like the
feel, so I return to the garage so the guys can make
some changes to the front sway bar and shocks. They
make the change and I go back out. But when I reach
Turn 2, the car refuses to turn.

I go straight into the wall at more than 170 miles per
hour and then the car slides across the track and hits the
inside wall just as hard, or so it seems, since I'm not
prepared or braced for the second impact.

Ty Norris, who is spotting for me today, calls to me on the radio. "Junior, are you OK? You OK, man?" I am, but I have no breath to answer.

As I sit there trying to catch my breath and clear my vision, I check to make sure everything is intact and I have no injuries. One of the safety guys comes rushing over and tries to take off my helmet with my head still in it. I quickly let him know he's going to break my fucking neck.

I get out of the car on my own and climb into the ambulance for the mandatory ride to the infield medical station. I'm back in the garage five minutes later and the team has the backup car out. I'm sore, I have a headache, I'm pissed off, but luckily I'm all right.

The team has only a couple of hours to make the backup car just as fast and race-ready as the primary car.

"The car just didn't turn," I tell Tony and Tony Jr. "The brakes locked and I went straight into the wall."

Because the crash happened after we made some changes, we all believe something broke or wasn't tightened correctly. Whatever caused the crash, the magical chassis that won the Winston is now ready for the scrap heap, or at best to return as a show car someday.

Dad and several other drivers come by to see if I'm OK. I'm sore but I tell them I'm fine. I sit down to relax, but several of the track doctors come into the garage looking for me.

"One of our safety workers believes that you were unconscious when they got to you," a doctor says to me.

"No way," I tell him. "I've been knocked out before, so I know what it's like. I was *not* knocked out."

"I'm sorry, but if they tell me that, I have to be sure that you get some tests taken before I can let you back in the car."

"No way, man, I'm OK."

"I'm sorry," the doctor says again, "but we are not going to clear you to drive unless we check you out. You need a CAT scan. We'll try to have you back here in time for happy hour. I promise."

I always knew the Pocono track was remote, but the nearest hospital is fifty miles from the track, in Allentown. In order to save time, we take the medical helicopter, but not before I make a quick stop at the motor coach to change into street clothes. Oh, and to suck down a couple of Winstons. *You* hit the wall that hard and tell me if you don't need a cigarette!

As we clear the track, we fly directly over Turn 2 and I look down and see my skid marks. They start midway through the corner and continue straight into the wall. It's eerie to see from this angle. Damn, I'm lucky.

We land at the hospital and I roll into the emergency room about the same time several other people arrive. They were injured in a highway crash. When they crashed, they were going a lot slower than I was, but right now I'm in a lot better shape than they are. This should be an advertisement for wearing your seat belt.

These people need medical attention a lot worse than I do, so I relax on the gurney while I wait to see a doctor. The emergency room staff apologizes for the wait. While I'm waiting, I go to sleep. A nap is always good.

The phones at the hospital light up.

"Is there a status report on Dale Jr.?"

"Has Ralph Dale Earnhardt been admitted?" the media ask over and over again, trying to get any scrap of news or information. The hospital staff is well trained, so they provide no information.

Jade, who flew in the helicopter with me, makes calls from a phone that the hospital provides near my examining room. He has a detailed emergency plan just for these situations, and he immediately calls my dad's motor coach, the NASCAR media staff, and Budweiser executives across the country. Everybody gets the same news—I'm fine, it's all just precautionary. He calls everyone on his list every thirty minutes or so.

After the injured people have been taken to operating rooms, the emergency room staff wheels me in for a CAT scan and some X-rays. Then we wait for a doctor to read the results.

The doctor on duty says they look good, but when a patient has lost consciousness, they like to keep him for at least twenty-four hours.

No way! I'll be about halfway through a five-hundred-mile race at this time tomorrow.

I insist again that I was never unconscious. But they insist that hospital policy is to get clearance from another doctor. Plus, they decide they should have X-rayed my kidney and pelvis area. Back we go down the hall to the X-ray room.

Finally the second doctor arrives and comes to the same conclusion. Everything is normal but we have to keep the patient. This is aggravating. I now have a headache, but mainly because I might not make it back to the track for the final practice today.

They need approval from a third doctor to release me. This time the hospital's top neurosurgeon, who had been enjoying the afternoon at home with his family, walks in with his two young boys. The kids are fans and we talk racing while their dad looks at the CAT scan and the X-rays. Same diagnosis, but he must be a race fan too, because he agrees to release me. Before I go, I sign a few autographs for the boys and the hospital staff, and the doctor writes a note to NASCAR, clearing me to drive today. I feel like I'm back in grade school or something, bringing a note to the principal that says, "Dale Jr. is allowed to attend the field trip to the racetrack. Please allow him to drive his car at a high rate of speed again."

After the helicopter takes us back to the track, I walk over to the NASCAR trailer and drop off my note from the doctor, like a good boy. I slide into the garage without being spotted and I hear another TV reporter asking Tony Eury if he knows about my condition or my injuries. Just then I walk into the camera shot, smile, wave, and then climb in the car. Surprise!

Even though I'm announced in fifteenth place during the driver introductions, NASCAR rules say I have to start at the back of the field since I'm not in the car that I qualified in on Friday. That means to get to the front of the pack, I have to pass forty-two cars. No problem.

In the first eight laps, I make up twelve positions, and after a pit stop on Lap 25, I move up another seven spots into twenty-fourth place. This is almost too easy. Starting at the back just makes it more interesting. The crew and I are wound pretty tight after the crash, but our mood improves each time I pass another car like it was standing still.

Then we lose a lot of what we'd gained when we have a problem with an air wrench on a pit stop. It looks like I'll have to pass the same guys again. Before the race reaches the halfway point, I am all the way back up to ninth place.

After a lot of early yellows, we run on green for a long time, so we need to start thinking about our fuel mileage. The guys in the pits figure and refigure and are confident that I won't need to pit before Lap 146. I get ready to come in on that exact lap, when a tire on my dad's car shreds, leaving debris on the track and bringing out another yellow. NASCAR closes the pits until the field can close up into single file. I now must milk at least one more lap—2.5 miles—out of the nearly empty fuel tank.

When the pits reopen, it's too late. The tank is dry and I have to coast around the final portion of the track. It takes forever. I don't remember the pit lane being *this* long! It seems like days before I roll quietly into the pit stall. When we get the engine restarted and the car back on the track, I'm in the thirtieth spot and I can't believe I have to pass these same bastards again!

I pass nineteen cars and get to eleventh place, but the tires are shot and in the closing laps our lap times fade. Rusty Wallace wins it on the last lap when Jeremy Mayfield's luck runs out and he blows a right front tire. We finish thirteenth.

But it's a hard-earned thirteenth. I feel like I passed two hundred cars today.

Now that the heat of battle is over, my adrenaline fades. Suddenly I begin to realize how hard I crashed yesterday. I need some aspirin. Or a Budweiser.

# Indianapolis, Indiana
## *Brickyard 400*

## A Lesser Driver Would Have Finished a Lap Down

After the drama at Pocono, everyone is relieved to have a weekend off from traveling. For the guys in the shop, it means their workload is increased, while much of my time is taken with appearances for Budweiser and my other sponsors.

Tonight's Budweiser appearance is in Rochester, New York, at Frontier Field, the home of the Rochester Red Wings minor league baseball team. The weather is damn near perfect and the ballpark is gorgeous. Even if baseball is not your idea of an exciting pastime, bring the family because this seems to be the place to be on a summer evening in upstate New York.

I arrive to find a line of fans stretching from inside the stadium all the way out to the parking lot. I go right to the table, sit down, and start signing. The line moves quickly, and soon I'm joined by a quartet of buxom Bud Girls. The girls are thrilled to hang with us in their town and let me know they already have some bars picked out for later on tonight.

Several of the girls teeter on the verge of tears when I tell them I'm flying home that very night. But they regain their smiles and strike their stylish model poses when a fan wants to get a photo of them.

After the signing is complete, we hustle down into the bowels of the stadium, past the locker rooms and into the home team's dugout. They give me an official Rochester jersey with my name on the back for throwing out the first pitch. One of the perks of my job is that I get to collect a lot of cool jerseys with my name and number 8 on the back. You name the sport, and I've probably got a badass jersey with my name on it.

My heart rate doesn't rise too much when I drive at top speed, or if I'm doing an autograph session or speaking in front of a big group of people, but throwing out a pitch in front of a crowd makes me nervous as hell! I hadn't practiced or warmed up or anything, but I get out there and hurl it as hard as I can. I won't give up my NASCAR license for a shot at the big leagues, but at least I reached the plate with the toss.

After the pitch, we venture immediately to the left-field VIP area to meet with the local media and the Budweiser VIP guests. I joke with the journalists who ask about my throwing motion. I hope I didn't look too lame.

The Bud Girls continue urging me to stay, but unfortunately I can't. But I do invite them all to fly back to North Carolina.

All eight eyes widen . . . and they squeal in excitement. I was kind of half teasing, but I still don't think they'll say yes. All four of 'em seem psyched to go, but on the limo ride back to the airport, reality sets in.

All four are on their cell phones . . . and then one by one, like slow-moving dominoes, they decline. The plane is wheels-up at eight-thirty . . . without any Bud Girls.

Oh well. It happens. Plus, I suppose, I should be concentrating on the race this week at Indy. It's one of the biggest races of our season.

I know millions of people who don't know anything about racing have heard of the Indy 500. Daytona and Darlington may have history and tradition going back to the 1940s, but this track opened in 1909. It has the same exact dimensions now as it did then. The surface was made with millions of bricks, which is why it's still called the Brickyard. Some of the original bricks are still left at the start/finish line. You can feel these bricks every time you roll over them. But the rest of the surface is now modern asphalt.

There are more than 250,000 permanent seats and lots of luxury suites high over the grandstands. There are more seats here than anywhere else we race. When you drive down the front straight, there are tall grandstands on both sides of the track, so it feels like you're driving down a hallway before you dive into Turn 1. The turns look wide, and maybe for the open-wheel cars they are, but for stock cars, the grooves in each corner are really narrow. In fact, compared to the Formula One cars that race here, our cars must look like Flintstones cars.

Tony George took over the track when his grandfather Tony Hulman died in 1977. George could see that Winston Cup was growing—he'd have had to be blind not to—and began working on a deal to get a race at the track. When the NASCAR Brickyard 400 ran in 1994, it was the first time that any race except for the Indy 500 had run on the track.

The Brickyard has been a great success with the fans, but the thing is . . . it's not great racing. The track is basically a rectangle with 9-degree banked turns. Believe me, in a race car, that almost feels flat. It also makes it incredibly hard to pass. So you get the kind of racing you see in Formula One—cars strung out in a line with very little passing. That's not NASCAR style. Our fans like to see us two-, three-, and even four-wide, banging and fighting each other to make a pass. That just doesn't happen here.

After qualifying, I feel good. We are sixth, which is much better than we expected. As the top rookie qualifier, I have to go to the media center for a news conference. I come in just after Dad left but I enjoy myself, doing the back and forth with the media.

One guy wants to know how it is between my father and me—they never leave that one alone for very long. He says that Big E has been saying I'm harder to give advice to since I won a couple of races.

"Yeah, well," I say, "things change, ya know. . . ."

The media love this father-versus-son verbal battle, so this line gets a big laugh.

"I've . . . I don't know," I kind of stammer, trying to come up with another good one. "He's not any easier . . . to talk to than he was a year ago, so I can't argue that point. I never feel like I can outcompete my father as far as knowledge and experience, it's just that sometimes he's hard to listen to."

This one really has everyone laughing. Sometimes I feel like they're in the palm of my hand. Plus, I feel good because we're back in the spotlight for something good instead of something like a string of shitty races.

On the day before the Brickyard, I put on my all-white IROC uniform and stroll out for the fourth and final race of the year. I'm not exactly up for the race, because I'm way behind in the points and because the race will most likely be boring due to the nature of the track. I've had two shitty races in a row—the bad engine at Talladega and the bad flu at Michigan—and I'm so far behind in the points that I have no shot at winning the championship. The only good part is that I get to start near the front of the field.

When we get rolling, I stay near the front, trying to be smooth and looking good in a violet Pontiac. Then the engine starts to go sour just like at Talladega. It sounds like a farting tuba, especially when I hear the rest of the healthy engines easily drive away from me. Dad has a chance to win the title today, but I'm so far back I can't see how he's doing. Thanks to a crash that takes out a few cars, I finish ninth in the race and tenth in the final point standings out of twelve drivers. Both suck.

My dad, meanwhile, clinches his fourth IROC championship. He *is* the man. I wonder if I should go find him, but I'm embarrassed about being so far back so I decide to go and hide in my motor coach.

On the way, Tony Jr. spots me and teases: "See, without us, you ain't shit." He almost falls over laughing, and then I counter. "Hey man," I jab back, "a lesser driver would have finished a full lap down!"

We laugh, and we continue to the motor coach. The problem is, the only thing between my home-away-from-home and every fan in the place is a thin white picket fence with an opening every ten feet or so. The opening is blocked by a single strand of plastic chain that must have been on sale at Kmart.

Jade and I decide to make a run for the lot by climbing over a short cement barrier at the far end of the garage, then slide in on the other side of the huge crowd. This is not a smart move.

The crowd sees my uniform and they run along the fence to get my autograph. The mad rush creates a bit of a panic. They trap us against the fence, and the crowd begins pushing closer and closer, knocking over several small children at the front of the crush. Unable to move more than a few inches at a time, we yell for the crowd to step back to let the kids up and to avoid anybody getting hurt. It is the scariest moment of the weekend for me.

Luckily, one of the security guards sees the mayhem and steps in with his three-hundred-plus–pound frame to help us out of the mess and toward the motor coach. Once we're there, the folks who didn't get an autograph or who want two or three more start knocking on the door and windows of my coach.

We sit inside and listen to the yelling and knocking.

I change clothes and then step back out to sign autographs for about an hour, spending extra time with several kids in wheelchairs.

Many of the fans want me to take photos with them, and I'm cool with that. For a few seconds anyway. I look over at a guy posing with me, flexing his bare bicep with a huge swastika tattoo. I wish I could have seen the look on my face when I spotted the tattoo.

I've had enough after that, and I walk back into the motor coach.

"Sonofabitch, man" I shout. "That guy had a swastika tattoo! Jesus—where could *that* photo end up? That's sick shit, man. . . . Who would do that? You don't think that will show up somewhere like the *Enquirer*, do you? Those bastards will print that shit!"

I decide that the swastika photo has replaced the falling children as the scariest moment of the weekend.

I have a guest coming in the night before the race. Susan Ward is the star of the movie *The In Crowd*. She's also been on television shows like *Sunset Beach*, where the producers must have looked for any excuse to put her in a bikini. The first I saw of her was in *Maxim* magazine's special "Hot 100 Women" issue. (She was number twenty-two, by the way. Fellas, you all probably remember. . . .) *FMH* magazine also called her one of the hottest women in the world. Her picture was stunning but what really got my attention was the caption that described her lifelong love of NASCAR.

Calls were made and she accepted my invitation to come to the race. The only hitch was that Ward could come only if her boyfriend could tag along. *Damn!* What are you gonna say? We already invited her. . . . "No. Leave him at home. Come alone. I'll be the guy in the red driving suit." (It doesn't hurt to dream sometimes, ya know.)

Ward is pretty damn hot in jeans and a T-shirt, and she's very nice when I give her the tour of the garage area and Gasoline Alley. The boyfriend turns out to be David Robinson, a movie producer and the son of James Robinson, who runs Morgan Creek Productions. They did *Ace Ventura, Major League,* and a lot of other big-time movies. He's so fucking cool I can't even hate him.

There is nothing to prepare you for the sensation of walking out of Gasoline Alley and onto pit lane on race day at Indianapolis. The grandstands stretch as far as you can see, with more than a quarter of a million fans cheering for you. It's awesome. OK, maybe I do see what these Indy 500 fans have been talking about.

After a crash yesterday that put Jeremy Mayfield out with a concussion, Kyle Petty is in his car as a relief driver, and because of NASCAR rules, he has to go to the back of the starting field. This means I move up one row. When the flag falls, I improve immediately and shoot into third place.

But I'm on the radio on the first lap telling them the car is real tight. The crew teases me about it later and say it's a record for the quickest complaint of the season.

I'm still third after fifteen laps but now Tony Jr. and the guys worry about a hot dog wrapper that had been blown onto the track and is caught on our radiator grille. Part of the grille is taped up for maximum aerodynamic help, but if the wrapper is covering an open air-intake area for the radiator, it could cause the car to overheat. The crew tells me to let Bill Elliott, who is running behind me, go past. Maybe the turbulence will dislodge the wrapper. But we get a yellow flag and don't need to let Elliott by. We're still third on the restart.

Then we pass Jerry Nadeau, take second, and are zooming in on Rusty Wallace in the "other beer" car. This is gonna be good when I pass him for the lead.

I'm the fastest car on the track. Too fast, in fact. I'm too aggressive and I wear out the tires. Before I can sweep triumphantly past Rusty for lead of the race, not to mention the glory of my sponsor and the delight of our supermodel guest, I start losing ground. To make matters worse, dark clouds roll in and temperatures start falling. Indy is known for the way the traction changes with the slightest shift in the weather. This is not what we need. The track cools off so much that my car gets real tight.

The chance to adjust comes on Lap 83, but the changes we make don't improve the car. I drop back to tenth. From the halfway point on, I run in almost the same position, lap after lap. There isn't much racing or much drama. The race just goes on and on and then it ends. We lose a few spots at the end and finish thirteenth. Just like we did last week. Now we are thir-teenth in the Winston Cup point standings. It's not exactly our lucky number.

Bobby Labonte strengthens his hold on the point lead by taking the victory. Dad finishes eighth and drops to third place, 145 points behind Labonte.

I'm disappointed being whooped again. I guess this is a good sign, because anyone happy with that type of performance should be looking for a new job.

## Watkins Glen, New York

### *Global Crossing at the Glen*

## A Video Game?

*Creative Loafing* is the hipster arts and entertainment magazine in the Charlotte area, and they selected me for several awards in their "Best of Charlotte" issue, which is on newsstands this week.

The staff selects me as the "Celebrity You'd Like to Know Personally," which is a cool thing, and shows that the publicity and all the media we've been doing is having an impact. (Although some of my buddies speculate that they're just looking for an invitation to have a cold Budweiser at Club E.)

The *Loafing* staff writes, "Who'd a-thought that Son of Terminator [*sic*] would turn out to be a pretty regular guy with a taste for music and a good-hearted nature? He's become almost as well-known for the parties in his basement as he is for his racin'."

Even better, the readers of the magazine vote for me as "Best New Driver, Winston Cup." It's nice to get recognized in your hometown, because sometimes it seems I see all the big Bud billboards with my picture everywhere we travel, but I never see one here in the Charlotte area.

Watkins Glen is one of the most famous road courses in America and a track that has been good to me. I finished ninth in the Busch race here in 1997, in only my third career Busch start. And I won the Busch race here last year. I hadn't led a single lap until I took the lead on the final lap of the race. But that's the lap that pays, and I won it with a pretty slick pass, if I do say so myself.

So people in the media wanted to know the "secret to my success" at Watkins Glen.

That's easy, I tell them. It's video games.

That's right. Video games.

I use several racing simulator games to do some serious training before we come here to race. The games help me with simple stuff, like the way the track goes left and right, but more importantly, where the shift points and braking points are. When I get out on the track, it's amazing how similar the real thing is to the game.

My success in the Busch Series means nothing now as we start the first practice session of the weekend. The spotter tells me Rusty Wallace reports oil on the track in Turn 9, a tricky corner. It was probably left there after Geoffrey Bodine crashed early in the day. A few seconds after the warning, I slide backwards through the grass. The car slams hard into the Styrofoam barrier and stops, with the shattered foam falling around me like flakes of snow. I'm not hurt, but the car sure is. The Styrofoam creates the illusion that you haven't hit the wall very hard, but when you climb out, the car looks like crap and reality sets in. Now we don't have much more than an hour to get the backup car ready for qualifying.

Back in the garage, I pitch in and help with the all-out thrash. As soon as the wrecked car arrives, everybody on the team descends on it like a pack of vultures and starts pulling the parts that aren't damaged so they can be installed on the backup chassis. I slide under the damaged car and start pulling suspension and transmission parts. I'm glad to be under the car, wrenching hard and getting greasy. It helps me get my mind off the wreck, and it's especially effective in keeping the media and the photographers back. I don't know any of 'em that would climb under the car with me. . . .

Almost everyone who works for DEI—not just the Bud crew—is pulling parts off the wrecked car. Steve Park is helping out. I see the DEI Busch Series driver Ron Hornaday carrying part of the transmission. Even Ty Norris, the general manager, slides under the car in his dress slacks and starched shirt.

We have to hurry to finish in time for qualifying. It may be tough to make a single lap with a car that has yet to turn a wheel, but I have faith that we can build a safe, fast car in record time. The other car looks like a carcass that was attacked by buzzards. Everything other than the chassis and the bent bodywork is gone. Big chunks of the Styrofoam are still wedged into many of the cracks and crevices of the smashed frame.

We finish prepping the backup car with a few seconds to spare. Just as I'm about to go back on the track to try to qualify, the rain starts falling hard and NASCAR decides to cancel qualifying. We'll start according to the owners' point standings.

We catch a break, and there's no need to risk crashing another car with a banzai qualifying lap.

We catch another break when the rain quits long enough for us to get in some practice laps. The backup car is set up better than the one I crashed, and about midway through the session, I let the crew know it handles like a dream.

As race time nears, I feel pretty good about the car that started the weekend as the backup. It ran great in the final practice and I look forward to getting out there today. But something is wrong. Something is missing.

I have no radio.

Crew member Brian Cram lets the crew know as they give the command to start the engines.

The car sits far down the front stretch near Turn 1, while the Bud pit area is located all the way up the track near the final corner. Brandon Blake, maybe because he is the youngest crew member or maybe because he is the fastest runner, arrives sprinting at top speed with a radio for the No. 8 car. He throws the radio into the car with only seconds to spare before we roll away from the grid.

It takes me less than a lap to barrel past three cars and barge my way into the eleventh spot. On the second lap, Jeff Gordon (who is trying to win his seventh consecutive Cup road-course race) and Tony Stewart make contact and Big E crashes hard into the barrier wall. I hope Dad is all right.

Too bad for Dad, but all these crashes work to my advantage. I'm up to eighth and the race is just three laps old.

We pull in for the first pit stop on Lap 32, but three laps later the crew notices an unusual sound when I speed past the pit. The car does not shift into third gear as I pick up speed. The engine revs above the usual limits, creating a screaming, hairy sound. This can't be good.

As I make it through Turn 1 and head toward Turn 2, I can't find third gear again, and then as I exit the turn, the gears lock up and the car spins and slams the Armco barrier. The crew look up at a huge video screen right behind the pit area and see me climbing out of the Bud car smashed against the fence right below a giant Bud sign. Well, at least we got some on-screen time for the sponsor.

I'm pretty pissed off, riding back to the infield in the ambulance. Up till that point there was a good chance we would have a strong finish. I'm cleared at the medical center and get back to the garage about the same time the car comes in looking like a rag doll. The team leaps into action to repair the car and get it back out on the track just like the day before.

"It wouldn't shift into third," I tell Tony. "It kept getting worse and worse. Then it was like the linkage was broken. I kept trying and trying to shift but it just locked up going into the esses, and then it just spun around, like it had been thrown into reverse."

Tony quickly discovers the problem. A broken shift linkage is hanging under the transmission like a limp flag. Some of the guys on the crew shake their heads and say that in all the time they've been racing, they've never seen that part fail. Until now.

They change the transmission, do an elementary wheel alignment, and I'm back on the track, down eleven laps to leader Steve Park.

Two laps later I'm hanging on for dear life and yelling into the radio that it feels like the car is breaking apart.

We've come a long way since Darlington, so the crew figures that if I say we have a major problem, we have a major problem. Tony tells me to bring it in.

Tony welds the thing together and I'm back on the track running fortieth. Twenty laps later the car gets stuck in first gear. I feel ridiculous driving the car off the track and then using the public roads in the infield to crawl back to the garage in first gear.

The car looks like it has been beaten with sledgehammers. You know how they have those old cars at the fair where you can hit 'em with a sledgehammer for a dollar? That's what it looks like, and with only one working gear, it's not much faster than an old beater either.

I'm disappointed, but soon realize that Steve Park and his team are running the race of their lives. Park holds off Mark Martin for his first Cup win, and as down as I feel about my day, I'm happy for Steve and his guys. Steve stops the Pennzoil car on the front stretch, climbs onto the roof, and bathes in the cheers like a man who has just scored the first Winston Cup win.

I join Dad, who had his own tough time on the track, in Victory Lane for the celebration.

It was not a good day for me or for Dad. But it's a great day for DEI.

# Brooklyn, Michigan
## *Pepsi 400*

## Big E, Little E, and Now Middle E

Before the race at Michigan, I do a bleach-blond job on my hair. It's sort of a ritual. I dyed my hair back in 1998 when I first ran here. This dye job really isn't all that outrageous. Some people act like they don't even notice.

They notice my qualifying time, though. No way they couldn't. We win the Bud Pole with a track record lap of 191.141 miles per hour. It is our second Bud Pole of the year, and it doesn't come a moment too soon. The car is awesome, and after wrecking two cars at the Glen, this is a great morale booster.

But my bleached hair and the pole aren't the only big news of the week. My brother Kerry is in the No. 71 Realtree-sponsored car that Dave Marcis, an old family friend, usually drives. If Kerry qualifies, it will be the first time a father and two sons start a NASCAR race since Lee Petty and his sons, Richard and Maurice, did it in 1960. It'll be the Three E's.

Kerry has a rough time on Friday, so he has to come

back and try to qualify in the second round on Saturday. The main reason Kerry has not been as successful as I have is that he's had difficulty getting good cars. Like my father found out when he first ran Winston Cup, if you don't have the equipment, it's impossible to win or even run up near the front. Kerry needs to get the right equipment and get the people behind him. That's been his problem for a long time. He has a family to take care of, so he's not really been able to put in the time needed to get the better rides. It's a vicious circle, but I think he can succeed if he finds the right situation.

This year Dad put Kerry in an ARCA car, and I think it's the best thing for him. It gives him an opportunity to drive with good equipment and to show he has talent. He won at Pocono in June, so he's got nothing to worry about from here on out as long as he can keep it off the wall and keep the car up front.

It's cool having him back at the track, just being able to hang out with him again and get our careers back parallel like when we started.

Kerry comes back on Saturday with a new engine and turns in the fastest lap of the session. He qualifies twenty-sixth, so he'll start ahead of Dad, who is way back in the pack at thirty-seventh. There will be Earnhardts front, back, and middle when the green flag drops. Little E, Big E, and now Middle E.

J. R. Rhodes, the man who has been Dad's PR guy for years and who worked with me in the Busch Series, comes to my motor coach to get me for a press conference after Kerry qualifies. I don't want to go. It's Kerry's moment. I don't want to take the spotlight from him. I tell J.R. "no" several times, but he insists that Dad will be there too. It's one of those situations where you might as well go, even though you don't want to.

So Dad, Kerry, and I sit up there taking questions.

Somebody asks me if I helped Kerry make his fast qualifying lap.

"Yeah," I say, "I talked with him about how to get around this place . . . but it's hard to explain, ya know, even to your brother."

"You didn't tell *me* how to run the lap," Dad interrupts. Like he's hurt and it's my fault he's so far in the back.

"You didn't ask," I say.

Once we are outside the media center, Dad gets on me about not wearing a sponsor's hat. I thought I was done for the day, so I didn't have my usual Bud gear on.

"Dontcha think this kid would wanna wear a sponsor's hat . . . to make his daddy happy?" Big E says. He's laughing, like everybody else around us, but it's real plain that he's serious too. "It would certainly make Budweiser really happy."

"I guess I'm a slow learner," I say.

"You weren't slow out on the track there," he snaps. "So dontcha think you'd wanna wear a sponsor hat like your dad and your older brother? Please wear that hat . . . Bud would love you for it."

When we're done, I find a spot on the fence, outside the garage area, and spend an hour or so out there signing autographs.


The next day is exciting. Racing with Dad and Kerry for the first time is great. The three of us pose for pictures on the grass beyond pit lane before the race. Kerry is nervous, but so am I. Even though I've been racing for a while, I still get nervous before I climb into the car. During the introductions, I'm still not wearing my Bud Pole hat—this doesn't please the Bud folks. But I don't want to mess up my hair until the last possible moment, when I put on that skull-and-eight-ball–covered helmet at the start of the race.

The green flag drops and I lead a race for the first time since all the way back in Dover. It feels like it's been years since we've been here. Then the yellow flag comes out on Lap 6. Kerry got loose and slid into the wall, and I can see the debris and the smashed-up No. 71 car when I come around. Thankfully, he's all right.

I lead until Lap 14, then drop back a few spots, but climb back to second place when Tony Stewart slices up through the field. Pretty soon we're side by side in Turn 2. Then he gets loose, tries to save it, and spins sideways. I make a move, out of pure instinct more than anything, to miss him. It works, but just barely.

For the next thirty laps, I hang with the top ten—passing one minute and sliding back the next. This wears the tires out and pretty soon I'm running as far back as sixteenth. I can't drive in the corners and for some reason it feels like I wrecked the car.

It gets so bad that when we get a yellow on Lap 77, we bring it into the pit and put an extra rubber in the right rear spring. It's a long pit stop, but the adjustments should help the car. We're so far back that we bring the car back in on the next lap for more work, while the race is still under yellow. When we go to green again, we run thirty-fifth.

The car is better and I start getting those spots back,

passing three-wide sometimes and making my spotter nervous.

We make our last stop on Lap 176, and hope to get the car back the way we'd had it when it was running fast. I go just a little more than a lap when Robby Gordon spins and hits the wall in front of me. I never see it coming and I don't get the usual warning from the spotter. I yank the wheel to get out of Robby's way and I'm off the track, sliding through the infield. Backwards.

"Sorry, guys," Dale Cagle, the spotter, radios. "I was changing batteries in the radio and didn't see the crash in time."

We pit. Change tires. And go down a lap. Now we are all the way back to thirty-second.

No point in getting on Cagle. Things happen and you can't go back and change anything. We need the crew to stay together after all the bad luck we've had.

I get by all the other cars that are a lap down, but with just eleven laps to go, the engine blows. We win the pole, dodge two major crashes, and now the best we can do is nurse it into the garage. It's so damn disappointing.

Rusty Wallace wins the race. I'm thirty-first, my dad comes in sixth, and Kerry finishes forty-third in his first Cup race. Not what you would call a real great day for the Three E's.

But I guess we all knew in our rookie year there would be days like this. We just didn't know there would be so many of them. Cry me a fucking river.

Weekends like these can have a huge impact on the team's morale. When things seem like they can't get any worse, somehow they do. It takes a toll on all of us. The only glimmer of light comes from my father. He lifts my spirits with just a few words of encouragement. Almost instantly he clears my head and gets my mind in position for the next race. He hammers home, "You need to go to the shop more often, see the guys, let them know your head is on straight."

I hide the fact that I'm so embarrassed with my performance that I'm afraid to show my face to the team. But somehow the next morning, I stagger into the shop and wait sheepishly for the first Eury to speak, giving me the OK that everyone is still dedicated to the cause. Maybe, hopefully, next week will be our shining moment, our next top ten.

# Bristol, Tennessee
## *Goracing.com 500*

## Poisoned and Pained

There is no question Bristol is one of the races on the calendar that everyone looks forward to. The night race at Bristol has a special energy and always seems to produce exciting action, controversial finishes (most involving my dad), and many crashes. The small track and the bright lights only help to make the more than 150,000 crazed fans even more vocal. It's like the largest college football crowd in the world.

Bristol is among my favorite tracks because it's so fast and so exciting. The fans are right on top of you, and the grandstands go up as far as they can build 'em. The crowd gets so loud you can hear them when we're under caution.

Though this is only a two-day race event instead of the usual three, the days seem to last forever. I am happy to record the twelfth-best time in Bud Pole qualifying, and then survive the Saturday morning and afternoon practice sessions without incident. The small track produces races that are more a survival test than an all-out speed contest, and we intend to be around late tonight when the five hundredth lap is run.

While I suit up for the race, I notice that the T-shirt I'm wearing is the No Fear brand and that always pisses off Dad. So I take a Sharpie and black out the logo. Then, with a little tip of the cap to Winston's "No Bull" ad campaign, I use the pen to write "100% NON BULL-SHIT" on the back of the shirt. I show it to some of my buddies and it breaks the tension a little before we have to go out and turn left one thousand times. Some of the Budweiser executives don't find the homemade logo quite so amusing.

In order to win, I need to drive to survive. Just stay in one piece until the last fifty laps and then go for it. Each lap lasts only about fifteen seconds, so there's *no* time to catch a breath anywhere on the track. There just isn't room to get away from the other cars. You have to be both patient and aggressive. It's especially hard to stay focused with the heat, the fumes, and the constant G-force of all those left turns. A lot of cars will get smashed, but the damage won't be enough to knock them out of the running. Undoubtedly it will look like an expensive junkyard by the end of the night. You just hope to avoid all contact, and try not to bend something that will put you out of commission.

Dad starts the race a couple of rows behind me, but he's right on my ass by the sixth lap, and we race nose-to-tail for a while before he passes me. I try to be patient. There is a long way to go and there are sure to be a lot of cautions.

We make adjustments to the car during each pit stop, and the car seems to run better, especially on long runs.

I manage to climb into the top ten by Lap 200 without taking any major chances. So far, so good. But muscling the car around the bullring is wearing me out.

I follow Dad around for a few laps and slip past him when he opens up the inside lane just a crack. Dad does not like to get passed, especially here at Bristol where he won his first Winston Cup race more than twenty years ago.

On Lap 352 all hell breaks loose in front of me, and cars spin all over the track. Somehow Dad and I both manage to make what one of my crew calls "a big avoidance." Most of the time when you miss one like that, it takes a lot of luck, but if you ask me, I say it's all skill and driving greatness.

After the pit stop, I'm in sixth place, right behind Dad.

Cagle, my spotter, says that Big E's spotter has passed along a message from Dad: "Be patient."

The advice irritates me. He may not like the way I passed him earlier. But damn, he left a hole and I took it. I had no choice, it was so big. I don't know if that message ever got relayed to him.

The carbon monoxide buildup inside the car also irritates me. My eyes hurt. My nose hurts. My head hurts. It feels like I'm slowly being poisoned.

The survival strategy almost collapses when Ted Musgrave and I make contact going into Turn 1 about twenty laps later and he almost spins me.

It's a typical Bristol moment. The car is OK, except for a big tire mark on the beautiful paint scheme, a special one-time-only Olympic theme.

Musgrave speeds off as I slow down to keep from

crashing. It takes me twenty laps to catch him again. I am faster than he is, and I get a run on the inside going into Turn 1 again. He tries the same move but this time he spins into the wall.

With fifty laps to go, I'm running eighth and Big E is ninth. Now is the time to charge.

Well . . . damn. It turns out to be a very short charge. Two laps, or thirty seconds to be precise. Coming out of Turn 4, the car gets loose, and when the rear of the car slides sideways, Ken Schrader runs into the back of me and I go spinning down the front stretch.

I refire the car and burn rubber to stay on the lead lap, but the slide has blown the left-side tires and I have to make an unscheduled pit stop. The crew struggles to get the jack under the car because of the flat tires. We lose a lap and any shot at the win and that Olympic bonus Budweiser is sponsoring. If I were to win tonight and Kenny Bernstein were to win his NHRA race next week, Bud would have split five million dollars between Kenny, me, the U.S. Olympic Committee and customer winner Kathy Millheim from Florida. Well, so much for that money.

With fresh tires, I manage to pass a lot of cars. But there are still twenty of them ahead of me when the race ends. Rusty Wallace, who always seems to kick butt at Bristol, wins his second consecutive race.

We were so close to a great finish, I could almost touch it. I am so disappointed, not to mention poisoned and pained. The whole team is down. We worked so hard to stay on the lead lap. We fought hard every lap, and then . . . the spin.

Dad is fourth. It isn't a win, but he's having a hell of

a season. I guess, looking back, I should have listened to him. I should have been more patient. All my life, my dad and I haven't seen eye to eye, but it always seems like his advice is the right call, no matter how much I disagree with it at the time.

# Darlington, South Carolina
## Southern 500

## Losing Is So Damn Cruel

There just isn't much to do in or around Darlington, South Carolina, so I ponder topics for the next few columns I'll write for NASCAR Online. It appears monthly, and I can write about whatever I want.

I think about dealing with the expectations of the team, the sponsors, and most of all, the fans. I start making notes and thinking of the pressures of my job.

Losing is so damn cruel. Deep down, my father is proud of me, no matter what I accomplish, but I still have these feelings and fears about the people I let down or disappoint when I do poorly.

How do you make that thirteen-year-old fan understand when you have a bad day? How do you explain to him the reasons you finished fortieth or thirty-first? This is the kid that's wearing my T-shirt, and his mom and dad spend all the money they have saved this year to come out here and see me race. Then I go out and crash or finish last? How do I deal with the hurt that kid must feel?

Growing up around the track, I've seen fans yank off their Earnhardt shirt if Dad had a shitty day. That always stuck in my mind—how cruel they are and how disappointed they are if their hero has a bad day.

Having to deal with these expectations takes its toll on the crew as well. These feelings really carry over when you are struggling like we have been. It helps to remember wins like the Winston. Those feelings that go along with a victory are so good that it feels good to remember that win—even if it seems like a long time ago.

With the pain and frustration of the Bristol night race still fresh in my mind, I sit down and write my next column for NASCAR.com. . . .

I could almost touch a decent finish—it was right there in front of me. We had fought so hard every single lap to stay up front at Bristol. Poisoned and pained, it all slipped away in a wicked slide down the front stretch. This month's column isn't about the race—it's about the pain of losing.

Failure is my worst fear. Pressure is the spark that fires that fear. I feel the pressure of expectations from myself, my team, the sponsors and the fans. I had a similar knot in the gut when I finished school. I had no direction. Through racing, I now have direction. But with that comes responsibility and the ongoing struggle to live up to expectations. It is a very grounding experience.

Every week is a new dose of reality. The reality of the NASCAR Winston Cup series is that you're not gonna be as good as you want to be right away.

Winning can spoil you. The look on my father's face after a win is worth all the money in the world. We've won two races so far and we snatched the Winston like some sort of bandit coming in to steal everyone's gold, but it means we got our butts whipped 20-some other weeks.

All that losing has a cruel, opposite effect. While I know my dad is proud of me no matter what, I can't help but wonder if I have let down my fans or my team. How do you make a young fan understand the reasons why you finished 40th?

Surrounded by the smoke and fireworks of the NASCAR circus, I feel like I am changing. I try to remain cool—but I am still not able to harness all of my emotions. I fight daily with a short temper. I know that with every snappy remark that blurts out of my mouth, I'm closer to finding out who my true friends are. We all have a breaking point, but the good ones learn how to harness that anger and emotion and use it as a motivational advantage.

When I drove late models around tracks in the Southeast, I wasn't winning much at all. Why didn't that bother me? Actually it did, but nothing like now. I remember when I wrecked my first car. My mind was clouded with the thought that I had just ended my racing career. I was naive. I was crazy about driving. That intensity has grown over the years; now it's an obsession. That obsession sometimes overshadows how much fun it is to do what I do.

Winning has afforded me an enjoyable life away from racing. It's not often, though, that I am away from racing. In order to be good at it, you must engulf yourself in it day in and day out. With what I have experienced this year, I will never doubt my ability as a driver. I don't doubt my ability to be a winner, and until it happens again, I learn more about how to handle losing.

I'm just tryin' to come real with it. Hopefully you understand that winning isn't everything to me, but it's a close second. Losing isn't something that I can just brush off and fake a smile to hide my frustration. It's that will and determination that I hope will get me where I want to go. In the time between, I hope this column becomes a hit. What's fun is writing this article. Admitting how I feel. Maybe it's more of a relief than fun. I know the more I reveal, the more responsibility I take. I may regret what I say down the road. That's something I have a hard time with. Wondering what's tasteful and what's not; knowing when to speak your piece and when to shut your mouth. A poor finish in a race can do the trick. The ride home from that race is a quiet one. The 24 hours after a crappy day at the track are the dullest times in my life. It tricks you into remembering the days where trophies kept popping up in the house on a regular basis.

Win a race, throw a party! Actually, we would party whether we won or not. Club E, as it's known, was getting a little popularity. It was always cocked and loaded with Bud for another throwdown. These days, though, I need a better excuse than just for the hell of it.

I will win again. The bad part is you never know

when. I have never thought before a race, "I am
gonna win this one." It's not something you know
is around the corner. You go week after week of
gettin' the crap kicked out of you and then one day
it's a trip into Victory Lane. It's the greatest feeling
I've ever known, and it makes it all worthwhile.

My two cents.

The Southern 500 is truly the "old granddad" race on
the tour. It's steeped in history and tradition. But on the
morning of the race, it is steeped in bad weather. The
skies look terrible as the race begins, and we make it to
Lap 37 before the race is stopped by rain. Everyone
just sits and waits for the rain to stop, but during the
two-hour break, the crew and I tune the satellite to the
first weekend of NFL action, specifically the Washing-
ton Redskins/Carolina Panthers game. Most of the
crew are fans of the hometown Panthers, but I'm still a
die-hard Redskins man. The guys give me a ton of shit
when the Panthers lead the game early on. I'm not too
concerned, but I am hungry. And so are the rest of the
guys. The Bud marketing team at the track today, Joe
Glynn and Jason Travis, get in a car and zoom out to
buy us four large pizzas, then deliver them directly to
our pit area.

Let it rain. We've got football and pizza.

The race restarts when the track is dry enough to
continue. We move up some, and run among the top
twenty for the first half of the race. The clouds come
and go, and once the race becomes official, nearly
every team assumes that the impending rain (and the
lack of lights at the racetrack) will force the end of the

race before the full distance is complete. Now strategy has less to do with handling and tire pressures, and more to do with gas mileage, the timing of the pit stops, and guessing about the weather.

Some teams just use a gut feeling, while some run to the NASCAR official trailer to look at the radar. Some teams use the assistance of their pilots, who can utilize the radar at the local airport to help predict when the rains may eventually come in and in one wet splash end the race.

On Lap 207 a light mist begins to spit. Tony Eury sees the moisture but has a feeling it won't last for long. Nearly everyone assumes the rain will end the race, so they refuse to give up their position and pit. But Tony is a gambler.

We pit and return to the racetrack near the back of the pack, which now runs slowly under the yellow flag due to the rain. When the rain eventually lightens and then finally stops, we are in perfect position. Practically all the other teams are now forced to make a pit stop for fuel and tires. When they do, we roll past and into the lead on Lap 225.

It's either a stroke of luck or brilliant pit strategy (maybe some of both), but we now launch out of the blocks. Suddenly the car is awesome. It's known as aero push. We had a decent car earlier today, but behind all of the traffic, it just wasn't very fast. Now, however, as the race leader, the car responds to the fresh air on the nose. The car is great, and we stretch out to a four-second lead.

*Now* we urge the rain to fall. Call the race now! Give

us the victory! We *neeeeeeeeed* a victory! C'mon, Mother Nature!

But there is another yellow flag on Lap 240. All of the leaders stop again. Our car is good for a lap or so, and then we realize that we have yet another set of unmatched tires. I hang in there as long as I can, but the tires eventually lose their grip, and we have to come in early on Lap 292. We hope the race continues long enough so that all of the other leaders will have to make a stop as well and we can retake the lead. However, it looks like the race may be called due to darkness rather than rain.

To our dismay, hard rains fall on Lap 328, flooding the track and stopping the race for good. Bobby Labonte leads at that time, and the points leader gains another victory. Dad stays close behind him with a third-place finish. We didn't get the break we needed at the end, but we manage to finish eleventh.

Not bad for a race that saw more twists and turns than a cheap carnival ride at the county fair. We led for sixteen laps and are the top-scoring rookie for the second consecutive race. But, if we have any hope of catching Kenseth for the Rookie of the Year award, we need to start finishing in the top five.

But I feel like we have something to work with from this run. With a chance to win so close to our fingers, I am disappointed that we didn't have a better finish, and I know the team is disappointed as well, but we learned a lot and we'll be more prepared the next time we race here.

As we leave the track, I can't help but think back to the last time we left Darlington with a demolished car

and the team in disarray. It was the low point of the
year for me: the team had no confidence in their driver
and the driver was questioning if he would keep his job
to even see the next race. In comparison to that,
eleventh place sounds pretty damn good.

# Richmond, Virginia
## *Chevrolet 400*

## We're Gonna Lap Everybody

Man I am so pumped up for this race. We won here in May, we had a great test session two weeks ago, and the team is eligible for a million-dollar bonus if we win. Winston sponsors the "No Bull Five" program at some of the best races each year, and if we win, we get a million dollars and one of Winston's customers wins a million as well. Not every car is eligible for the prize: you had to have finished in the top five in the previous No Bull race. We were fourth at Charlotte in May, so we're in, along with Dad and Matt Kenseth, Bobby Labonte, and Dale Jarrett.

This is the first time Matt and I are eligible for the No Bull payday, so we're both pretty excited. Guys like my dad and Bobby have done this thing umpteen times, but this is new for us rookies. Pairing up with a race fan for the bonus money is a little bit more pressure. I had a similar deal with Bud at Bristol, and it was kind of weird meeting the winning fan. Hey, I can win them a million bucks—but I can also be the guy that for the rest of their life will cause them to say, "Damn, he coulda won a million for me if the jerk didn't lose that race."

I have to do an appearance of some sort for Budweiser every weekend, and they are usually pretty sedate. I'll go to a luxury suite and sign autographs for about twenty to thirty corporate guests or maybe I'll go to a tent with a hundred or more guests and answer questions for fifteen or twenty minutes. It's pretty efficient and because we do it every week, we have the procedures down pretty well at most tracks. Smooth in, smooth during, and smooth out.

However, Friday afternoon several reps from Chevrolet show up and ask if I'm ready for my appearance. I haven't a clue what they're talking about and neither does Jade.

So Jade quickly huddles with the reps and they walk off to try and contact Steve Crisp at DEI to work out the confusion.

They return with this proposition: "If you'll do this today, it will count as an official appearance."

In other words, my contract with Chevy requires me to make a certain number of public appearances across the country each year. If I visit their VIPs today, it means I won't have to take a whole day later in the season to fly to a dealership somewhere in the middle of Montana. Or Arkansas. (Pick your least favorite state—no matter *what* damn state I pick, I'll piss someone off!) So I say, "Sure! Let's do it!"

The Richmond track is located at the fairgrounds, and the appearance is in a building quite a distance away.

Joe Glynn, the Bud marketing guy, drives me to the appearance across the fairgrounds.

We hop on the red Bud golf cart that's painted to look like my race car and head off. Most of the time, when I'm in street clothes and riding in a golf cart, people don't recognize me until it's too late. They see me go by, and then they turn and yell, "Junior!" They do this for one of two reasons. The first is based on wishful thinking. They hope that I'll stop and go back to sign autographs. The other reason is that they want to tell their friends they saw me first. I don't mean to sound cynical, but people really do get pissed off each week if I don't stop the cart to come back. Hey, folks, I love you all, but I'm sorry, I have somewhere to go.

Today some dude just doesn't get it. He's decked out in a redneck-style summertime outfit, which means he's wearing nothing but old tennis shoes and too-short cut-off jeans. He looks like he hasn't cut or combed his hair in months.

He spots me on the cart and when we don't stop he runs after us at full speed. Now, 99 percent of the fans are harmless, but when a crazy-eyed scruffy dude like this starts chasing you, you don't want to take a chance.

Joe Glynn, who relishes moments like this, floors the gas pedal. This is fine until we reach a very crowded area where hundreds of spectators are streaming in toward their reserved seats.

Glynn pretends to be David Pearson or Tim Richmond and keeps his foot on the gas and begins dodging cars and pedestrians like they are orange cones on an obstacle course. Joe is a good guy, but he scares the shit outta me when he does this.

Somehow, someway, we make it to the auditorium. He slides to a stop and we hop off and run inside. The element of surprise is good, as the fans don't catch on until we're in the building. Getting out, however, will be a different story.

We are escorted to a roped-off area in the middle of the cavernous arena. It looks like ten or twelve companies have their guests inside this compound. I am whisked to the center of the Chevy area where their four hundred guests crowd around a small card table.

Jade then attempts to introduce me to the crowd using a megaphone that serves as a primitive PA system. He sounds like he's talking through the world's worst drive-through restaurant speaker system. I can't understand a word he says, and neither can the crowd.

The front row starts clapping, which prompts the crowd to press closer to the flimsy card table that I am standing behind. I wave, and we open it for questions from the audience.

"Dale! Will you autograph my die-cast car?"

The Chevy reps scold the guy: "No autographs!"

"Are ya gonna kick ass tonight, Junior?"

"Yeah, sure!"

No response. They can't hear a word I'm saying. They stand in silence, with their jaws slightly open, like they can't believe they're seeing me.

Next question . . .

"Will you autograph my T-shirt?"

The Chevy folks scold another patron.

After a couple more humiliating minutes, Jade grabs the megaphone again and says, "OK, oflflofookksls, msaltisins *he's gotta go* kdg sjsuiytaina lnwelkjwkj ttttankkkk youuuuuuu . . ." At least that's what I think he says. We're out of here.

Joe had already scoped out an alternative escape route, so we exit through the kitchen. Except, no one told the kitchen workers.

When they see our gang of three start to walk through their food prep area, they yell.

Like a cat, one of the big guys steps in our path, and little Joe knocks him back onto a table with a swift elbow and forearm. As the big chef fights back, he sees it's me, and he relaxes his straining muscles and lets Joe slide past and toward the door.

I give the chef a high five and we run out the door.

Looks like it's pretty clear, until we start to roll. Around the corner comes our old friend in the cutoffs. He yells and runs after us again.

Just like before, Joe guns the golf cart. We're close to escaping when Joe slams on the brakes. We've been cut off by traffic. With nowhere to go, we grind to a squealing stop. Unfortunately, our brakes are much better than those of our pursuer, who proceeds to fall into the cart at full speed and sprawl across me. It's one smelly, sweaty mess.

"Junnnnyrrrrrrrr, Junnnnnnyerr," he slurs. "Yagotta ssssssssign thissss fer me."

Duuuuude. Just chill.

He pulls an old T-shirt out of his back pocket, and it's one of my shirts from the ACDelco Busch Series. I sign as fast as I can, and we get going again.

It's appearances like this one that make me appreciate Budweiser even more, especially the way they take care of me for their functions. Like I said, 99 percent of the fans are great . . . but in a crowd of 100,000, that means you gotta watch out for those 1,000 that are the bad apples, and a little preplanning always pays off.

Even though we won here a few months ago, Tony and the guys decide we should test for two days to see if we can find some more speed. With an extra million on the line, you do whatever it takes. Richmond has always been a good track for us—we won twice here in the Busch car—and no matter what series we've entered here, we've finished in the top ten every time but one. The test helps us find an even better setup for the race. We are second fastest among all of the teams that test.

However, when we go out to qualify, something is horribly wrong, and we only turn the thirty-first-best lap.

Thirty-first?

At Richmond?

Whoa!

Tony, Tony Jr., and I put our heads together with the rest of the guys to try to figure out why we are so slow. When the happy-hour session begins, we put a different set of tires on the car, and instantly it's back to our old magic. The car is wonderful—we are not only superfast at the start of each run, but we are able to maintain a lot of speed after a number of laps while the rest of the field falls off dramatically.

I may be starting at the back of the field, but I am confident that the fans will enjoy it immensely when I slice through the field into the lead and then lap the field easily and grab that big Winston chunk of cash. I can close my eyes and see it now. I can almost start counting the big bills. The car is that good.

Then the green flag falls and I wake up from the daydream. The same setup as before is now a nightmare—the tires are horrendous. I do well just to survive and hold our position as the front tires hop, skip, and chatter across the pavement in each corner. I feel like I'm hanging on to the ledge of a cliff with just my fingertips. If I lose any more grip, I'm gonna fall a long way, and it's gonna hurt.

Somehow I manage to stay on the lead lap for the first 245 laps (out of 400 total), when I fall one lap behind the leaders. Kiss that million goodbye. . . . But we finally change to a set of tires that the car likes and it's back to speed. Suddenly we are seven tenths of a second per lap faster, and we begin picking off cars one after another! Using some aggressive pit strategy, we even get the red No. 8 Bud car into the lead for five laps.

However, we don't get the benefit of a yellow flag, and we eventually drop back to one lap behind the leaders after taking a pit stop.

As the race comes to a close, Steve Park and Dad wage one helluva battle for second place. I know Dad has the fastest car, and if he had been able to get past Park earlier, he probably could have passed the eventual winner Jeff Gordon and not only won the race but won the million-dollar bonus. But when he hired Steve Park to drive for DEI, he didn't hire him to just move over and not put up a fight—not even against the car owner.

We end up thirteenth. We passed a lot of cars on the final 150 laps, but I can't draw any satisfaction from that or from the fact that we are the top-scoring rookie team for the third consecutive race. We knew we could win, so everything else is crap.

The car was almost perfect in happy hour, but it was a total mystery to me during most of the race. Nobody understands why the car was seven tenths of a second quicker per lap on one set of tires versus another.

We fought and gouged and struggled and sucked, but on the bright side we hung in there and we got a decent finish. But we're not here to be "decent" for our sponsors, our fans, and especially ourselves. We want to win, and right now we all wonder when the next victory will come. Decent sucks.

## Loudon, New Hampshire
### *Dura Lube 300*

## Like Paying to Drive a Go-Kart

Friday of the Loudon weekend is dreary, cold, and rainy. No one wants to be here after what happened to Adam Petty and Kenny Irwin. The mood is black and it only gets worse with the weather.

There are a few rays of sunshine though. MTV, one of my favorite TV networks, has sent producer Bill Richmond and a small crew to begin videotaping a special show called "True Life: My Life as a Race Car Driver." They are searching for a driver to focus on, and Jade is pushing hard to make me the main subject of the documentary. He shows them the *Rolling Stone* story and the *Charlotte Observer* story that called me a "hottie."

They come out to my motor coach in the rain to get a preliminary interview out of the way. It goes so well that Richmond and his assistant, Jonathan Kane, a young hip guy from MTV News, decide that they want to follow me around for the remainder of the season.

Jade also has some behind-the-scenes discussions

with NASCAR regarding interest in me as one of a handful of drivers being considered for *People* magazine's "Sexiest Men" special issue. While our on-track performance continues to decay week by week, somehow the media outside of the sport continue to take note of Opie, this fair-haired, fair-skinned kid from Mooresville. Amazing.

In an effort to prevent another tragedy from occurring at this track, NASCAR has mandated restrictor plates on all of the cars this weekend.

The change pisses off Dad. He can't understand why we are being slowed down so much—this is the premiere series in America, and we shouldn't be puttering around this place at granny speeds while the relatively crude but fast NASCAR modifieds blast around at incredible speeds.

I try to remain neutral when the media tries to draw me into the fight over the restrictor plates. Dad's job as the veteran is to lead the charge almost like a politician—he's the guy everyone looks to for advice and leadership. (He also has to pay for the extra R&D and manpower needed at DEI to change over all of the engines in a week's time when the rule change is announced.) I'm happily a rookie and they just pay me to drive the car no matter what's under the hood. I'm sure that if I stick around for a while, I'll be one of the guys who speaks up and battles NASCAR about rules changes, but for now that's a fight I'm happy to avoid.

Speaking of happy, during the first practice, I'm not

happy at all about the feel of the race car with these power-robbing plates. It's like paying to drive a go-kart.

Despite complaining that the engine feels real flat and sounds funny, we qualify twentieth best for Sunday's race. It turns out all of the engines sound and feel that way with the restrictor plates.

Saturday morning's practice session produces a helluva scare. As I dive into Turn 3, the throttle sticks open for a split second. This is the same corner that claimed Petty and Irwin earlier this year, so I'm a little freaked out. This is no time to mess around, so I get off the track and pull into the garage immediately. This is bullshit. I talk with Tony Jr. and Tony Sr. but I'm not happy with their feedback.

"Get Daddy over here," I yell.

Soon, Big E walks over and leans in the car. I tell him what happened, and he offers some advice that cuts right to the heart of the matter.

"Don't go back out in this car unless they get it fixed," he says.

The throttle is fixed, and we're able to make a couple of runs to ensure the car is ready for Sunday's race.

In the meantime the MTV guys follow me everywhere. They ride along on the golf cart to my Budweiser appearance Sunday morning and see the crowd of people cheer when I arrive. They even follow me to the Porta-John before the race. It's a cool thought that I'll have a show on MTV—but this part might not be so cool.

The impact of the restrictor plate is unknown—no one is quite sure what will happen when the three-hundred-lap event begins. It will certainly help fuel mileage, but will anyone be able to pass? Is the restrictor plate going to bunch up the field on a flat track that is already incredibly difficult to pass on? To add to the uncertainty, it is very chilly. To help warm the engines and brakes, NASCAR allows a few extra warm-up laps before the race begins.

Starting on the outside of row 10, I floor it at the green flag, and even though the restrictor plate makes the engine think it has asthma, it gives me enough power to make a big run in the outside groove. Some other drivers take a more cautious approach to the first few corners, so in less than ten laps I launch myself into twelfth place, moving past a series of cars in concert with Jeff Gordon and Tony Stewart. We're like a multicolored three-car convoy, moving up in tandem past slower cars. All three of us pass Steve Park, and now we're in the top ten after only thirteen laps.

As a general rule in NASCAR, the closer to the front you climb, each successive car becomes tougher to pass. Usually, if a guy is running thirtieth, he's not having a good day, so he's easier to pass than somebody that's fifteenth. As you get closer to first place, it really gets tough.

So once I reach tenth place, my progress becomes more gradual, as I eventually climb to seventh place by Lap 40. By the time I reach sixth place on Lap 51, I have not said a single word to the crew on the radio.

Suddenly my right thumb is pushing the Talk button.

"Somebody's oiling the track down!" I shout. "There's shit all over this track!"

The liquid on the track ruins my rhythm, and I drop back. As Darrell Waltrip exits the pits on Lap 73, the retiring legend and I make hard contact. Whoa! Luckily, we both speed off again with only superficial damage.

The race continues with very little action. Jeff Burton leads easily, while the rest of us—on the track and in the grandstands—fall into a hypnotic, snooze-inducing rhythm. To everyone's relief, the boredom is preferable to the tragic alternative. Occasionally, I try to spice up the action with some intentional bump drafting with Dave Blaney, but by the halfway point, we're just cruising along in ninth position.

I'm bored, echoing what I'm sure is the feeling of just about everyone in attendance. I try to think of things like race strategy to keep my brain engaged. How great is our tire wear? Should we think about gambling later on? Maybe taking two tires is the best way to pass the guys in front of us. With the restrictor plates, we can't pull enough power to spin the rear tires, so they last much longer.

As the race lurches along, we manage to hold on to the lead lap as Burton passes all but the top thirteen cars by Lap 200. We hang in there, but the boredom soon goes out the window when a mysterious problem develops.

After Lap 200 the team can't hear me when I talk on the radio, and I have trouble hearing the spotter and the crew when they speak with me. As the final pit stops approaches, and with a top-ten finish in our grasp, the inability to communicate angers and frustrates everyone.

We switch to our backup channel, but after a yellow flag slows the field on Lap 215, the radio problems take a strange new turn.

We hear a crackling voice that breaks in on the frequency. "Uh . . . can someone find Steve so he can approve this credit card purchase?"

What?

"Do we have more of those?"

The voice on the radio is unknown, but it's clear that it is not someone on our team. It seems the radio problems are caused by interference from one of the souvenir vendors using the same or similar frequencies.

I'm not happy with the interference, so I snap, "Hey, Steve! Get your people off this fucking radio! We're trying to win a race here!"

The team summons Pat Froussard (also known as Major Pat) from Racing Radios to try to solve the problem as the race restarts. He jumps into action, but the interference continues, like the scene in the movie *This Is Spinal Tap* where the lead guitar solo is drowned out by inane radio chatter from his wireless pickup.

The race is now fifty laps from completion, and no one can hear anyone else, other than a T-shirt vendor confirming another sale of a shirt that's probably a bootleg anyway. I'm sure in a few weeks we'll all laugh about it, but the humor of it all is lost on us in the heat of the moment.

Radio communication is critical, and not having a solid connection with the spotter and the guys in the pits is distracting and dangerous. Out of nowhere I slam the lapped car of Bill Elliott. Elliott crashes hard, and I quickly apologize for the contact.

A few laps later, it's like a replay—this time I whack Jimmy Spencer. Spencer can be a grouchy ol' broke-ass bastard, so when another yellow flag flies I worry about retaliation. My dad is still considered the Intimidator, but Spencer is certainly one of the roughest drivers out here. He's like a coiled cobra—you really don't want to be in the area when the rotund Spencer gets angry and lashes out.

The radio problems aren't totally solved, but they seem to improve as we enter the final thirty laps. Even though we haven't had a top-ten finish since the first week of June, and even with a smashed-up car, we all smell a good result. I show little (if any) patience as I bump and grind my way past lapped cars.

With twenty-two laps to go, Steve Park crashes, bringing out another yellow flag. Tony Sr. decides to leave me on the track to improve our track position for the final lunge to the finish. It's a strategy move I agree with.

"We've got a good car," I say. "I just can't get the track position. It's tough to pass these guys without bumpin' 'em outta the way. I just can't do that to every car or do it every lap. I have to wait for a mistake as we get closer to the front."

"Uh . . . yeah, we're ready to shut 'er down. . . ." The interference is back.

"Did Steve fix the credit card machine?"

The voices are back, cutting me off in midsentence.

"Goddamn! Get off the radio!" I beg. "Man! This sucks . . . this is worse than a damn Internet chat room where everybody's talkin' at once. . . ."

The green flag is out—and we have fourteen laps to improve from eleventh place. However, before we can even get through the first corner, Jerry Nadeau and Mark Martin get together right in front of me, and they spin toward the outside wall. I have a fraction of a second to decide which way to point the car . . . and I choose wrong. Almost instantly, I hit the outside wall.

A top ten down the drain. Damn it.

A broken radiator spits steam and water into the air, and signals I'm done for the day. I hop out and climb into an ambulance for the mandatory trip to see the track doctor. It's a bitter ride after struggling so hard for 286 laps. After the doc gives me the OK, I sadly walk from the care center to look at the crumpled car, which now rests in a heap near the transporter.

I feel really bad for the guys. They work so hard to give me a good car and then I make a judgment call that is all wrong. Just like a damn rookie.

I do my best to apologize but I'm not sure it lessens the level of frustration everyone is feeling.

Tony Jr. walks off to help the guys grind and crunch the remains of the car just so they can prop it up and into the transporter for the trip home. I turn around and the only one left is the MTV guy, camera in hand.

"At least now you'll see the highs and the lows," I tell him. "It's just one of those deals where we do fine and then we have junk-ass problems like this. I don't know what I did or how I could have avoided the wreck. . . .

"We had a good car today—we were as fast as the leaders, but we just couldn't get track position to get up there to challenge them. I don't know what I've done to get all this bad luck. We were set for a great day—it looked like we were gonna gain in points and in the Rookie [of the Year] deal."

Jeff Burton leads the final laps to complete a flag-to-flag win. He is the first driver to lead every lap of a Win-

ston Cup race since 1978. It is the most boring—but one
of the safest—races of the year.

I'm anxious to get the hell out of New Hampshire so
I can forget all this bullshit. Dad is usually the first one
in his street clothes and raisin' hell if I'm lagging behind him on the way to the helicopter, but since we
crashed before the race ended, I have to sit on the back
of his hauler waiting for him. It feels like yet another
low point for the season. Just when I didn't think I
could feel any shittier, another race comes along to
prove me wrong.

Dad comes out of his hauler and we walk toward the
helipad. He can tell I'm down, so he throws an arm
around me and tells me about a point early in his career
when he was lower than ever. Then he tells me how
things do and will get better. For some reason, I feel a
helluva lot better as I climb into the copter.

## Note to Self: Don't Cuss at Stiffy

No matter how shitty things are on the track, it's always great to be reminded about what is really important in my life. My biggest fan and supporter has always been my sister Kelley. She was always there for me, loaning me money nearly every day for lunch and snacks when we attended military school. She even loaned me enough money to buy my first PC. When I was in high school, I was just a five-foot-four-inch kid that kept to himself, and she was the only one who insisted that once I matured, the girls would go crazy for me. I never did believe her, but she supported me completely, no matter what.

This week Kelley gave birth to her first child, Karsyn Kingslee. Karsyn was born September 18, 2000, and I can't describe the feeling I had holding my sister's little girl in my arms. Unbelievable. I can't wait to be able to hold my own child sometime soon.

• • •

Later that week, at the invitation of one of my sponsors, Remington Arms, I was flown to a site in Virginia to check out the usually off-limits Secret Service school where all the security personnel for the U. S. President are trained. Remington, who supplies many law enforcement agencies in the United States, provided me with a bad-ass custom handmade sniper rifle to try a few shots on the range. At a distance of one thousand yards, I can't believe I can even see the target, let alone hit it. It's not quite as awesome a feeling as holding my new niece, but it's pretty damn cool to take a rifle and put a bullet through the forehead of a cardboard mannequin more than three hundred yards away. The target was so far away that you had time to look through binoculars before the bullet hit the target.

The cardboard head, with a single bullet hole in the center of the forehead, was brought to the track to be on display for the rest of the weekend in my motor coach, along with a bowling pin that I blew into a twisted shell.

One of the perks of my job is getting to do cool stuff like that, and they even promise to make me my own sniper rifle to use for target practice back in the woods at home.

Another perk is getting to do things like the MTV documentary. But this weekend something even better happens. A writer and a photo crew from *People* magazine arrive at the track to shoot photos for the "Sexiest Men" issue. This is *huge!* The issue is one of the most popular of the year, as *People* selects the guys they think are the sexiest men in the world. They have space for only a few NASCAR drivers, so I'm surprised but pretty excited that they chose me, Matt Kenseth, and my buddy Hank Parker Jr.

Bill and Jonathan from MTV are at the track again, and they shoot footage of me until some prospective new sponsors from InterAct, a computer and video gaming accessories company, come to meet with me.

At the same time, details for a trip to Los Angeles begin to take shape, as Jade discusses bookings with *The X Show* on the FX network, and a talk show on the Comedy Central network called *Turn Ben Stein On*. Working these into my schedule is like trying to finish a large jigsaw puzzle. We also have some discussions with VH1, but they lead nowhere. While the network would like me to appear on any number of their shows, most notably *The List* (where celebrities present their lists for topics like "Best Rock Song" and so on), most of their programs tape on the weekends in Los Angeles, so it is impossible for me to attend during the race season.

Kristine Chin, a photo editor from *Sports Illustrated,* also calls to arrange a photo session with my latest purchase: a cool red 1971 Corvette. A date and location is set, and she asks if I would be willing to wear some 1970s clothing to match the era of the car. . . .

Hell yeah, this is right up my alley.

I also agree to meet with Robert Edelstein of *TV Guide* next weekend during the Martinsville event. Believe it or not, I'm uncomfortable with all of the attention swirling around me. I've always been suspicious that most of the attention is because of who my dad is, and now I'm even more suspicious because of how bad we've been doing in the races lately. It makes me more determined than ever to turn the on-track performance in the right direction. Instead of being a distraction, all of this new media interest is a great motivator.

During Friday morning's first practice session, the car is not fast at all, but I try hard to be more confident and assertive with the remedies I suggest. As I huddle with Tony Jr. and the crew, my body language and gestures are animated as I try to mimic the lumbering race car without bitching or yelling. I don't expect much when it's my time to qualify, but I'm pleasantly surprised by the changes that have been made to the car. We are thirteenth best, and it's not exactly the Bud Pole position. And that's my fault.

I didn't drive the car hard enough because I didn't expect it would be that good. We have a great car but I just didn't use it.

The next morning, practice is rained out, so I use the time to do photos for *People* magazine. In addition to a photographer, *People* brings along a stylist and a makeup artist. They tell me that many of the other drivers had put up some serious resistance to the wardrobe, but I think some of the clothes are cool as hell.

My first choice is a nightclub-ready combination of blue leather pants, red shirt, blue leather vest, and vintage-style blue sneakers. When I emerge from the transporter, I'm met with laughter from the less stylish in attendance. The crew members are laughing as they go back and forth between the transporter and the garage, while Matt nearly falls over when he sees my outfit. He can laugh all he wants. I think it looks cool.

Next I emerge head-to-toe in brown: leather S&M

pants with multiple zippers and a shiny shirt. I like this look, and so do the people from *People*. At this stage my publicist and I are actively flirting with the attractive stylist, Sarah Parlow, who tells me that I am perfect model size. And that the clothes fit me great. I imagine my sister in high school, telling me that the girls would eventually go for me, and maybe, for once, I start to believe she may have been a little bit right.

The rain stops, so the photographer insists I roll a racing tire through the garage area. While many fans watch in stunned disbelief, I stroll my way through the garage, to the delight of the crew, who have never seen their driver in leather S&M pants before.

The shoot is finally over, and Rochelle Jones, the writer from *People,* joins me and some of the guys in the lounge. With the team in attendance, I try to be as funny and entertaining as I can when Jones asks me about what it means to me to be considered a "hottie."

"It's tough for me," I say with my best poker face. "I can't seem to refer to myself in that way or in those terms. I really think . . . [*thoughtful pause here for fake dramatic effect*] by admitting that you're a 'hottie,' you tend to remove yourself from 'hottie' status."

The crew erupts in laughter and Jones smiles sheepishly as she writes the quip into her notebook.

The rain finally subsides for the day, and we're able to get an extended final practice. I hate the tires Goodyear has provided for the weekend. It's like we have damn plastic Hot Wheels tires. They slide all over the damn place. The car is chattering all around the track, and the tires are junk.

The Dover garage is one of the smallest and most dangerous anywhere, and as I slowly pull out of the garage for my final laps of the day, I'm greeted by a large contingent of women waving and screaming at me as I make my way toward the track. They are only inches from me.

I've never seen so many hoochie mamas at a racetrack at one time, so at least I can forget about the tires for a few seconds.

When the session is over, I compare complaints about the tires with Steve Park. Big E ambles over and puts his long arms around both of us and agrees the tires suck.

Right before the race, I wander toward my car after being introduced to the giant Dover crowd (hoochie mamas included). I can't help but think how well the crew responded when I tried to be more direct and forceful with my feedback before qualifying. I hope I can do the same today during the race. I ask one of the crewmen for some Day-Glo red tape, borrow a Sharpie, and begin writing. I stick the piece of tape on the dashboard next to the gauges.

*Note to self,* it says. *Do not cuss at Stiffy!*

Stiffy, which is Tony Jr.'s nickname, sees the message and begins laughing. He asks for the tape and begins writing his own message.

*Note to self,* Stiffy begins, *I don't give a fuck.*

Though everyone laughs at the joke, I'm still apprehensive before I climb in, wondering if we have the right setup.

I say hello to my niece Karsyn during my prerace interview on TNN, and then I settle in for the start of the race. As the race begins, I follow Jeff Burton through traffic and into the top ten until NASCAR throws a "mandatory yellow flag." Under the yellow, each team is required to make a pit stop to make sure the worrisome tires are holding up. Better safe than sorry, I guess.

As I head into my pit, I find a red car already there. Like some sort of "Goldilocks and the Three Bears" episode gone wrong ("Who's been stopping in my pit stall?"), I'm unable to stop fast enough before I slam hard into the rear of Bill Elliott's car.

Elliott became confused as he turned toward his McDonald's pit area, which is beside our pit and painted in a similar red color. He stopped in our stall instead, and nearly hit two of my crew as he finally lurched forward to his own stall. The incident costs us ten positions, and we drop to twentieth place.

When racing resumes, I find myself dicing with my father for seventeenth place. He bumps me like we're both trying to win the race on the final lap. We make contact several times, to the delight of the crowd. But I am not delighted at all, because he's just screwing with me.

It's gonna be a long ride home if he keeps this up, but I try to get my mind back on the race ahead of me.

For almost a hundred laps, I hike forward, picking off many of the positions we lost in the bizarre Elliott incident. I take a very high line around the track, passing cars on the outside. It's fast, but it's killing the tires.

The team warns me about running so high, because they know I might blow a tire. No sooner do they say that than Jeff Burton blows a tire and slams the wall very hard.

I can't go as fast on the bottom of the track, but after

seeing what happens to Burton, I'll try and keep the car down there.

I race hard with Matt for a few laps, and I can't resist taking another shot at Dad.

"That's fun running with Matt," I say. "He's my friend, and at least I know I can trust him."

When it's just us two rookies, we both stay in the top ten until I begin racing hard again with Dad. Trying too hard, it seems, because I get very close to the wall off of Turn 4, and Big E goes by.

The abuse is more than the tires can handle, and the car begins slowing down, no matter what I do. Tony Stewart, the leader, laps me with less than fifty laps to go. Stewart wins again to sweep the two Dover races this year, while Kenseth finishes thirteenth and I finish sixteenth, one spot ahead of Dad, who had problems late in the race as well.

Neither of us is happy, and no doubt it will be a long, quiet, solitary ride home in the jet.

## Martinsville, Virginia
## NAPA 500

## Like Some Sort of Stunt Show

The track at Martinsville is the closest Winston Cup racing gets to what people see at local tracks around the country. It's a short track, a half mile long, the same length as Bristol, but there is hardly any banking in the turns. It's the slowest track we run all season. If you pass here, what you usually have to do is give somebody a polite little slam with your front bumper. We call it "the chrome horn." Dad always said if you weren't supposed to use 'em, they wouldn't call 'em bumpers!

There will be gleaming, spotless cars starting this race. You never know how many will finish, but you can count on one thing—none of the cars will be gleaming and spotless by the end of the race. They'll look like they came from the boneyard somewhere.

Actually, the beating and the banging that goes on at Martinsville is kind of fun. You expect it, so you prepare for it. You have to be careful not to get spun out, and you can forget all the talk about patience. Try running five hundred laps at this place on a hot Sunday afternoon, slamming on the brakes and turning hard left a thousand times, with forty-two other guys trying to bash you out of their way, and there is no way you are going to be patient.

My last race at Martinsville was my first time on the track, and we didn't do too badly. We were a lot more competitive than the finish showed.

When the race starts, we stay out of trouble for the most part, but I can tell that we are abusing the right front tire. It holds up all right until the fifty-second lap—when it blows and the car slides straight up into the wall. Less than thirty miles of racing, and already we're junk.

The damage isn't terminal, and the crew fixes the car so we can get back on the track. I'm ten laps down and it looks like our shitty luck stays with us. I wonder if we'll ever break out of this slump.

The No. 8 looks more like an advertisement for red duct tape than Budweiser, but we soldier on, just hanging until Lap 187, when Sterling Marlin, who is leading, backs off the throttle and lets some other cars get a lap back. It's a nice gesture, but it causes a big traffic jam behind him and I'm right in the middle of it. When I try to keep from hitting Sterling, I smash into another car. More damage.

I'm ready to just go home, but the crew insists on repairing the car again. So I leave the track and take the car straight to the garage. Once I get behind the pit wall, I make contact *again*. This time with a wrecker that's trying to haul another car into the garage. It's like a scene out of *Days of Thunder*. I'm hitting everything but the pace car. It's sort of funny and pathetic.

The car looks like it has finished a demolition derby.

The crew does its thing and the car is ready to get back to the wars. Because this is the slowest track, aerodynamics don't mean much. Otherwise we'd never be able to keep up at all. I'm not thrilled about driving this ill-handling wreck, but I make it back around the track, lap by endless lap, until I spin out again on Lap 379. Nobody else is involved in this one and I don't even smash into the wall, so I can keep running without another major effort from the crew.

Then, with the finish in sight, almost within reach of my tired arms, I get into *another* crash. This is a big one. My car is already so beat up that the front bodywork is gone completely, leaving the left front tire exposed. A car in front of me spins, so I slow down but still make contact with Dave Blaney. My exposed tire touches one of his tires, and before I know it, I'm airborne. It's hard to steer or brake when you're off the ground, so I sail straight into the wall. It's a relatively slow track, and to the spectators it probably doesn't look like much of a crash, but it hurts like hell. Even though I slow down a little, I'm probably going eighty or ninety miles per hour when I slam into the barrier.

I feel for all of my limbs. Check—they all seem intact. I catch my breath and then climb out of the car. Even though it was a wild ride, it's pretty cool once I think about it. It feels like some sort of stunt show or daredevil act. After all it has been through today, this poor car is finally history, and so am I.

Tony Stewart wins, with Dad chasing him to the finish. Dad still hangs in there on the points, but he'll need to win a couple of races and get some other help if he's going to win that eighth Winston Cup this season. Still, he's having his best year in a while, and everyone is say-ing, "He's back." I think his neck injury the last couple of years hurt him more than he was willing to admit. But now that he's had surgery, he's strong, healthy, and still tough as hell.

We're having an up-and-down year but today we were literally up and then down in that last crash. I have never been in more wrecks in one month than I was on this single afternoon.

Some of the crew say consider it the low point of our season.

I'm not going to argue. Again, it promises to be a long, silent trip home.

# Charlotte, North Carolina
## UAW-GM 500

## Seems Like It Was Five Years Ago

This is a great time for us to race at Charlotte. Home again.

We need a good run. We've been struggling just to get a good finish, so I think this is the right place for us. You can't imagine how much it hurts to work as hard as this team does and then only to crash or have a bad race. We showed what we could do here in May. Winning the Winston was awesome, plus we set a track record and earned the Bud Pole position. Another run like that is all we need to get back on track.

But right now May seems like it was five years ago.

Another advantage to racing near home is that many of the crew members from all the different teams bring their wives and/or girlfriends to the track. These guys are competitive in everything, so it's a badge of honor to bring the best-looking woman to the track. This leads to a larger than usual assortment of well-dressed, attractive women in the garage area. It increases the amount of rubbernecking that goes on.

But I'm without a female "guest" this week. Somebody asked me why, and rather than tell him that I've been too busy to date, I tell him, "Why bring sand to the beach?"

Although the car is pretty decent, when we go out for our qualifying lap, we can't match our record lap time from May. No one else can either because Goodyear has brought another new tire compound. Now we have to throw out the setups from May and start again. It's ridiculous: Goodyear just can't seem to get it right. After this monkey wrench is thrown into the equation, we qualify thirteenth. Not great, but we can definitely still win from there.

After today's practice session, I head home as soon as I can. I invite some friends to the house to play the new computer game NASCAR Heat. The game is the latest and greatest NASCAR simulation, and it features a video segment of me within the game as well as some superb graphics.

In my computer room there are four desks bolted together in a large diamond formation. Each desk holds a superfast computer optimized for gaming. Each computer is linked to the other three and also has a direct connection to the Internet through my personal T-1 line. A T-1 line is usually used by large companies to connect an entire office building to the Internet, but I pay a large fee each month to have my personal ultra-high-speed connection to the world. It makes it easy to play games and race online against people from around the globe.

That's how I met TJ Majors, who helped with my on-line computer racing skills. To repay the favor, I sponsor Majors in his first season behind a real steering wheel in a series called Cup Lites in the northeastern United States. TJ's a great young guy, and he shows some promise, winning the Rookie of the Year award in the series.

TJ is at the house along with Shane Hmeil (another promising young racer and the son of Steve Hmeil, DEI technical director) and they are racing head-to-head on the computers when I get there. Another friend, Terrill Hinson (a.k.a. T-Dogg) also joins in the action. I sit down at my computer to make it four players and we choose the Talladega track. To make it more interesting, we all pick drivers that we think are the worst, and just for the fun of it, we all start at the back of the starting lineup.

We start the race and barrel our way forward, trash-talking to each other across the room, even zooming past the digital Dale Jr. until someone makes a wrong move and starts a huge crash. Before the crash can even finish, I reach up and hit the reset button on my key-board. There are several advantages to computer racing versus the real thing: the crashes don't hurt, they cost a lot less, and the reset button starts it all over again. Oh, and you can have a cold Bud or two while you're racing on the computer.

We start the race over and over again, rarely making it much farther than two or three laps at a time. The joy is in the trash-talking and cussing and crashing each other more than it is in winning the game. This is fun, and it puts me in a great mood. I'm much more relaxed than I am at the racetrack. The rough season is forgotten, at least for the night.

Tomorrow is an off day, so I don't have to be at the track. This allows me to make a few publicity appearances. The afternoon starts with a visit from the MTV crew to my house. Since the CBS show featured Club E, Dad insisted that I not allow any more media near my home. He says I say and show way too much. But the MTV documentary is such an important project for me, I secretly arrange for them to make a quick visit to my house.

When they arrive with their small digital cameras, I take them outside to look at my ever-growing assortment of vehicles—the '71 Corvette, the big-ass pickup, the '99 'Vette, the Impala . . . and my newest ride, a white Chevy Tahoe that will be towed behind my new motor coach during the 2001 season. Each car has a cheesy nickname (the Tahoe is "the Ho" and so on), and each is kept in pristine condition.

MTV's Bill Richmond and I hop in the '71 'Vette, top down, and zoom off for some on-the-road footage. Soon after we hit the road, my mood brightens as we speed along.

Following the joy ride, the MTV guys and the entire Dirty MoPosse crew prepare to head to the racetrack for an autograph session at one of the huge souvenir rigs that carry nothing but Dale Jr. and Budweiser merchandise. There were some questions early in the week as to whether I was going to do an autograph session, but if I don't sign autographs, I know everyone will think I'm an asshole.

When we arrive at the track, there is a line stretching

past the trailer and down Highway 49. The souvenir staff handed out a limited number of tickets for the session, so if you don't have a ticket, you're out of luck. In the line are a number of fans that regularly post messages on the Dale Jr. Pit Stop web site. The Pit Stoppers hang out together at the side of the trailer and politely ask if I'll pose for a photo or two with them when I'm done. I wish all of my appearances were this organized and this mellow.

After ninety minutes of signing, I hop out of the trailer, smile for the photos, and then I'm on the move again (with MTV cameras following me every step of the way). We head toward uptown Charlotte to "106.5 The End," our local alternative/new-rock radio station. Kristen Honeycutt hosts "The Budweiser Lounge" afternoon drive-time radio show, and she asks me to co-host.

I prepare a list of songs that I think are appropriate for the show. The mix is eclectic, and includes local favorites like Ben Folds Five, alt-rock stars Radiohead, Collective Soul, and Soul Asylum, and even obscure songs by bands that I really enjoy, like Treble Charger and the Matthew Good Band—who I think are the best band in the world right now. Kristen enthusiastically plays several of the selections on-air, and jokes with me constantly while taking a large number of phone calls from listeners. At several points during the show, the station's switchboard is completely lit.

A call comes in from a mother trying to set her daughter up with me. "She's very pretty and she wants to know what bar you're going to tonight," says the proud mother. Though I'm very single and sort of flattered at some level, I try to be polite but evasive about our plans for the remainder of the evening.

Kristen asks if I know Shannon Wiseman, a very attractive intern who works at the station. She is somewhat well known in the area because she was the runner-up in an MTV contest called "Wanna Be a VJ."

"Oh yeah! I know her, and I even asked her out, but she told me she had a boyfriend," I answer, on the air.

As soon as the next commercial begins, the "hotline" in the studio rings. It's Shannon calling to scold me about my comment.

"He just didn't try hard enough," she tells Kristin. Then Shannon and I flirt and argue for a few minutes until we're back on the air. She's pretty cool, so maybe she's right. Maybe I should try harder.

Though my appearance is scheduled to last only an hour, we have so much fun and the show goes so well that I stay for the entire two hours, complaining that I don't get to play enough music because the traffic report takes up too much time.

On the way back home, we swing the Tahoe into downtown Concord, a town near the Speedway, to show the MTV guys my blue and black 1969 Camaro that is being tweaked and customized at the local garage. Trust me on this: it's a sweet ride.

Because there was no Winston Cup practice yesterday, nearly everyone in the garage heard all or some of my radio appearance. I am thrilled it's the talk of the paddock area, but I'm less pleased with the way the Bud car handles. I don't know what's wrong with this car, but something just ain't right.

The entire team discusses the problem. While some drivers and car chiefs talk one-on-one, separating themselves from the rest of the team, our crew usually crowds together, four or five or six at a time like some sort of football huddle. Today that huddle consists of a bunch of grown men scratching their heads as we try to figure out how the car could be so bad all of a sudden.

"Let's try *something*," Tony Jr. says. "Anybody got an idea? I ain't gotta damn clue. . . ."

I return for the afternoon happy-hour session and am thrilled with the way the car responds to the changes the crew made. It is the most comfortable the car has been all week.

After the session, we learn that Goodyear has announced that there may not be enough tires to go around for all of the teams for tomorrow's race. Now not only are they changing the tire compounds each week, they aren't even making enough of them! We were so invincible at this track only several months ago, and now we are forced to take wild guesses in the dark!

Without fresh tires, we'll all be out there slipping and sliding and crashing. This is not a good thing. It's my ass on the line out there, and I am not in any mood to hear that I may have to drive all day on old tires.

I need to get away again.

Tonight there is a live show at a nearby bar featuring Bridge, a local band that I have financed completely for more than a year. The MTV crew and a wide assortment of hangers-on and fans expect that I will attend this

evening. However, with a five-hundred-mile race tomorrow, I don't want the team to think I'm out partying
on the night before a race.

I tell everyone at the track that I'm tired and that I'm
not going to attend. Plus, I'm pissed off at one of the
band members, who has taken advantage of my goodwill
and generosity. This looks like the end of the line for my
support for these guys.

However, once I get home, I'm unable to sit still, so I
slip out for an hour or two of the show. Once there, I'm
approached by a stream of well-wishers for photos and
autographs. I handle it all with patience, but soon I'm
ready to get home and think about tomorrow's race.

Starting thirteenth, we are not the focus of nearly as
much hoopla as we were before the May race, but I still
receive the second-loudest cheer when I'm introduced. I
pay attention to those things because I want to be liked
by the fans. My dad receives the loudest ovation—no
matter where we race.

It's a very cold and overcast day, and the crowd is
surprisingly sparse. (Sparse is a relative term, as there
are easily more than 150,000 fans on hand.) There is an
NFL game going on across town, and the clash of
schedules has hurt both the Carolina Panthers crowd
and the race attendance. This doesn't bother me as
soon as the race starts, and I try to make my usual aggressive start and jump into the top ten on the second
lap.

When the first yellow flag comes out, I'm a little
concerned about the engine. It doesn't sound good running under the caution.

But it sounds good at full speed, and I roar around

easily in the first fifty laps, running eighth while Dad takes the lead. However, Big E soon has a problem with a broken shock absorber and begins to drop back.

After a pit stop under a yellow flag on Lap 88, tires are still very much a concern to the team. And soon the right tire won't stay underneath me, and the car gets loose.

The crew watches helplessly as our once fast car drops to twenty-fourth in less than thirty laps. Mercifully a yellow flag flies on Lap 130, and I bring the car in for a new set of skins.

When they change the tires, they discover the right rear wheel was not attached tightly. This is what caused the vibration and ill handling.

"Thank God, I'm not going crazy," I breathe. "For one lap that car felt as good as the Winston car, then it just went to hell. . . ."

When the race resumes, the car is fast again, and I feel like the same driver that won the Winston. We zoom back to twelfth place in less than 10 laps.

I find myself talking on the radio more as the car improves.

"Andy [Houston] is family," I say at one point about Houston, who is making one of his first Cup starts today. (Andy is Teresa Earnhardt's cousin.) "He's good people. But damn, he's trying some weird shit out here." Houston and his team struggle all day with the tires, and Goodyear officials later release a statement that Houston's team was running the tires with air pressures well below the recommended level. How's that for sending a team under the bus?

On Lap 159, Rusty Wallace slams into the back of

Dale Jarrett, and Jarrett spins right in front of me. With a split-second instinctual move, I somehow avoid the carnage.

After a blazing pit stop, we're in sixth place, and quickly improve to fifth at the restart, barging past Mark Martin. After the earlier troubles, it looks like we could pull off a repeat of the Winston. The car is fast, the team is confident, and now we're gonna look to take the lead.

Seconds later that plan changes. Another tire is loose.

Four laps later the car is simply not drivable, and I turn it into pit lane for an unscheduled pit stop. We will lose at least one lap.

As we stop for service, a NASCAR official steps in front of the Bud car. I slid into the pits a little too fast and NASCAR catches me speeding. The official holds his palm out for fifteen seconds after the work is completed. Each second seems like an hour as the other cars go zooming past. I rev the engine in anger and frustration, and then do a tire-smoking burnout when the official steps aside. I am now two full laps behind the leaders.

"Be cool . . . be cool," insists Tony Jr. "You were right again. The left rear tire was loose."

I say nothing. Right now I'm angry and ready to snap. We drop all the way to thirtieth position. The car is still wickedly fast, so all we can do is try to make up the two laps we lost.

While Bobby Labonte and Ricky Rudd battle for the lead of the race, I pass and then pull away from them easily. We regain one of our lost laps when a car dumps oil in Turn 3, causing another yellow flag. The new set of tires, borrowed from Robby Gordon's team, is not nearly as good as the previous set. Once again, there is a vibration.

I manage to hang on until yet another caution slows the pace on Lap 306. On the restart, I go for it and make my way in front of the race leaders again, getting back on the tail end of the lead lap. If a yellow flag comes out now, we can move up a handful of positions, but it's too little, too late. The laps are running out.

Bobby Labonte leaps closer toward his first Winston Cup title as he takes the victory. It is his fourth win of the 2000 season, and he extends his championship lead to 252 points with five races to go. While we were fighting with loose tires, Labonte was one of thirteen different leaders who swapped the top spot forty-six times in the 334-lap race. Despite our comeback, we only move up to finish nineteenth.

After the race, I'm exhausted from driving my ass off. When we were racing to get our laps back, we were ahead of the leaders for more than fifty laps as well as the last twenty-five laps. This sucks, because it means we could have won if we didn't have two loose wheels and an unscheduled pit stop.

The slump continues.

On the way home, feeling sorry for myself, I remember that when I was practicing for one of my early Busch races at Charlotte in 1997, I lost control and wrecked the car. This was before I had a full-time ride, and we only had one car. I went back home to my double-wide trailer with a few friends and just sat there in disbelief. I pondered my racing future when the back door flew open and my father walked in, looking about ten feet tall. One look at his face and my buddies were on their way out the front door.

Dad asked me to join him on the back porch, and we spent more than an hour out there, talking. He told me about the frustrations he'd experienced in the early days of his racing career, and while everyone knows about his glory years, he had to go through his tough times to get there.

Just as he was getting started in racing, his father died of a heart attack. They had only raced together once, and Ralph was pushing and crashing into Dad during the race just to teach him who was still the boss.

So while we stood out on the porch of the double-wide, Dad told me that instead of brooding over the car I'd just wrecked, I needed to look forward to my next opportunity to race and think about that. Somewhere in the conversation, he assured me of his love and his hope that I'd be successful in whatever I did. Since then, I've never worried about my mistakes. I just looked forward to the chance to redeem them.

# Talladega, Alabama
## Winston 500

## The Big One

It's hard to be the center of attention wherever I walk at the racetrack. I don't mind signing autographs, but sometimes the crowds get to be too pushy. Photographers are the same way. It seems that they are always hovering around trying to catch you looking like shit. When things go well, I suppose I don't mind it as much, but a lot of times I feel like they are mocking me. All of those lenses pointed at me: "Hey, boy, what are you going to do now?" "Why the hell did you suck last week?" "Why did you crash the car?"

I get a lot of looks on pit lane in Talladega when I come out to qualify. Just like usual, but today the looks are a little different. It's a mix of confusion and amusement on people's faces. It must be the Budweiser bandanna I'm wearing on my head—do-rag style, like all the coolest rappers or the guys in the NFL. I figure rappers wear 'em, so why not? But it's not really what people expect to see on a NASCAR pit lane, so it upsets some folks who don't like anything new or different from what they've known for fifty years. Screw 'em. I like it, my team likes it, and my buddies like it, so I'm wearin' the do-rag.

Well, anything to break the tension of Talladega. The biggest, fastest track of all, where everybody knows that an epic crash is just waiting to happen. They've even got a name for it—The Big One.

I remember the first time I ever drove this place, back before I ever started running Winston Cup or even Busch Series. I was still in late models and my dad called me and said, "Don't tell anyone, but you're coming with us tomorrow morning. Just be at the shop."

So we flew off to Talladega, where they were testing some new engine parts or something. Dad put me in the car and said, "Whatever you do, just don't let off the throttle in the corners. You have to keep it to the floor or you'll crash hard."

Damn, I'd never even been in one of these cars and he sends me out on the fastest track of all . . . and I'm not supposed to lift?

I was scared at first but I just continued repeating what Dad had said: "Don't lift . . . don't lift . . . don't lift . . ." I was hauling ass down the backstraight, holding my foot down. The third turn seemed like it was a mile away and then the banking started coming into focus. It looked like a big wall. I held my breath as the car curved into the banked turn. I figured I was either gonna have the biggest crash of my life or I was gonna set a new track record! The car curved around the banking with no problem.

After a few laps, I thought I was really getting with it. I thought this was easy. I was carving the most beautiful, arching turns through the corners, flat out, foot to the floor, and I thought I was the smoothest thing anyone had ever seen. But when I came in and looked at my lap times, they were terrible. I just didn't understand.

So Dave Marcis comes over and tells me that this place is so big and the track is so wide that you don't really have to use all of it. He tells me that if you swing out wide, like they teach you to do at almost every other track, you'll add hundreds of extra feet to the total distance of the lap.

So I went back and started cutting the corners tighter and tighter, still foot to the floor, and my lap times got better and better. By the end of the day, I was just as fast as the other guys out there testing.

Talladega is so big and so fast that NASCAR implements special rules and equipment to slow the cars down. We not only race with restrictor plates just like we do at Daytona, but for this race, NASCAR has added some new tricks to try to slow us down. By making the aerodynamics of the cars "dirty" by disrupting the usual smooth airflow over the car, they hope that the speeds will slow down dramatically—so much for all of that time and money spent in the wind tunnels to make these cars sleek and fast.

For this race, cars will carry an extended flange—called a "wickerbill" or "Gurney Flap" (named for American racing legend Dan Gurney, who was the first to steal the idea of a flap on the back of a wing from airplane designs)—on top of the rear spoiler and a vertical roof deflector. It's a one-and-three-eighths-inch flap on the roof of the car that makes it look like a police cruiser or a taxi cab from the front. Also, the ground clearance on the cars has been raised for this race.

All of the changes are supposed to slow the cars down and bring back passing. Especially "slingshot" passing, where a car gets into the draft of the car in front of it and starts picking up speed as it gets closer. The driver uses that speed when he ducks under the front car to whip right past, like he'd been shot from the barrel of a Remington rifle. It's an old NASCAR move that made superspeedway racing awesome in the 1960s, 70s, and 80s, long before the days of restrictor plates.

One thing you don't have to worry about here is tire wear. "As long as they've got air in them," our tire specialist, Keith Mansch, says, "they're okay."

Fine with me.

Our car is awesome—it's the same one we had at Daytona in July. I'm third best when qualifying is done, so I head to the media center for the required news conference. We've been running like crap for so long, it seems like it's been months since I had to go to one of these things. I look forward to some tough questions or at least interesting ones. But all of the questions are really boring. It's like these media guys are just phoning it in. I guess they're just as burnt out as the rest of us. Or maybe it's because we've sucked lately. Hopefully this is the week when this changes, and I can do something to change their apathy.


The next day, it's kind of chilly, so I decide to wear a black stocking cap instead of the do-rag. A little less wild, but still pretty damn cool.

If Saturday morning practice is a preview of what we can expect with the new rules changes, then it's going to be a wild one. The closing speeds (the speed that you catch the car in front of you) are faster than ever, so you get clumps of eight to twelve cars running in a tight pack. You can't help wondering what it'll be like out there on race day when all of us are lumped together. And we will be—the new rules mean the cars cut a huge hole in the air and make it almost impossible to lose the draft. I could probably go out there in my new Chevy pickup and run in the draft, it's so strong.

Some of the cars, including Jeff Gordon's ride, get tangled together during the morning practice, and it has a lot of people on pit row, including some in the Bud team, a little nervous. Maybe a lot nervous.

As a result, NASCAR calls a special, drivers-only meeting that afternoon to inform us that the restrictor plates will be adjusted again to cut down on the closing speeds. A lot of the crew chiefs and engine men are screaming in protest, but what are you going to do? No matter what crap NASCAR throws at us, we feel like we've got one badass race car. We're fast whether we're out front, leading the pack, or drafting somewhere in the middle of a long line of cars.

I give the MTV crew a briefing on what to expect tomorrow.

"I love restrictor-plate racing, because it's all-out, hairy shit," I tell them. "At Talladega, you know you're seeing guys out there with their right foot mashed to the floor and driving as fast as they can. The restrictor plate makes it like a chess match—you really have to plan ahead and try to outthink the other guys.

"I think the guys with the most common sense are gonna end up in the top ten. I hope that means that we're happy tomorrow. We just have to be patient and wait for our turn. You have to avoid trouble. There'll be a lotta chances to pass and lead the race."

Just like they're nervous about me wandering around with a do-rag on my head, NASCAR is nervous about the MTV crew wandering through the Talladega infield with their cameras. This is like the home turf of the throwbacks—the drunken, unwashed fans from NASCAR's redneck roots. There are a lot of bad jokes about the Talladega infield. You know, like "What has forty legs and ten teeth? The ticket line for the infield at Talladega." Stuff like that. The Talladega infield can be a scary place (especially if you are a girl), and the areas surrounding the track are not much better. The local hotels are like mold factories, yet they can look you in the face while charging you three hundred dollars a night. It makes me happy I have my motor coach here. It is *not* the image NASCAR wants MTV to portray. I guess I'll try my best to keep their focus on the excitement on the track.

"The Big One" is a real, live presence at Talladega. There are a lot of fans who hope and wish and pray to see and cheer The Big One. But in the garage area, it's something everyone fears because most of them have already seen it. The Big One is that grinding, multicar crash that takes out a huge chunk of the field and looks almost like the work of some big, angry, invisible hand that reaches out and starts smashing things. There's an element of danger anywhere you race, but nerves are on edge here more than anywhere else because we all know that The Big One is always lurking. One bad move can bring it out like an ill-tempered overgrown child smashing his blocks to the ground after building a tall tower of pieces.

"TBO" might be bigger than ever today. There is so much uncertainty with the new rules, the tension in the garage area is greater than ever. Like a lot of the other drivers, I go to the Motor Racing Outreach chapel service after the drivers' meeting to listen to my friend Dale Beaver give the sermon. I don't usually attend these, but everyone is looking for a little something extra to take comfort in this morning.

Race time approaches, and while I strap into the car, Teresa comes by and says a few words. So does Richard Childress. They urge me to be safe and careful. They really didn't need to say anything. I can see it in their eyes. Everybody's heart is pumping a little harder today.

I attach the in-car radio to my helmet, then key the mike and call up to the spotter, Dale Cagle, and let him know I don't want him to stop talking to me from the green flag to the checkers.

The spotter is a huge key here. We'll be racing three-wide for five hundred miles, and I need to know what's happening everywhere around me. We've even got a secondary spotter near Turn 4 to pick up the action where Cagle can't see the track.

All the cars are slowly rolling around on the pace lap when I call the crew.

"I know it's a long race, guys, and I'm gonna do my best. I ain't gonna push the envelope . . . until the end."

Well, easy for me to *say*. Doing it is something else. So, of course, I'm leading the race by the end of the first lap. But the new aerodynamics make it hard to stay in front for long, and a flock of cars line up and draft past, so by the third lap I'm back to nineteenth. Yeah, nineteenth! It's going to be that kind of race. They want passing, then we'll give 'em passing.

At the ten-lap mark, my first Talladega teacher, Dave Marcis, is leading a race for the first time in what seems like forever. My dad and I are working together, slicing back through the field. I'm behind him and slamming into his rear bumper—"bump drafting," it's called—to give him a little extra speed down the straights. We'll be trying anything and everything, especially since my dad is one of five drivers still eligible for Winston's "No Bull" $1 million bonus.

By Lap 40 pit stop negotiations are going on up and down pit lane. You have to make deals with guys because the draft is so important. A single car—no matter how fast—can't pit and rejoin the front of the pack without help. You need drafting partners and the pit crews have runners out making offers.

Early in a race, you usually go to teams that are "friendly." Teammates, family members, or just a team where the crew chief is your buddy. Later on, the dealing becomes more complex and a little desperate. You'll deal with the devil himself if you think it will get you a win. Ordinarily a Chevrolet team won't ask a Ford team for help. But they might get to be real good temporary friends near the finish if it looks like the two drivers are working well together. Whatever it takes.

On Lap 49, it's me and my teammate Steve Park,

along with Dad and his teammate Mike Skinner. We come in and go out together. Right now we're all still friends. But it's early.

The three-wide action goes to four-wide at some spots on the track. It's both exciting and scary, and I'm told that the guys in my pit area can hardly stand to look. I can feel The Big One coming.

I'm working with my father and I'm in the top ten. But then I make one wrong move and almost instantly fall all the way back to twenty-fourth.

"Nothing I can fucking do right now," I'm screaming. "What do y'all want me to do? Tony? Tony Jr.? Anybody?"

Tony Jr. comes on the radio and tries to calm me down a little. "Whichever lane moves," he says, "take it one spot at a time. That's how your daddy moved up there. One at a time."

I try it and lose a couple of more spots. Then I make a move to the middle lane and in three laps I'm back to running eighth. Hell yeah.

So much for patience and taking them one at a time.

As the sun moves across the sky, it creates blind spots for the spotters. For a split second, Cagle loses the action in the glare and I almost crash into two other cars.

"What the hell is going on inside of me?" I shout.

"It's a long race," Tony Jr. says. "Don't get frustrated."

When the second pit stops come around, I'm running second.

Then we get a yellow flag. Not TBO, though, just debris on the track. Regardless, it's a chance to catch a breath. But you can't stop worrying or paying total attention. Slow speeds have their own peculiar dangers. They can be harder on these highly tuned engines than hot laps, and this track is so big it takes us four full minutes to get around it under yellow. Time to talk and worry.

"I can't do it like Daddy does," I tell Tony Jr. "I just don't know when to go and when not to. If I fuck up, I'll look like a dumb ass."

"Your daddy looked like an asshole twenty years ago," Tony says, and I can hear the crew laughing through the radio.

"I just don't like running near the very bottom," I say to the spotter, hoping he can help keep me in the middle or outside line of cars. "You can get trapped there—you can't move. If I'm in the middle or the high line, I feel like I can move around."

The stop is quick as we change only two tires, but I'm slow out of the pits because I'm surprised when they tell me to go.

At Lap 120 it's rookie time. Matt and I swap the lead back and forth a few times. This is like the good ol' days of last year. Then we both fall back out of the top ten and start clawing our way back up again. It's like climbing one of those indoor rock-climbing machines: you keep struggling to go up one treacherous step at a time, but the damn thing keeps moving and pushing you down. Today I have help on the wall, and working with Dad, we push and gouge back into the top five, but we both find resistance from Mike Skinner. Skinner (who once said he'd "wreck his mom to win one of these things") chooses not to work with either of us, and we're pushed back in the field again.

I drop off to seventeenth and Tony Jr. can sense my frustration.

"Just chill," he says. "Ride a bit."

So just like before when he told me to relax, I charge. Soon it's three of us young guns out front again. Me, Matt, and one of my favorite guys, Elliott Sadler. At the end of 150 laps (of 200), the top thirty-one cars are within two seconds of each other.

As the end of the race nears, the urgency to be up front increases, and the huge pack breaks apart and the top five cars get into a single-file breakaway. I'm in the lead, pulling Bobby Labonte right behind me. I admire Bobby a lot, so I'm glad that it's him on my back bumper, and we start working together with less than thirty laps to go. He's the points leader, so when I help him, I hurt Dad's chances for his eighth championship because he is second in points to Bobby right now. But when it gets to this stage in the race, you don't think friends and family. You think winning.

"Tell him to hit me," I tell the spotter. I want him to relay the message through Labonte's spotter. "If he bumps me, we'll get away."

With twenty laps to go, we get a yellow flag for a three-car crash. Nerves are frayed on the track and in the pits.

The spotter and Tony are on the radio at the same time, and I can't make out what either one of them is saying.

"I can't understand anything if y'all keep stepping on each other," I holler. "Talk in short sentences. Are the pits open?"

"Are the pits open?" Tony repeats the question.

"Ten-four," the spotter says, nice and crisp.

"Two tires," Tony yells. "Two tires."

It takes the guys 7.91 seconds to put on two new Goodyear Eagles and add fuel. We should easily be the first car back on track.

I'm in the lead. In the pits the only people not standing are the ones who are drained by the tension. My guys can barely stand to watch. They're exhausted—but not because of physical exertion. The stress is that powerful.

Labonte bumps me like I asked, and we run first and second with eight laps to go. With less than five left, all hell starts breaking loose. The Big One is in the house. He's coming up the stairs like in a bad horror movie. Kenseth runs off into the grass on the backstretch—all I see in the mirror is a big cloud of dirt flying—but he gets it gathered up and falls back in line. I can't see Dad at all now.

Skinner, who is third, can't stand it anymore and he breaks out of single file and challenges Labonte for second. This opens the floodgates and every driver on the track decides to make his move. We go two-wide, then three-wide, then four-wide.

Holy shit.

Tony Jr., who has been trying to keep me calm all day, roars into the radio, *"Go get 'em!"*

With two laps to go, from out of nowhere, here comes the black No. 3. When Skinner made it an every-man-for-himself race, my dad started working with Kenny Wallace. Wallace looks like he is welded to Dad's bumper because he knows it's his best hope to move to the front.

Now I'm fighting with Big E, John Andretti, and Skinner for the lead. We head for the white flag like a pack of angry, snarling dogs, and if I'm going to do something, it has to be this moment.

I jerk the car hard to the left and it sends me down into no-man's-land along the apron on the inside of the front stretch. I get a tap from Labonte, who is still trying to help, but this time it gets me sideways.

Now I'm on the apron heading toward Turn 1 at nearly two hundred miles per hour and this simply will not work. I'm either going to slide across the track into the lead ahead of Skinner, or be forced to let off and drop back or . . . well, I'll be the guy who causes The Big One.

I still get a run on Skinner but I run out of room into Turn 1. I get wild outta shape and I think I'm gonna end up upside down. It's insane—I can't believe I saved the car.

Every driver on the track is holding on to his own spot. It's every man for himself, and nobody is interested in letting some crazy rookie back into line.

Imagine being in bumper-to-bumper traffic for five hundred miles, surrounded by drivers that want nothing more than to get to their destination before you do. No CD player. No air-conditioning. No stops for a cool drink and snack. Imagine your mood at this point in the afternoon, with the late-day sun glaring in your eyes. Now imagine that scenario except that you're traveling more than one hundred yards every second instead of creeping along, and that there's huge prize money for getting there first. And, for Dad and four others in the race, an extra million dollars from Winston. Would *you* let someone back in line?

I don't have any choice. I back off the throttle and I creep back into traffic on the banking of Turn 1. I manage to escape The Big One, but I also drop all the way to fourteenth. Just like that.

While all this is going on, Big E has blasted into the lead. With Wallace and Joe Nemechek on his bumper, the three break away from the now-scrambled pack and streak to the finish line. Amazing—Dad wins the race and the million-dollar bonus. After forty-nine lead changes among twenty-one drivers, he rallies from eighteenth place with less than five laps to go. He kicks our asses. Again. It's easily one of the most exciting races ever—not just at Talladega, but in the history of NASCAR.

Just to make it a complete Talladega experience, there is a wreck at the checkered flag. It's like The Big One gives us a little flip of his finger and sends a few cars spinning down the track, slamming into each other. No one is hurt, but there are some seriously bent-up cars when all the dust settles.

I manage to escape the wreck and, all things considered, no one is too disappointed with how we did here. We finish fourteenth in a wild race. We had what we think was one of the top three cars all day. I passed eleven cars in one lap—and I did that *twice*. I was in the race to win, right until that last banzai move. I fucked up, but the car was strong all day and we led a lot of laps. It was just like the decision at the Winston—we could have been comfortable and finished in the top ten, but we're racers and we wanna win. I was trying to win when I made the move, so we go home with fourteenth instead of fifth or sixth.

"That was nuts, wasn't it?" I say after crawling from the car. "I don't know what it looked like for the fans, but that was a blast from where I sat!"

The first man I look for is Bobby Labonte, to apologize for costing him a chance for the win with my kamikaze move.

For the first time in a long time, the crew gives me high fives as they straggle one by one back to the transporter.

My eyes widen when I see the crowd of media around me, wanting to hear what I have to say about the race and my dad.

"I knew I was a sitting duck there in the lead," I explain. "I was fine with that—I liked leading the race—but I was a bit nervous thinking about how I was going to run the last couple of laps. I trust Bobby and he's a good guy to race with. He was helping me and I apologized to him after the race for maybe taking him out of a chance to win. I think we're gonna win one of these [restrictor-plate] races. I like these races but I just don't know if I'm very good at it yet. I didn't want to look like a dumb ass if I screwed up, but we were up front nearly all day. We like that—that looks good."

But not as good as the badass in the black car. This isn't my day—it belongs to him. It's unbelievable what he did out there. Even he says he couldn't believe it. Anybody who knows anything about racing knows they saw something magical today. Like everybody else who saw the race or ran in it, I am in awe of him.

He picks up some points on Labonte (who could have

crashed me big time but let off the throttle). His eighth Winston Cup is still possible. It's a long shot but no one is counting Dad out.

Dad tells the media, "It was a pretty good day, seeing that kind of racing side by side and three- and four-wide. And nobody got in trouble. It was good, hard racing. But I still don't like restrictor-plate racing. I'm not that good at it."

· If he's not that good at it, then what does that say about the rest of us?

# Rockingham, North Carolina
## *Pop Secret 400*

## I Know a Man
## and Leave That Kid Alone

For a few weeks, I had been tossing around an idea for one of my columns for NASCAR Online. It was tough to come up with something new every month that was impactful or interesting, and I thought about how I could do a cool story about my dad. I wanted to describe him and give my own view of him, but I wanted to write it so that you really didn't know who I was talking about until the very end. You know, lay it all out there without really saying it was Dad.

One night I felt inspired, so I sat down and started typing. It all fell out at once—I was typing along and the words just came tumbling out. To a lot of people, my dad is the Intimidator and a great driver and all that, but for me, growing up where he was not around too much and now getting to be with him and race with him every week, he is Superman—invincible. I wanted to let him know how much I loved him and how much he meant to me.

I finished it late, late one night and e-mailed it to Jade, who did his usual editing stuff, like correcting a few spelling errors or moving a sentence here and there. Before we sent it out, I knew I had to show my dad. I was proud of how it had turned out, and I wanted him to see it before anyone else did.

It was usually really hard to get time with him—you know, just him and me, without a bunch of people or activity around—but I was able to take it to him in his office at DEI a day or two after it was written. It was just me and him sitting there.

"I want you to see this before we send it to NASCAR Online," I told him.

He sat down to read it and got a strange look on his face. He got up and walked right over to me, right in my face. He gave me a hug and told me how much he liked it and I thought for a second we were both gonna cry, which doesn't happen at all with the Earnhardt men. No matter if he told me he loved me a hundred times, or I told him, it was really the first time in my life that I could put it into words in a way that really hit home.

In no time, he was back to ol' Big E, running the show and telling me what I should do.

"This is too damn good to just be put on some Internet deal," he said. "You need to save this for something big, like a book."

I thought about that for a few days but decided that it was just too much to keep under wraps. The online column seemed to be reaching a growing number of people, and so I felt like it was worthy of being out there in the public. If I could put it in a book later, well, that was a bonus . . .

**"I know a man . . ."**
I know a man whose hands are so calloused that

gloves aren't necessary. Once, while cutting down a tree, he cut the back of his hand to the bone with a chainsaw. He didn't even stop to look until the job was done.

I've seen him get thrown from a tractor. The tractor, as large as a small home, was flipped by the trunk of a stubborn oak tree. His first thought was not fear, but how quickly he could get the tractor back on its tracks to complete the task. He has suffered broken bones and never had one complaint. Not to anyone, not even to himself.

This man could lead the world's finest army. He has wisdom that knows no bounds. No fire could burn his character, no stone could break it. He maintains a private existence. One that shelters his most coveted thoughts from the world.

His upbringing was no controlled creation. His hard-working family was like many from that era. He gained his knowledge in hard dirt and second-hand tools, from his toys as a child to the trucks he drove in his twenties. From that natural upbringing, he has an incredible sense of good and bad. He sees it before it sees him, in people, in anything imaginable. Where did he learn this? How does he know so many things?

I've seen this man create many things. With no blueprints, he has carved and produced wonders upon wonders. His résumé shows he has created major companies. He has hammered out deal upon deal—always being as fair as God would have it. He has taken land with thick shrubs and deep valleys and molded it into a frontier fit for heaven. He has built homes that kings couldn't fathom.

Solving problems is as easy as breathing for him. They are thrown his way like the morning paper. People surround him daily, wanting solutions. He hands them out with pride and passion. Each solution is a battle won. He calculates his every action, demanding the same from everyone else. He is honest in letting you know your end of the bargain.

His friendship is the greatest gift you could ever obtain. Out of all his attributes, it is the most impressive. He trusts only a few with this gift. If you ever break that trust, it is over. He accepts few apologies. Many have crossed him, and they leave with only regret for their actions. In every result, he stands as an example of what hard work and dedication will achieve. Even his enemies know this.

I have had the pleasure of joining him on the battlefield. I have experienced his intimidating wrath. That may sound strong, but I know what I am talking about. He roams like a lion, king of his jungle. His jungle is his and his alone. Every step he takes has purpose. Every walk has reason.

He praises God, loves his family, enjoys his friends.

I wonder what his future holds. He has so much to be proud of. To this point, he's only barely satisfied. His eyes see much more than my imagination could produce. He is Dale Earnhardt.

Dad, the world's finest army awaits.

The response was huge, and people seemed really impressed with the piece. Some hinted or insisted that it was so good that I hadn't written it myself, but I didn't care because I knew Dad was proud of it and it was special to him.

Steve Crisp looks like he's in heaven. He's been working at DEI for years and he's sort of a jack-of-all-trades. He works with sponsors and does scheduling and takes care of whatever it is that needs to be done. He was my right-hand man when I was in the Busch Series, and he's funnier than hell.

But what Steve Crisp really loves is cars. Chevrolets, to be precise. Two days after the race at Talladega, he is as happy as a pig in shit. He's on stage at DEI to introduce a Chevrolet right out of his dreams—the Camaro Intimidator SS. This is a kick-butt, haul-ass Chevy that has been tricked up into a snarling, 381-horsepower street-legal machine. This limited-edition car will be sold at Dale Earnhardt Chevrolet, the dealership Dad owns in Newton, North Carolina. The car has been one of Steve's pet projects and he's like a proud father.

The "buff books"—magazine for car enthusiasts— have sent reporters to cover the event, and there are also some top Chevrolet executives attending. They're here not just for the Camaro announcement but also to unveil their plans for Dad and me to join the factory Corvette team at the 2001 Rolex 24 Hours of Daytona, one of the world's most prestigious endurance races.

The 24 Hours of Daytona makes running six hundred miles at Charlotte look like a drive down the street to downtown Mooresville. Heavyweight manufacturers like Chevy and Chrysler go head-to-head for bragging rights that get turned into big-money marketing campaigns. Dad and I will be teaming up with Andy Pilgrim, a road racer, and taking turns at the wheel, like a tag team. This will be the first time that I team up with my dad instead of racing against him.

There is a yellow and white Corvette, like the one we'll be running in the 24 Hours, on display with the silver and black Intimidator Camaro. The 'Vette looks awesome, even though they spelled the last name wrong above the door. "Earnhart" will do for now. . . . The car is like a big cat, ready to pounce. All low-slung and looking wicked fast. I can't keep my eyes off that car. Some wiseass says that's because it's nine-thirty in the morning—the bright yellow paint job is the *only* thing that can keep my eyes propped open.

My dad is still amped up from the win at Talladega. When it's his time to talk, he says, "Kenny Wallace will be getting a nice Christmas gift this year."

Then he talks about the future.

"I'm looking forward to the 24 Hours and racing with Andy and Dale Jr. I didn't want to do this deal unless I thought we had a shot to win the thing. I've been impressed with Andy and the whole Chevy effort."

Then, because he can't pass up a chance to needle me in front of so many people, he says, "I think we'll let Dale Jr. drive at night since he's up all night most of the time anyway."

After the news conference, we head out to Lowe's Motor Speedway with some of the journalists and Chevy execs. They'll get a chance to drive the Intimidator SS around the tight, twisting infield road course. And

I'll take a few of them as passengers and put the SS through some fast laps.

This thing really hauls and I really have fun throwing it around the tight corners. But my boots are too wide to brake and also use the clutch and gas pedal at the same time, so after my first drive, I stop to take them off. After the next passenger hops in, I peel out in just my socks. It makes it easier to corner faster. At least until the engine starts to wheeze and sputter and clank. I can't believe it. I've blown the engine. I'm starting to think I'm jinxed.

On Friday, walking out of the garage on my way to qualify at Rockingham, Ward Burton stops me.

"What were you doin' on the apron last week? You about took us all out there."

Hard to know how to handle this. I'm still a rookie but I can't back down.

"I was in control the whole time," I tell Burton.

He turns and walks back to his car, although something tells me I didn't convince him.

I forget about Ward immediately because I have my own problems to deal with. The car is awful. Really shitty. I didn't think the car could get any worse until now. We are forty-fourth quickest . . . if you can call that quick.

After the lap, I sit in the garage with the crew while they tear the car down. Sometimes the problem is obvious and sometimes it's not. Today it's not. The crew decides to change just about everything. Later in the day, the car runs a lot better.

After practice I give each member of the crew a do-rag to show my appreciation and support for the way they work their butts off and for getting the car running again. The crew will be competing in their first Union 76 World Championship Pit Crew later in the day, so I figure they can wear the rags as a kind of badge of honor.

As Dad and I wait for our turn, we talk about the shitty track surface. "Look at that," my dad says. "If you ran your hand across that track, it would cut your hand. Look at all the seashells and crap in there . . ."

"The power of the rag!" Steve Wolfe, the rear-tire changer, shouts as my dressed-in-do-rags crew leaps over the wall to complete a brutally quick stop in world-record time. It is the best time ever in the history of the event, but we wait, holding our breath while a NASCAR official checks to make sure each lug nut is tight. (Each loose nut is a penalty.) When he stands up and says, "No penalties," we start cheering and giving high fives. It's a great moment for them.

Their glory lasts only a few seconds as the record gets broken and then broken again by the next two teams. When the day is over, the Bud crew is fourth best out of thirty-five teams.

"Not bad for our first year in it," says Tony Jr. "They knew we were here. They'd better watch out for us in the future."

We decide not to go out and requalify Saturday afternoon. We need the time to work on the race-day setup, so we take a provisional starting spot for the first time. The way it works is, the first thirty-six spots in any race are based on qualifying speed. The rest—thirty-seven to forty-three—are awarded on Winston Cup points standing. And, if you want to get *really* technical, there is even a "past champion's provisional" that allows former Winston Cup champions to get in the field. Guys have been calling that the "Darrell Waltrip rule," poking fun at Darrell, who's one of the best ever but he's been saddled with a noncompetitive team the past few seasons. The rules assure the fans that even if one of the top drivers has a terrible qualifying session, he'll still be in the race on Sunday.

Nobody likes to get in a race by using a provisional, so I'm in a down mood Sunday afternoon, standing next to the car and waiting for the race to start. It's a new view for us. We are so far back I can't even see the cars up at the front of the line.

Dad comes over to give me a little encouragement.

"Two words," he says. "Tire. Management."

I just wanna get this race over with. The only comeback I can think of is, "Two words. Cold . . . beer."

Something tells me I'm probably gonna enjoy the ride home more than I'm gonna enjoy starting this far back.

Right now my mind is on the week off that is coming up right after this race. Not a good place for a racer's head to be right before the green flag.

Tony Jr. reads my mood and tries to get me to lighten up a little and get my head in the race.

"All right, any fans listening in on this frequency," he says into the radio, "there is a big party after the race at my house."

"Nah, man," I say, "*my* house. The beer is colder and the TV is bigger."

"We'll need to do a tape measure on the TVs," Tony Jr. says. "I think mine is the same size. . . ."

"Yeah," I say, "but I've got *two*."

I feel a little better about things when the race starts, and after a few laps I feel real good. The car is damn fast. I pick up more than a dozen spots before I come in for the second pit stop of the day. The pit area at Rockingham curves around Turns 1 and 2, and we're in the middle of the arc, so it's hard to turn straight into our stall. When I slide too far forward, the stop is delayed and I lose a lot of what I'd gained in the first hundred laps.

The crew makes the right changes to the car, though, and I get by ten cars before the next yellow flag.

This pit stop is slow too, because I have to avoid hitting a guy from Tony Stewart's crew and also because Robert Pressley stalls right in front of me.

Tony Sr. is hot. We've got a fast car—thanks to the crew's hard work—and we're losing it in the pits. Tony thinks Stewart's guy ran in front of me on purpose.

"Knock that son of a bitch outta the way," he's yelling. "Ya knock one of them on their ass, they'll learn."

"Tony," I say, "since you just suggested it on the radio, I think we'd be charged with premeditated murder."

There's a switch, me trying to cool Tony down. Usually it's the other way around.

I need his help when I get a little impatient on Lap 173. Coming out of Turn 2, I bump into the rear of Jimmy Spencer's car. He spins and gets into Mark Martin. They both crash hard. Jimmy Spencer is *not* the guy to run into, believe me!

"Did he check up or what?" I ask the spotter with a

hint of panic or at least looking for support for my side of the story. "I'm sorry—tell him I didn't mean to hit him. I wasn't ready for him to check up there."

I have a fresh dent in the left front fender, but the Bud car is still fast and I'm back in the top ten when the yellow comes out on Lap 210. The pit angle bites me again and I get too close to the wall for the jackman to completely lift the car and change the left-side tires. We drop to the back of the lead lap. Tony decides to make another stop to work on the bent fender.

I'm out of patience now—the pit stops have bit us three times—and I start catching cars one by one until Lap 234, when I get hit from behind. By a *rookie*.

Kurt Busch is making one of his first starts in Winston Cup, and the tap is like the one I gave Spencer earlier in the race. I hit the wall hard, just like Spencer did.

I'm able to refire the car and drive it back to the garage, knocking over pylons and trash cans like some kind of angry drunk at closing time.

When I'm out of the car, waiting while the crew tries to fix it, a reporter asks me if I'm going to retaliate.

"Nah, it's not like I'm gonna go out there and kill him. He was racing hard and I guess I did that a lot when I was young."

It's funny, talking about another driver that way. Now I'm playing the role of the pissed-off veteran, fifty-eight laps down because some rookie got into me.

Some of the people on the Kurt Busch team don't hear my comment correctly, and one of their guys runs over to Jade and asks, "Did Junior say he was gonna kill him?"

Nah . . .

When the car is deemed safe enough to return, they put on four fresh tires and push me back toward pit lane. Purely by coincidence, I'm right behind Kurt Busch when I get back out on the track. With fresh rubber, it's no problem to close right up on him and fill his mirrors. I'm sure people think I'm gonna crash Busch like he did me, but I swear I would spin out and crash my own car before I'd run into him. But it's cool to follow him so closely—real closely—for a while, just to let him know I was there.

I get on Busch's rear bumper like I'm welded to it. Lap after lap, where he goes, I'm right there with him. High, low, anywhere he goes on this track, he's pulling me along, a couple of inches behind. It looks like I'm doing an Intimidator imitation.

Finally somebody from NASCAR notifies Ty Norris, DEI's general manager, that this is going to have to stop.

"Dale Jr.," Norris says, "NASCAR says back off."

I don't answer.

One lap later, Norris tells me again.

"Lay off. They say if *anything* happens to Busch's car, we will be severely penalized."

"Can't hear ya," I say. "Radio problems. You're breaking up."

The team loves that.

"Dale Jr., they will penalize you if *anything* happens to that 97 car," Norris is saying, a lot louder now.

"You're breaking up," I radio back, still hanging on Busch's bumper.

A NASCAR official waves Tony Eury down to the pit wall to emphasize their point.

"Goddamnit, Junior!" Tony screams into the radio. "I

*know* you can hear me. Now leave that fucking kid alone."

I don't answer.

"Quit fucking with that kid," Tony yells so loud I almost don't need the radio.

"I'm not doing anything," I say, probably sounding like a little boy caught in the act.

"You heard me," Tony says. "Quit it. Right now. NASCAR is chewing on my ass."

The fun ends just about the time a huge fire breaks out in Kenseth's pit area, leaving a horrifying cloud over pit lane. I think all of us in racing, no matter how macho, are scared of fire, and this one looks like trouble. Luckily, no one is seriously injured. But it sure changes our mood.

After a few more laps, I'm still far enough behind that I can't make up any more positions, so we pull it into the pits and call it a day. One more race that started out real promising but ends with a smashed car and a full load of disappointment.

On the bright side, I've got a week off.

## Phoenix, Arizona
## Checker 500

## I Admire Your Style

The CART FedEx Championship Series is the top open-wheel category in the United States. CART is great racing but has crappy promotion and marketing in the United States. They are successful throughout the world, but there are very few American drivers in the series. Some people point to the lack of recognizable American names as a reason for their fading glory in the U.S., so someone suggested that the best thing they could do would be to hire me or Tony Stewart away from NASCAR to bring our fans to their series. Although I'd like to drive one of the CART cars someday just to see how it feels, I have no interest in racing those kind of things.

Jon Ferrey is a photographer with the Allsport photography agency, and he looks just like me. Sometimes I laugh when I see him and say "Hey, Dale . . ." or shit like that. When he shoots photos at a NASCAR event, heads usually turn when he goes by, as fans do a double take.

Ferrey shoots at CART events too, so they asked him

if he'd participate in a charity event at the race in Fontana with drivers and team members performing ridiculous skits dressed in goofy costumes. It's Halloween weekend, so I guess it makes sense.

Through Budweiser, which is also the official beer of CART, Ferry gets ahold of one of my Bud uniforms, and walks on stage in the middle of the show to proclaim that he ("Dale Jr.") has decided to leave NASCAR and join CART. He waves and smiles and receives a big ovation. He makes fun of my southern accent and gives a speech like he's from *The Beverly Hillbillies*. He says, "I hear ya need some 'Mericans to race in them thar funny cars without fenders." The joke is met with applause and laughter, but not everyone gets the joke.

Backstage, still wearing the uniform and a "Little E" hat, Ferrey is greeted by an assortment of guests, who are thrilled that a new young American driver is coming to their series.

"We'd love to see ya over here," three-time Indy 500 winner Bobby Unser tells Ferrey.

"I admire your style," says CART team owner Paul Newman. Yes—*that* Paul Newman.

Ferrey poses for a series of photos with many of the VIP guests and is even asked for some autographs.

"For a few minutes, I could understand what you must go through," Ferry says when he tells me the story.

My Halloween is pretty damn cool too. I go as Dirk Diggler from the movie *Boogie Nights,* and me, Shannon (that's right, the same Shannon from the radio station. I took her advice and tried a little harder), and the boys go out and tear up several of the finer nightspots in Charlotte. The costume is a hit: I wear some seventies-era clothes that I got in the *Sports Illustrated* shoot with my '71 'Vette, and a big-ass Afro fright wig. When we get home at some ungodly hour, I take off the wig and throw it on the hood of my truck.

Several hours (or maybe several minutes) later, Jade arrives to wake me up for a flight to Seattle. It's still dark when he arrives, and as he walks around the truck to come to the door, he catches the big wig out of the corner of his eye. Convinced he is being attacked by some vicious furry creature, he jumps away from the truck immediately. He is still laughing by the time I stumble to the door to let him in . . . which is about ten minutes after he started knocking.

I haven't had much (if any) sleep, but I manage to get dressed and packed in time to catch the long flight to Seattle. It's a bigger suitcase than usual, because after the Budweiser appearance in Seattle, we fly to Phoenix late tonight and then to Los Angeles after Sunday's race before I head home to North Carolina.

Once we're in Seattle (I slept through the entire flight), I call my buddy Shane and we confer on "Operation Flowerbed," a thinly veiled reference to the flowers that I want him to deliver to Shannon while I'm gone. I hate being away from home anyway, but this trip seems like it will last months and months.

After touring the city and spending a few hours in the Experience Music Project, an interactive rock-and-roll museum created by Microsoft cofounder Paul Allen, I am brought to a local indoor karting center, where I sign autographs and pose for photos with local Bud employees and VIP guests. As usual, I'm nervous about the appearance and I'm tentative around the strangers until I become more comfortable with the surroundings.

When the autographs are completed, I drive a racing kart that has been painted to match my Winston Cup Bud car. I take it on the track by myself and promptly spin out—an all too familiar feeling. So much for the big shot.

When the appearance is over, they shuttle us back to the airport to catch a flight south to Phoenix for this weekend's race. By the time the Alaska Air flight lands in Phoenix, it is well after midnight on the West Coast, making it a twenty-four-hour day from start to finish . . . all this with a massive Halloween hangover.

"Let's see it," is the first thing I say the next morning when I spot the magazine in Jade's hand.

The *People* magazine "Sexiest Man" issue is scheduled to be on the newsstands the next day, but we get a sneak preview one day early.

"Page 175," he tells me, as I tear past the cover photo of some unknown dude named Brad Pitt to find out how it looks.

"Cool!" I say, as it turns out to be a helluva lot cooler than I expected. My photo is even spread across two pages. Sweet.

After a few seconds of looking, I turn and ask, "It *is* cool, isn't it?" I guess I needed validation that the photo of me rolling a racing tire through a wet garage area in leather pants is a good thing.

Soon the crew crowds around me, and they hoot and

holler at the photo. After falling to the ground in spasms of laughter, they assure me that it is, indeed, cool.

While there are a handful of NASCAR drivers pictured in the issue (including my buddies Hank Parker Jr. and Matt), my photo is the first and the largest. Very cool.

When the laughter dies down, the crew goes back to work, and I chill out in the transporter. My motor coach is not here, so I make the best of the small couch, using my jacket as a pillow. I'm asleep within seconds.

I try to catch up from my twenty-four-hour marathon the day before, but I'm jolted awake when the door opens.

"NASCAR wants you in the big red truck. . . ."

Oh shit. What now? It's usually not good when you're called into the NASCAR trailer.

As I approach, I see Kurt Busch waiting, and now I know why we're here.

After last week's on-track extracurricular activities, Kurt and I cleared the air, but NASCAR wants to make sure.

They scold us like we're children in the principal's office, and we assure them that everything is fine between us. They make us admit that we were both too aggressive and they make us promise we won't pull another stunt like that.

The crew seems to be in decent spirits, teasing me about the magazine, but inside the garage they're just going through the motions. The usual energy and laughter is nowhere to be found. The grind of the past few months has taken a toll on all of us—but the long trip west has taken the last bit of energy out of everyone on the team.

When practice begins, the energy level drops further as the car is unbelievably slow. We are only able to muster the forty-sixth-best time out of the forty-eight cars that make laps. After practice, I'm so disheartened that I don't stick around with the crew for very long.

When I get back to the garage later in the day, the team makes dramatic changes to the car, and their attitudes. They overhaul the entire setup and switch the engine in an all-out effort to find the lost speed. I jump underneath the car and begin wrenching and helping however I can.

At one point, I stand up and Kurt Busch sneaks behind me. When I turn, he turns, and when I step forward, he steps forward. It gets a big laugh out of the guys.

Somehow, some way, the changes help, and when we qualify, we leap to eighteenth quickest in the session. Thank God.


The next morning, the sexiest man in NASCAR is the sickest man in NASCAR. I have a bad case of the flu. I'm sure the all-night Halloween bash followed by a twenty-four-hour day on planes to Seattle and Phoenix has beaten up my immune system pretty good.

The entire crew seems even less energetic today, yawning and drooping in the Phoenix heat.

When happy hour arrives, the car is again a handful. There's no traction.

I roll into the garage, climb out of the car while Tony Jr. and the crew stand silently, looking at the ground.

"Nothing makes sense to me anymore," Tony Jr. says. "That's the God's honest truth. . . ."

With my health failing and the mood dropping below ground level, I'm in no state of mind or body to participate in an afternoon promotion for EA Sports, the video game company. Though I love to be one of the first people to see and play with the new Sony PlayStation 2, I go back to the hotel to sleep for the rest of the day and night.

"Damn, he passed up video games?" Tony Jr. says, "He *is* sick. . . ."

The hours and hours of sleep help me feel better on race morning, but I smile weakly and say only that I'm "80 percent better" than yesterday. I walk to the chapel service after the drivers' meeting and listen to Dale Beaver give a sermon that mocks the "Sexiest Man" issue. It's pretty funny when he nominates Jesus over Russell Crowe and Brad Pitt.

Before the green flag falls, a handful of team members congregate in the transporter, watching the prerace coverage on TNN. Because of the new television contracts that begin in 2001, this is the final Winston Cup race that TNN will televise, and they show a retrospective of some of the finest racing moments of the past decade. As highlights are shown of the Winston from years past, we all cheer, yell, and joke about each memorable moment. When the footage turns to our victory in May, the room turns quiet. It's like everyone suddenly realizes the historical context of our victory. It's something that they—and the race fans that watched that night—will remember for years and years to come. In the midst of a season, it's hard to fully appreciate the long-term significance of what you have done until the event is slightly further from view.

I start eighteenth today, with serious doubts that we will make more history at this particular race. But in our usual manner, the car is good early on. I progress past Matt and rookie Ryan Newman, who is making his first Winston Cup start. The day's first yellow flag, on Lap 36, allows us to make a pit stop, but there is trouble with the right rear tire, and the stop takes longer than planned. We lose fifteen spots.

When the green flies again, I know right away something is very wrong. Immediately, it's all I can do to hang on and I drop back to last place. I radio in a panic, "The right front is flat!"

Dale Cagle, spotting today high above the front straight, takes a look at the tire from his vantage point. "It looks OK . . . looks like it's up," he says.

The tire is not flat, though I am still unable to make the car turn. We have to make an unscheduled stop to fix what is wrong.

Tony and Tony Jr. are barely able to contain themselves when they discover the right-side tires have been put on the left side of the car and vice versa. Although the tires look the same to the naked eye, they are vastly different from left to right side. Somehow the tires were inverted on their tire stands before the pit stop. The unbalanced set makes the car feel like it's traveling on flat tires with no brakes.

By the time we return to the race, we are more than a full lap behind. But surprisingly, the car responds to the correct tires, and the Bud car is suddenly the fastest on the track, moving from last place to thirty-first and even gaining the lap back when the leaders pit again. As the race progresses, my frustration grows and grows. We have a good car but we fall too far behind to contend for any hope of a top finish. It's become a recurring theme this year, and I am tired of this feeling.

"It's tight," I say on Lap 162.

"It's way way way tight" is the call on Lap 164.

"It's fucking tight!" I yell on Lap 165.

When I get no response from the crew, my anger grows.

"Hello?" I spit. "Is this radio working? I might've flat-spotted these tires on a restart!"

After pitting on Lap 252, I return to the track with red wheels—not the usual black wheels. After the tire switch, the team ran out of "matching" tires, so they borrowed some from Bobby Hamilton's No. 4 Kodak team. They tell me the Bud car looks odd with the red wheels. After so many weeks of black wheels, it's jarring to see something different.

The team regroups and manages to rip off two really good stops (less than fifteen seconds each) in the late stages of the race. Not since the win in Texas have the times been that good. The race restarts for the final time with only twelve laps left, and even though I'm a lap down again, I'm in the midst of an all-out battle, often racing three-wide on a track that is notorious for having only one fast groove.

Jeff Burton crosses the finish line for his fourth victory of the season, while we finish twenty-seventh, one lap behind Burton. My teammate Steve Park finishes third, which continues his hot streak since he won at Watkins Glen. It only makes it more frustrating for us to see our more experienced teammates do so well while we struggle and shoot ourselves in the foot week after week.

No one is kidding anyone—we blew it again. And we slide further behind Kenseth for top rookie honors. But I try to keep a happy face after the race when I talk to the guys. I let them know we had a fast car that was able to run with the leaders, but once we got down a lap there was just not much we could do.

There's no usual postrace rush to find my father for the ride home today. I'm actually able to relax for a few minutes, as I'm on a flight later tonight to Los Angeles for two days of national television appearances. All I want to do is go home, but that'll have to wait.

When I arrive at the hotel room in L.A. late that evening, the phone is ringing. It's a local radio show called *Speed Freaks,* and they have tracked me down to see if I could chat with them on the air for a while. I'm too tired to say no, so I spend half an hour on the phone, joking and laughing with them before I go to bed. It has been a long week, and there's more fun (hopefully) ahead tomorrow.

# Homestead, Florida
## Pennzoil 400

## Too Sexy for One Page

My first appearance of the day is on *The X Show,* which runs on the FX Network. FX is a part of the new NASCAR TV package in 2001, and the network is trying to educate the twenty-something audience and get them up to speed on the sport. I'm the first driver chosen to appear on the show, which includes hot models and a wild audience (made up mostly of out-of-work actors who get forty bucks a day to hang out and eat bad snacks between takes). My race car will be making an appearance too.

It requires several takes to get the opening segments of the show right. Finally they get it done, and after a couple of comedy skits, it's my turn. Not much makes me nervous, but this show is pretty unpredictable and I wonder if I'm really ready for this sort of thing.

Craig Jackson, one of the cohosts, wants to talk about *People* magazine's "Sexiest Man" issue, which is on the newsstands right now. We talk about my picture and the two-page spread.

"I guess I'm sexier than most," I say. "Too sexy for one page."

That gets some laughs.

Then we move over to the car and I take Jackson around and answer some basic questions about the engine and tires and stuff like that. We finish the segment talking about what the drivers wear, and a blond model hops out of the car wearing my Bud uniform that she really fills up. She is called Icy, but not because she isn't hot. Turns out she's from Iceland.

Then another model runs out on stage wearing long underwear to simulate the Nomex fireproof underwear that some drivers wear under their uniforms. I explain that I don't usually wear that because it's hot and uncomfortable, and that I prefer a T-shirt and my lucky boxer shorts. That's the cue for a third model to come out in a tiny T-shirt and some colorful boxers. The three models then simulate a victory celebration. They're all pretty hot, but they need a lot more practice opening champagne bottles.

It's a fun time and I think the segment will look good on the air and show that NASCAR drivers are cool.

Next I meet up with Riki Rachtman. He and I hook up with Benji Kaze, a motor sports producer at Fox Sports Network. Kaze wants to do something different than a typical interview, so he has a crew follow the action while Rachtman and I are racing each other at the NASCAR Silicon Speedway at Universal Studies. These computer simulators are as close as most people will ever get to driving a real race car. I don't think it's too impressive, but it *is* fun as hell. You race against other people and computer-controlled opponents. I handle both of 'em but Rachtman struggles.

When the cyber-racing is over, Rachtman takes me to Sunset Boulevard to get some dinner and see some of the sights. We eat at the Rainbow, an icon of the L.A. rock-and-roll scene. There are photos and posters from the big-hair, heavy-metal eighties all over the walls of the restaurant. The signatures on the wall include John Lennon, Keith Moon, members of the Doors, and lots of other legendary partyers. A lot of them are dead now, which adds to the weird feeling inside the club, which is almost totally empty. It is early on a Monday evening and there is nobody in the joint except for the group of us. Behind the bar is a bartender with freakish, gigantic, "only-in-Los-Angeles" breasts.

We decide to walk down Sunset Boulevard to see if anything else is happening. The Whiskey—which was originally the Whiskey-A-Go-Go, where many of L.A.'s greatest bands, from the Doors to Motley Crue, got their start—is closed tonight. So we walk on, past the gaudy *Hustler* magazine sex shop with all the neon lights, to check out the Viper Room. Johnny Depp owns the club and it has a reputation as the cool spot to hang.

The guy at the door recognizes Rachtman right away and whisks us in. We're on the list, I'm told. That seems to be very important in L.A. The downstairs bar is not much larger than my bedroom, and it's full of people trying hard not to be seen looking around to see what other cool people are here. Upstairs there is a special screening of a documentary on the career of an obscure eighties death-metal band called Stormtroopers of Death, or S.O.D. Most of the people watching look like they're still wearing the same clothes they wore back in the eighties. Rachtman works the room a little, schmoozing with musicians like Corey Parks, the six-foot-six female bassist who quit the band Nashville Pussy a few weeks ago.

It's an entertaining scene, I guess, in a freakish sort of way. The whole thing seems like it's all hype and no substance.

"This is no different than clubs back home," I say to the Los Angeles dudes.

We walk back to the Rainbow for Riki's pickup. It's painted black and has decals that make it look sorta like my dad's Goodwrench race car. While we're waiting for valet parking, we see a couple more celebs. Everlast, the rapper, and B-Real from the group Cypress Hill.

"I guess it's kind of cool," I tell Riki on the way back to the hotel. "But L.A. gives me a headache . . . too many lights, too much hype."


The next day is Election Day. While the world is wondering who is going to be the next President, I'm a guest on the comedy Central show *Turn Ben Stein On*. Stein played the teacher in *Ferris Bueller's Day Off* and he also has a game show called *Win Ben Stein's Money*. A lot of people don't know that he used to write speeches for President Richard Nixon and is a serious political guy.

"Oh my God," he says when he first sees me. "You look so young. You're just a child."

The house band for the show is G. Love and Special Sauce. The drummer is wearing an ol' beat up Amoco racing hat with Dave Blaney's number 93 on the side.

They are shocked I know their signature song, "Cold Beverage."

I was nervous before the *X Show* taping, but now I'm really nervous. I'm the only guest for a full thirty minutes and this guy is so smart. I hope he doesn't ask me anything that will make me look like an ass.

But Stein is working hard to make me comfortable and he starts out by showing me this Cadillac he owns. I tell him what he'd have to do to get it NASCAR-ready. (A helluva lot!) Then we go back on the set, where he asks me what it's like to be a third-generation racer.

During the first commercial break, G. Love and Special Sauce kick in with "Cold Beverage." It's cool that they play my request, and the small audience seems to enjoy it as well. Stein, who is ducking backstage to check the election results, goes back and forth, his mood changing as the results in Florida are projected and changed and debated. But he's back in form when the cameras roll. We close the show by racing radio-controlled cars around the set and then doing twenty push-ups.

Seems he closes every show with the push-ups.

And that's it for L.A. I catch the red-eye, and when I get back to North Carolina the next morning, the election is still undecided. I wonder how Stein is holding up.

• • •

The Homestead/Miami track is the tropical stop on the NASCAR circuit. Everything is pastel and art deco, and while you're more than an hour from downtown Miami, if you squint your eyes, you might swear you're still in South Beach. Well, not really, but it's hot and humid as hell, just like South Beach.

It's the first Winston Cup race here for the Bud team, but we're familiar with the track, having clinched two straight Busch championships at Homestead. We definitely have a positive feeling about this place. A positive feeling, yes, but we still do a lot of guessing because the Winston Cup car handles much differently than the Busch car.

But we must be guessing right, because we're fifth best in the first practice session.

When it comes time to qualify, we're the twelfth-fastest car. Steve Park gets the Bud Pole and if somebody else has to get it, then it might as well be my teammate. We borrow some of the data and setups from his team and feel confident going into the race.

We get a little extra thrill just before the race, when WWF wrestler Sergeant Slaughter stops by the transporter. A lot of the guys on the team are big wrestling fans, so it's a kick for them. He has a wife and son with him and the kid is a big Dale Jr. fan, so when I pose for a picture with his son, Sergeant Slaughter is ecstatic.

Just before the start of the race, Dale Cagle radios a warning down to me. "A few of the guys around you are new at this game," he says. "So be careful." He's talking about Kurt Busch and another rookie, Casey Atwood.

Everybody is behaving well at the start, and the whole field drops into single file. The banking and the shape of Homestead don't allow for much two-by-two racing. Even though they changed the track configuration a couple of times, it's still a track where most of the races are boring as hell. I try to change that boring trend with a three-wide pass on Lap 53, but then I learn why it's just not done, as Rusty Wallace gets by me in the next corner.

When you push the car as far as it can go, even a minor problem can feel severe when you dive into a corner. On Lap 130, I radio the crew.

"We might have a tire going down!"

A lap or two later I call them again after I've tiptoed around a few times.

"OK. I really don't think so. But the car is rolling over on the right front, big time."

Cagle calls down to tell me that no cars are close to passing me.

"No pressure," he says. "No pressure . . ."

"Lotsa pressure," I snap. "Lotsa pressure here. We gotta get this thing tightened up."

"Ten-four," says Jeff Clark, the engine guy.

"I need to hear that from my crew chief!" I say. Tempers get short at the end of a long season. We all just want to go home.

Tony Stewart is dominating the race, and when he laps me on 145, I come in for tires. Back on the track, I'm suddenly two seconds faster each time around.

I get the lap back when Stewart pits. But the new leader, Ricky Rudd, is in my mirror. I hold him off for five laps. Then six. And I'm able to hold him off for eleven laps until he finally passes me.

Tony Jr. decides to bring the car in earlier than expected, on Lap 204, to keep up with the other cars that are a lap down. The strategy backfires almost immediately when a yellow comes out four laps later, and we go two laps behind. The race is no longer fun.

Although things do get a little more interesting when Rusty Wallace and I race side by side for a few laps. But he has a faster car right now. You fight as hard as you can, but sometimes you just have to let a faster guy go to help preserve your tires.

When we come out of the pits after another stop, we beat Wallace to the line, but he takes a shortcut across the grass to get ahead of me.

"The 2 car cut across!" I'm screaming into the radio. "Make sure he's penalized for that. Cheatin' fucker!"

This minor controversy energizes me, and I make it my mission to close in on Wallace lap after lap. Tony Stewart and Ricky Rudd are kicking everyone's ass, but I'm faster than anyone else.

But the day belongs to race winner Tony Stewart and his teammate at Joe Gibbs Racing, Bobby Labonte, who finishes fourth and clinches the Winston Cup trophy for 2000. My dad hung close all season and made a good run of it. I thought he had a real shot at it, but it just didn't happen. I'm really happy for Bobby, who is one of the coolest guys around. He was a Busch champion like I was, and he really was the best this year. He's always laid back—he never crashes, gets excited, or makes mistakes. Off the track he's like that too— he's a guy that I can approach pretty easily.

We finish two laps down, in thirteenth place, and it seems pretty empty to see another team celebrating a championship when we had done the same thing here the last two years. It was a pretty boring race from my seat. Not too much fun. We just kinda rode around. We could pass people, but on a flat track like this, everyone gets strung out and there's not much action.

It's the fifth time this season we've run thirteenth, and I guess that says something about our luck since the Winston way back in May. Next week's race in Atlanta is the last one of the season. Yeah! It's about damn time. For me, and I'm sure the rest of the team, the end can't come soon enough.

## Atlanta, Georgia
### NAPA 500

## Put Us Outta Our Misery,
## Know What I Mean?

The final race. The end of my rookie season in Winston Cup. It seemed like the end would never get there, and as awful as we ran the final months of the season, we all *really* look forward to this final event. Put us outta our misery, ya know what I mean?

Although I knew we would have some hardships as a first-year team, I didn't expect the year to be as disappointing as it was. Everyone says, "Dude, three wins! Quit whining! You should be happy!" Well, not this dude. I didn't run as well as I expected the second half of the season. My driving was not what it should have been, and our race cars weren't as good as they should have been either. Too often it was a struggle mounted on frustration and recklessness.

The majority of the time, my crew and I were on the same page. Then there were times when we weren't even reading the same book or speaking the same language. It's mainly due to lack of communication. Communication. Man, am I tired of hearing that word. I shudder at even typing it. It's a word that came up repeatedly throughout the year.

But I discovered that communication is a two-way street. I didn't always talk things out when I should, and sometimes I got pissed and sulked when I should have worked to find a solution. In truth, I'm happy Tony Sr. had enough confidence in me and didn't slug me in the face when I wasn't acting my age.

I learned a lot about leadership and attitude this season. When things are going badly, I need to be a more positive force, instead of getting pissed off and walking back to my motor coach to relax. When everyone works hard for so many months, everyone gets burnt out and it's very easy in the heat of the moment to lose sight of the bigger picture. The crew guys saw Tony Jr. and me arguing and thought things were worse than they really were. Hey, Tony Jr. and I have known each other most of our lives, and we always fight and scrap like cats and dogs, but once it's done, it's done and forgotten. But it's hard to motivate an entire team when all they see is disagreement and head butting.

Each of the fellas on the team has a job, and they each did it extremely well. They are individuals, but they are a much more powerful unit when they stick together and work as a team. They are unmatched by any team when on top of their game, but it takes only a speck of animosity to destroy team unity. Next year I know we'll all work better, so all the other teams had better look out!

As much as I'm glad it's over, I can't wait to see what's ahead for 2001.

I think that our team has great potential for next season. We will be more consistent, and if so, I think we will be a top-ten—hell, maybe even a top-five—team in points. As proud as I am of what we've done, we all know that we need to grow ten times in maturity and focus more clearly on what we need to do as a team.

As for this weekend, it starts off like crap. The car was awful in practice, and we needed a fresh engine for qualifying. To relieve the stress, I decided to go back to the coach and go through some in-car camera footage from this season. Whenever there is an in-car camera in my car, the network records the whole race from that point of view. Then they give me a copy of the tape so I can watch it with the team.

I choose to watch some of the best races of the year: Talladega, Texas, Charlotte, even Bristol, where I crashed. It is fun as hell to relive those races with my buddies. I can point out the best shit for them. We all laugh and hoot as we watch me pass guys like mad. It's been so long since I've been able to do that for real, it feels like years ago that we were winning those races.

Earlier in the year when we raced at this track, we were the car to beat, but Goodyear has a new tire, so we're struggling just to learn how to run with these new wheels. We qualify twenty-eighth. This is embarrassing even if we can use the new tires as an excuse.

The rest of the weekend is equally miserable: it's cold, it's raining, and so mostly I just hide out in the motor coach with Shannon and some of the guys.

InterAct, our newest sponsor, has spent big bucks to host a news conference Saturday to announce that I will be endorsing their "Blue Thunder" steering wheels for video and computer games. The conference is a hit, and I go to their private suite and get to race against journalists from all the hip electronics web sites and magazines. Unfortunately for them, they don't get to see a single lap of racing on Sunday. Constant rain washes out all activities, and their guests all have to catch planes back home without seeing any real action.

The season can't end soon enough for many of us, but now Mother Nature has made us stay yet another day to prolong the pain. The season concludes on Monday.

NASCAR chooses to start the race at 10 A.M. I don't like to get up that early for anything, so things are mostly a blur as we go out into the clear, cold morning to celebrate Darrell Waltrip's final Winston Cup start. He's had a great career, and I know he'll be great at his new profession as a race announcer.

It's cold as hell, so we have to be careful to warm up the tires and take it easy for a lap or two to make sure they are at the proper temperature. It's days like this where a lot of guys get too eager on cold tires and tear up their car. Even though we may not be very fast, maybe we can move up as the rest of the field crashes out.

Well, at least that's the plan, because I see an opening on the first lap and go three-wide to take two spots right away. I'm not happy with the car—it wants to wreck me every turn—but we move up through the field. We make a couple of pit stops and get into the top fifteen, but Tony is mad as hell that I'm not getting out of the pits as quick as usual after the crew have finished their work.

"Did someone forget to wake his ass up this morning?" he yells. "Is he still sleeping?"

We just hang on for much of the first hundred laps, moving up or back occasionally, but always around twentieth position or so. When a yellow flag comes out on Lap 110, we try to solve the problem.

"The car's vibrating like the tires are made of concrete," I explain. "Something has happened, because they're chattering real bad."

"We need to do something," Tony grouses. "Because we suck right now."

As we leave the pits, I get on the gas hard, and the car breaks loose on the cold tires. I slide right into the back of John Andretti's car, which is sitting still in its pit stall. The contact peels back the right rear corner of Andretti's car like a can opener.

"I can't fucking believe that!" Tony yells into his radio. "Come in this lap and we'll try to fix it."

The damage to my car is cosmetic but any hope we had of ending the year on an up note goes to hell with one dumb move in the pits. We return on the lead lap, but we're thirtieth or twenty-eighth or something. It's hard to stay focused when you're so far back.

My focus comes back on Lap 222, when something in the rear of the car breaks loose and I have to dive into the pits. It looks like problems with a wheel, and we're four laps down by the time we return. I just try to keep the car intact for the rest of the day, and, thanks to attrition on the part of the field, I finish twentieth.

Jerry Nadeau becomes the fourth first-time winner of the season. This is a Winston Cup record as he joins me, Matt, and Steve Park as first-time winners.

The season is finally completed, and I can look down the long list of numbers that sum up what we accomplished: three wins, two pole positions (both track records), sixteenth place in the Winston Cup point standings, and more than $2.6 million in prize money. We led ten races and led more than 425 laps overall throughout the season. And, perhaps most disappointing of all, we finish second to my buddy Kenseth in the rookie standings. We had more victories than Matt, but he had a more consistent season. All of the numbers look good, but at the end of the day, they really don't mean shit. The season was a disappointment for the team and me. We began the year with high hopes but failed to live up to our expectations as the season unfolded.

We know what challenges lie ahead for the 2001 season, so we need to focus right away on the things that can make us more competitive every race and help us win our first Winston Cup title.

# Epilogue

$S$peedweeks 2001 at Daytona were some of the best days of my life. I raced as a teammate with my dad for the first time in the 24 Hours of Daytona. One week later I raced against him in my first Budweiser Shootout, and then I ran really well in the 125-mile qualifying race where I lost out in a photo finish with Mike Skinner. My car was great again in the Daytona 500. I even had a dream of winning at Daytona that was so real in the weeks prior to the race that I was bold enough to tell the media about it.

"I'll see you in Victory Lane," I told 'em.

I completely believed that the dream would come true. Then the last lap of the race turned that dream into a nightmare.

I lost the greatest man I ever knew, my dad.

There were no guidebooks, no rules, no script about how to act or how to grieve. The first three or four days after the crash were the emptiest days of my life. I don't know how I remained strong. I had such a weight on my chest. But my family was there for me, and I was there for them. I had Kelley and I had my mom, who had moved back to North Carolina from Virginia to help take care of Kelley's baby. Yet I still felt alone.

I worried that I would have to take over DEI. But Teresa stood tall and kept her rightful place in charge of the business. Not a lot of people gave her the due she deserved for the success of DEI before my dad's death, but they will now when they see what a great business-woman she is.

I was worried that all of my sponsors would leave me. I had assumed they were all supporting me because of who my dad was. Now that he was gone, I thought they would walk away.

I was worried about my teammate Michael Waltrip, whose first Winston Cup win will always be tainted in tragedy.

As I walked out of the memorial service for Dad on a bitterly cold, dreary, rainy day, I felt like I was walking into my future. I was now on my own, just like my dad had been when his dad died and left him to carry on. When Ralph died, Dad was almost the same age as I am now.

I was sad that my dad would never get to meet my future wife . . . would never play with my kids . . . or help me make it through the rest of my life just like he had done for the previous twenty-six years. But I knew he had raised me to be my own person and that somehow I would find the strength and the guts to carry on like he did.

The decision to go back to racing right away was one everyone at DEI agreed with. It's what we, as racers, do, and it's where we felt closest to our friends. If I hadn't raced that first weekend, I would have felt so much more helpless and miserable. I really didn't want to be *any-where*—but being at the track seemed like the best place.

Kyle Petty, who had lost his son Adam only months before, stopped by the transporter at Rockingham on the Friday following Dad's death. He assured me that my best role for the sport, and for DEI, was as a driver and that I should just do what I was best at, and not worry about taking on a new role that was beyond my limited business skills.

The weeks after Dad's death were a blur. I was surrounded by people all of the time, but it was like being on a raft in the ocean: surrounded by water but unable to drink any of it. I missed my dad every moment.

Slowly I began doing things like I had done before: public appearances, interviews, and such. I woke up every day and asked myself, "How would Dad do this?" or "How would Dad do that?"

At autograph sessions or in the garage area, people meant well, but they'd bring odd items for me to autograph, like photos of Dad. They wanted me to sign them, as if that would make it better or something. They gave me copies of pictures or drawings they had done of Dad or of his car. Some days I was fine, and then one of these moments would just set me back days and days and send me into depression. Some fans insisted on giving me their most prized possession, like an old No. 3 hat or T-shirt or poster. I didn't get it. Why would someone want my signature on Dad's merchandise? I began to understand how John Kennedy Jr. must have lived his life: being asked or reminded about his father's death every day. Every week, the media and the fans asked the same questions. I understood this would go on for the rest of my life, but I was sick of talking about my dad every day.

I also didn't get it when psycho fans threatened Sterling Marlin because they thought he caused the crash. That hurt me, and I went out of my way that first week to provide support for him and send a message to race fans that I would not tolerate crap like that.

The worst was all the bootleg merchandise that some sick folks created to take advantage of Dad's death. Fans would bring up this crap at autograph sessions for me to sign. It took less energy to just sign it and get them out of there than to tell 'em they were ripping off my family. Somehow, signing my autograph on anything that said 1951–2001 made it seem somehow more permanent, more final. The circus in Florida over the autopsy photos was painful as well. Teresa was awesome—she kicked their asses. I was convinced that my dad was indestructible, but now I'm beginning to think Teresa is the one that is strongest.

The race team struggled for a few races, although we were much better than we showed on the scoreboard. We had a top-five car at Las Vegas before we were penalized in the pits, and we had a lot of little shit go wrong that stopped us from getting the finishes we deserved. Everyone at DEI stuck together and stepped up bigger than they ever had before. No one could replace Dad, so we all tried to pick up our own little corner and lift together.

Tony Eury Sr., who had been a friend to Dad for longer than I had been alive, kept the team, and me, together and gave us a reason to continue. Tony is a guy you want to be loyal to and someone who you want to work hard for. Slowly the little problems began to disappear on the track, and we began piling up top-five finishes and climbing the points chart.

Everyone knew (although it was unspoken) that we would be going back to Daytona again in July. I wanted to go back. It's a great track with a lot of history, and I could think of no better place to go back and win a race. Dad loved that place and so do I.

I went to Daytona Beach a week before the race. I packed up some buddies and rented a secluded house where we could chill, drink a lot of beer, and just forget about the rest of the world. A few days before the race, I drove them all to the speedway to show them around. We drove out on the track and talked to some of the workers who were preparing the facility for the Pepsi 400.

I took them around the 2.5-mile track and into Turn 4, where Dad's accident occurred. I looked at the skid marks that still hadn't been washed off the track and I looked at the point where his car hit the wall. I sat and thought quietly for a while. I somehow felt closer to my dad at that moment.

My first lap behind the wheel of the race car at Daytona two days later was the hardest lap of the weekend. I drove the car out onto pit lane, where I had to wait in line to go on the track. I just sat there silently, thinking about everything. I was shaky and emotional on the first lap, but once I got to thinking only about the race car, I started to relax and get my mind back on winning. We had a good car, hell, a *great* car, and we had a shot to win.

All of the guys worked their asses off on that car. Every time Tony Jr. and I talked about it, his eyes lit up. He poured his heart into that machine. We knew we would be good, just like we were in February when we finished second, but I think everyone else found out how good we were in the final practice session on Friday night before the race. I was able to drop back in a pack of cars and then easily work my way to the front. I was also able to maintain speed once I was in front.

When the race started, we chilled out for a while to let the field settle down. Then we marched forward. Once we got to the front of the pack, we were able to stay there much of the night. The car was a dream. The engine department found a few more horsepower since February, so we were screaming down the straights as well.

When the race fell under a late caution flag, we decided to take four tires on our last pit stop. A handful of teams chose to only change two tires or none at all. They got out of the pits ahead of us. We restarted in sixth place and it looked bleak for a while, until they threw the green flag.

I got a great start, and with that momentum, I found that the guys who didn't have four fresh tires like we did couldn't keep up. I got into the lead in Turn 4 and tried not to look back. As the finish neared, my mirrors filled with blue and yellow as Michael Waltrip's car came up behind me just like I had done for him a few months before. With his help, we streaked across the finish line first and second, just like the Daytona 500, but this time I was in front.

As we went down the backstraight on the cool-down

lap, Matt came up and tried to give my car a "donut," or a black mark made by slamming the sidewall of one of his tires into the sheet metal of my car. It was one of my dad's signature postrace moves. It's kind of like a rough and manly way of saying "Congrats." Matt got into the side of my car and then our wheels touched. It was funnier than hell, and it's why my car had long black streaks down the passenger-side door! (Some idiots in the media suggested that I had damaged the car by slamming it into the Turn 4 wall in some sort of act of defiance to the concrete wall that took my dad.)

It was a great feeling, so great, in fact, that I had to do something to let the joy out. If I drove right into the sterile and controlled Victory Lane, my chest would have exploded. So I did my best attempt at a burnout in the front-stretch grass, and jumped out of the car to salute all of the fans, who were still standing and cheering. It was awesome—and it only got better when Michael slid to a stop a few feet from my car.

We hugged and laughed and smiled and were soon drowning among our crews and what seemed like a thousand people surrounding us on the grass.

In Victory Lane, Steve Park came by, Ken Schrader came over, and then Dale Jarrett came by to congratulate me. "That reminded me of someone I once knew," he said while we embraced.

Kelley's new husband, Ray Holm, a member of Ricky Rudd's crew, came over and hugged me. Then Mike Helton, NASCAR's president, did the same. For a while I thought every damn body was gonna come over there and say congratulations to me and Tony and Tony Jr. and everyone else who had made it happen.

We celebrated and sprayed beer all over each other, poured a few on the ground in honor of my dad, and then, when all of the media interviews were done, we went back to my motor coach. The local Budweiser people had brought some big tubs of Bud, and all of my friends were there as well as Michael, Steve Park, musician Edwin McCain, and so many others. We just sat and bathed in the victory until the beer was gone. Then, at 5 A.M., we all went to our motor coaches and went to bed.

It was just like what I had dreamed so vividly before the season started. I dreamed that I was out front for much of the race before I was able to win my first race at Daytona. The dream felt so real. I thought I was dreaming about the 500, but maybe it was predicting this victory.

When I told the media about the dream in January, one journalist asked, "Where was your dad in the dream?"

"He wasn't there," I said.

Or was he?